There is a certain sense of irony to the fact that Pete Dye and I both dabbled in the insurance business in our younger days. Because in so many ways, it was Pete who provided me what might be called a life *assurance* policy. Were it not for Pete Dye, Jack Nicklaus the golf course designer might never have existed. Instead, in part because of Pete, I am fortunate to say that I have had two careers, both of which I have enjoyed enormously as they played out parallel to each other, and one which, even today, still enthuses me, motivates me, challenges me, and, most important, provides me a deep-rooted sense of satisfaction.

Pete and I became friends, on and off the golf course, when we were both still amateur golfers. We would occasionally tangle on the golf course, and, in fact, Pete remains proud of the fact he beat me by a couple of strokes in the first two rounds of the 1957 U.S. Open—my first appearance in a major championship. To his credit, Pete also has never forgotten that I beat him the next year in the semifinals of the Trans-Mississippi Amateur. Yet, most important, it was our days as amateur golfers that provided the genesis of the professional and personal relationship that I cherish today.

It was more than forty years ago when that relationship led to the start of my second career as a course designer. In the mid-1960s, Pete was working on The Golf Club in my hometown of Columbus, and he asked me to come out to

take a look at what he was doing. I was reluctant to do so at first, but Pete eventually convinced me. In the end, he was very receptive to my comments, and I think I gave him some ideas that he appreciated and even implemented. Shortly thereafter, we collaborated on Harbour Town, the beginning of a partnership that saw us collaborate on several courses that opened between 1969 and 1972. Before long, an avocation for me became a vocation.

A few hundred courses later, what began quite casually one day on a visit with Pete has given me a career that's taken me well beyond my golf game. It has allowed me to create a business that has not only benefited my family but involved them. It is a business that has allowed me to give back to the game I so dearly love by perhaps shaping the game for years to come. It has created a legacy that will last beyond anything I have done on the golf course. Just as golf was once my vehicle to competition, golf course design now provides me that challenge and competition, whether it is with a piece of dirt or my own creative limits. And I have Pete to thank.

Working with Pete early in my career was a wonderful learning experience, and great fun. I absorbed a tremendous amount from Pete, and much of my philosophy on design can be traced back to what I learned from him. One of Pete's philosophies is that golf is a more pleasant game

Donald Ross once wrote, "My work will tell my story," and that's how I hope to be remembered. I find the greatest satisfaction in believing that I have somehow contributed in making the game I love a more exciting one to play. **Pete Dye**

Pete Dye

Golf Courses

Fifty Years of Visionary Design

Joel Zuckerman

With Appreciations by

Jack Nicklaus,

Arnold Palmer,

and

Greg Norman

Abrams, New York

To Pete, Alice, and the entire Dye family of architects, who have created hundreds of wonderful courses the world over.

And especially to Perry O. Dye, who created the incredible opportunity that allowed me the privilege of writing this book.

Contents

Page 1: Destination Kohler, Irish, 6th hole
Pages 4–5: The Honors Course, 15th hole
Above: The Dye Preserve, 6th hole

Acknowledgments

It might best be described as a metallurgical medley. Writing this book was a golden opportunity, resulted in platinum-level frequent flyer status, yet my iron game was a constant source of disappointment. Over 28,000 air miles. Over 6,000 road miles. Three dozen flights. It's easy to chronicle now, after the fact. But while it was happening, it was a hectic blur of tee times, airline connections, Advil, audiotapes, interviews, and a seemingly unending string of double bogeys, "others," and a couple of out-of-the-blue eagles, to be candid, from New England to Hawaii to the Dominican Republic, and back again.

There were two basic reactions from friends, colleagues, and neighbors who got wind of this once-in-a-lifetime assignment: jealousy and sympathy. An example of the former: "You're getting *paid* to play all of these world-class courses? Where can I get a gig like that?" An example of the latter: "*Every* course is a Dye design? Which expense is greater—golf balls or psychiatry sessions?"

The effort extended in writing this book is a penny on the dollar compared to what Pete Dye and company went through to make these courses a reality. And the talent level? The dedication to the task? To pen 600 to 800 semi-informative or entertaining words on each course is perhaps one-thousandth the effort it took Pete, and in many cases, Alice, Perry, P.B., Matt, Andy, or Cynthia Dye to conjure the courses on which I comment. But then, Pete made his mark over 50 years. This book was written in 50 weeks.

The year 2007 was all Dye all day. Of course, being a vagabond golfer, I had a bit of wiggle room once in a while. But even when I very occasionally strayed from a Dye-designed fairway, Pete was generally close at hand.

One long 36-hole day in Palm Springs featured Dye at dawn and Doak at midday (but Tom Doak, one of golf architecture's hottest names, spent three years learning the trade under the Dyes). On a weekend visit to eastern Tennessee, it was my honor to play the Honors Course a few times, but only after venturing crosstown to play a Seth Raynor classic (one of Pete Dye's early influences). In Hawaii, I surrounded Dye course visits with trips to courses designed by Jack Nicklaus (who began his architectural career as a design consultant at Pete Dye's Harbour Town) and Robin Nelson (long a Dye admirer). Well, you get the idea.

Along the way, there have been a number of folks who made this often arduous assignment pleasurable. In Florida, I credit Billy Detlaff in Ponte Vedra, J.J. Sehlke in Fort Lauderdale, Laurie and Kevin Hammer in Delray Beach, Joe Webster in Jupiter, and Michael Gibson in Palm Beach Gardens. In Tennessee, my thanks to Joel Richardson. In Indiana, I was lucky to spend some time with Dave Bego at Maple Creek, Tony Pancake at Crooked Stick, Jon Chapple and Bob Barriger at The Fort, and, of course, a memorable lunchtime visit with Pete and Alice themselves. In Ohio, I had great hosts in Joe Regner at The Golf Club and Ron Klingle at Avalon Lakes. In Utah and Las Vegas, I was happy to have the Birdman, Brian Oar, as my running buddy and chauffeur. Same scenario in Maryland, when Tim Riviere pulled driving duty to and from Philadelphia on a 15-hour, 36-hole buffet. In Oklahoma City, it was a pleasure to be hosted by Tony and Michelle Maranto. In the Dominican Republic, I owe the Rainieri family in Punta Cana and Kim Hutchinson and Gilles Gagnon at Casa de Campo. And I would be remiss in not crediting one of the finest souls in this business, Dan Shepherd of Buffalo Communications, who was instrumental in facilitating Dye visits for me in California, Hawaii, and Louisiana. Others who deserve credit include longtime Dye photographer Ken May, who contributed many of the images in this book, and coordinated the rest. Editor Margaret L. Kaplan of Abrams Books has been a terrific sounding board during this entire process. Brady McNamara did a wonderful design job. Writing colleagues Brad King and Shane Sharp did some vital legwork for me, and their expertise and guidance was much appreciated. I must also recognize author Mark Shaw, who collaborated with Pete on his mid-1990s biography, *Bury Me in a Pot Bunker*. If one can consider the writing of this book as a real-world classroom (or perhaps year-long field trip might be a better analogy), then *Bury Me* served as an absolutely indispensable textbook.

As one can imagine, I've fielded plenty of questions about Pete Dye—his courses and his career. The most common question is whether I actually enjoy, or just endure, his courses. These typically come from folks who have tangled unsuccessfully with Pete's most notorious creations—and found no safe shelter at Harbour Town, been run over at The Brickyard, been mauled by the Teeth of the Dog, etc., and have come to the harsh realization that their game isn't quite at the level they had hoped. There's a simple answer to this question, and a picture, as they say, is worth a thousand words. Check out the author photo on this book's jacket. That's all one needs to know.

Joel Zuckerman
Savannah, Georgia
Autumn 2008

Pete Dye's Championship Venues

One of the reasons for Pete Dye's architectural eminence is the fact that his golf courses have so often served or will eventually be serving as the site of major competitions. Bear in mind that in addition to the extensive list below, The Players Championship, considered one of professional golf's most prestigious titles, has been contested at the Dye-designed Stadium Course at TPC Sawgrass every spring since 1982. Furthermore, The Heritage, one of the preeminent Invitational tournaments on the PGA Tour, has been contested at Harbour Town Golf Links annually since 1969!

1974 US Senior Amateur Harbour Town, South Carolina

1974 Men's World Amateur Team Championship
Teeth of the Dog, Dominican Republic

1974 Women's World Amateur Team Championship
Teeth of the Dog, Dominican Republic

1983 US Senior Amateur Crooked Stick, Indiana

1984 US Amateur Oak Tree Golf Club, Oklahoma

1988 PGA Championship Oak Tree Golf Club, Oklahoma

1989 US Mid-Amateur Crooked Stick, Indiana

1989 NCAA Golf Championship Oak Tree Golf Club, Oklahoma

1991 PGA Championship Crooked Stick Golf Club, Indiana

1991 Ryder Cup Matches Ocean Course, South Carolina

1991 US Amateur Honors Course, Tennessee

1991 US Mid-Amateur Long Cove, South Carolina

1992 US Women's Mid-Amateur Old Marsh, Florida

1993 US Women's Open Crooked Stick, Indiana

1994 US Amateur TPC Sawgrass—Stadium, Florida

1994 Curtis Cup Matches Honors Course, Tennessee

1996 NCAA Golf Championship Honors Course, Tennessee

1996 US Women's Amateur Firethorn, Nebraska

1997 US Amateur Public Links Kearney Hills, Kentucky

1997 World Cup Ocean Course, South Carolina

1998 US Women's Open Blackwolf Run, Wisconsin

1999 US Senior Open Des Moines Country Club, Iowa

2003 US Women's Mid-Amateur Long Cove, South Carolina

2003 World Cup Ocean Course, South Carolina

2004 PGA Championship Whistling Straits, Wisconsin

2005 US Mid-Amateur Honors Course, Tennessee

2005 LPGA Championship Bulle Rock, Maryland

2005 Solheim Cup Crooked Stick, Indiana

2006 LPGA Championship Bulle Rock, Maryland

2006 Senior PGA Championship Oak Tree Golf Course, Oklahoma

2007 Senior PGA Championship Ocean Course, South Carolina

2007 LPGA Championship Bulle Rock, Maryland

2007 US Senior Open Whistling Straits, Wisconsin

2007 US Women's Amateur Public Links Kearney Hills, Kentucky

2007 US Women's Amateur Crooked Stick, Indiana

2008 NCAA Golf Championship Kampen Course, Indiana

2008 LPGA Championship Bulle Rock, Maryland

2009 US Mid-Amateur Ocean Course, South Carolina

2009 US Senior Open Crooked Stick, Indiana

2009 LPGA Championship Bulle Rock, Maryland

2010 NCAA Golf Championship Honors Course, Tennessee

2010 PGA Championship Whistling Straits, Wisconsin

2012 US Women's Open Blackwolf Run, Wisconsin

2012 PGA Championship Ocean Course, South Carolina

2015 PGA Championship Whistling Straits, Wisconsin

2020 Ryder Cup Matches Whistling Straits, Wisconsin

Introduction

There are more than 300,000 independent insurance agents in the United States. There are about 200 members of the American Society of Golf Course Architects. But there is only one Pete Dye.

It was the eighteenth-century novelist George Eliot who said, "It's never too late to be who you might have been." Pete Dye may never have read Eliot's better-known novels, but he has been living her credo since the day he gave up the insurance business forever and turned his full attention to golf course design. Here's the Cliffs Notes version of how it all transpired:

There are two major reasons why Pete Dye became a household name in golf. The first was being born the son of Paul "Pink" Dye, in 1925. The second was meeting and marrying Alice O'Neal.

Pete's work ethic likely came from his father. Nicknamed Pink because of the shock of red hair he sported in his youth, he was a politician, bar owner, insurance agent, and postmaster in Pete's hometown of Urbana, Ohio. He also loved golf, and had his son swinging a cut-down club at age five.

"The game was born and bred into me by my dad," recalls the architect, who also served as an occasional caddy for his mother, Elizabeth. "And I've always been grateful for his choice of sport."

While Pink Dye won the club championship at Urbana Country Club several times in the early 1930s, his playing record was eclipsed by his son. Pete eventually won the Ohio High School Championship, captained the golf team at Rollins College, won the Indiana State Amateur, played in a U.S. Open, several U.S. Amateurs, and, most important at least from an architectural standpoint, played in the British Amateur. But, beyond the love of playing the game, his father also sparked in Pete an interest in golf course maintenance and construction.

Pink Dye, tired of traveling to outlying courses in the surrounding communities, convinced his wife to donate 60 acres of farmland to the cause. He could not enlist the services of a name architect, so in 1922, three years before his namesake son was born, he designed and constructed the Urbana Country Club. (Note: The given name of the man we know today as Pete Dye is actually Paul, after his dad. But to distinguish the two generations, the son was called by his initials. P.D. morphed to Pede, which eventually became Pete.)

It took almost a year for Pink and his makeshift construction crew to rough out six holes. Three more were added several years later. As a youngster, Pete helped with routine maintenance like mowing greens and running sprinklers.

Pete with Jack Nicklaus

When World War II broke out and all the able-bodied Urbana men went off to war, the fifteen-year-old took over the maintenance of the golf course entirely.

In his youth, accompanied by his dad, Pete played some of the finest courses in his home state, all within reasonable driving distance. These included Scioto in Columbus, Cincinnati's Camargo Club, and Inverness in Toledo. But his golfer's education went to a whole new level during his military service. He won the base championship and tended the golf course at Georgia's Fort Benning. Then, when he was stationed at Fort Bragg in North Carolina as a member of the Army Paratroops 82nd Airborne Division, he was just forty miles from Pinehurst. Despite his military duties, he found time to play its famed Number 2 course regularly. Speaking of the Donald Ross masterpiece, the designer-to-be has said, "Pinehurst Number 2 impressed me more than any other golf course I had ever seen."

Pete Dye met his future wife at Rollins College in 1946. Alice O'Neal was a fine player then, and became a great player in the ensuing decades. Her trophy case includes nine Indiana Women's Amateur titles, eleven Indianapolis City Championships, the Women's Eastern, the North and South, and a pair of USGA Senior Amateur Championships, among many other significant titles, both individual and team. Though Alice became instrumental in her husband's architectural career, Pete did not mind getting the lion's share of the credit. "Hell no," he once told a reporter, only half-jokingly. "I played second fiddle to Alice for so many years in Indianapolis, it's finally my turn!"

It was 1955, five years into their marriage, when Pete first entertained the idea of getting into golf course design. Timing-wise, it was a curious decision. From the early 1930s until the mid-1950s, course closures outnumbered openings by a ratio of 3 to 1. The stock market crash, the ensuing Depression, bank foreclosures, World War II, and the seizure of golf properties to make way for the burgeoning interstate highway system all contributed to the marked attrition of courses nationwide. Pete was a successful insurance agent in Indianapolis at the time, having followed Alice into the field. The Dyes had parlayed their local golf prominence into a thriving insurance business. But despite his membership in the million-dollar roundtable, it was his membership at the Country Club of Indianapolis that veered him into an entirely different direction.

Pete began using the club grounds as a living laboratory. There were serious maintenance issues at the club, and as an enthusiastic greens committee chairman, he dove into the job full force. He transplanted saplings after disease killed off the elm trees. He tinkered with bunkers and added curvature to fairway mowing patterns. His interest piqued, he started commuting to classes at the Purdue University School of Agronomy, where he learned about grasses, turf, pesticides, and fungicides. A little knowledge can be a dangerous thing. Pete managed to kill what little grass there was on some of his club's fairways. He built a "lifetime" bridge that collapsed in the first spring rain. To his surprise, he was never kicked out of the club or even removed as head of the committee, and with the encouragement of his wife, he remained undaunted as he attempted to forge a new career.

El Dorado in Indianapolis was Pete and Alice's first official design, which was a real mom-and-pop shop. They had to hand-mix the soil, sand, and peat mixture for the USGA-specified greens in a local barn. They grew bent grass in their yard, bought a sod-cutter, and transported sections to the course in the trunk of their Oldsmobile. The nine-hole course, which is now an eighteen-hole facility known as Dye's Walk, opened in 1961. Pete's penchant for making a golfer sweat was evident right from the beginning. Richard Tufts, friend to the Dyes and a former USGA president, wrote them with some helpful advice. "I certainly enjoyed looking at your routing, but don't you think crossing the creek *thirteen* times in nine holes is a bit much?"

The Dyes built their first eighteen-hole course a year later in Indianapolis. It was named Heather Hills and eventually renamed Maple Creek. More work followed, most of it on a local level. The architect wondered whether his amateur status as a golfer would be affected by his new profession, but it was a moot point. As his design career flourished, the seven-days-a-week, in-the-trenches regimen made his brief foray into big-time amateur golf only a fond memory.

There was one notable exception. When thirty-eight-year-old Pete Dye qualified for the 1963 British Amateur, he and Alice seized the opportunity to visit the great courses of Scotland. He regretted his impetuous disparagement of the Old Course at St. Andrews, after a single round, as a "goat ranch." Seven rounds later, thanks to his strong showing in the event, he realized it was one of the world's great tracks. The Dyes used this inaugural overseas jaunt to study and play more than thirty Scottish classics. This seminal visit helped clarify and articulate their vision of vibrantly memorable golf course designs.

They were particularly impressed by the Old Course, Turnberry, Prestwick, Carnoustie, Royal Dornoch, Muirfield, Troon, Nairn, Gullane, Western Gailes, and North Berwick. They came back to the Midwest eager to build courses with small greens and wide, undulating fairways. They wanted to incorporate pot bunkers, railroad ties, and blind holes into their work, experiment with contrasting grass mixes, and add gorselike vegetation to frame fairways.

It's probably no coincidence that Pete Dye's inaugural masterpiece, Crooked Stick in Carmel, Indiana, was the first course he designed after his initial foray to the British Isles. Up to that point, Dye had produced ten courses and made revisions on a dozen others. But Crooked Stick, which the Dyes refer to as their "firstborn," truly put Pete on the map. He got on a roll thereafter, creating The Golf Club in New Albany, Ohio, and Harbour Town Golf Links on Hilton Head Island in short order. All three courses remain on most worldwide Top 100 lists.

One triumph followed another, usually with Alice, who became known as "the patron saint of forward tees," by his side, offering valuable input. It's been said that despite the fact she was never seen lifting a shovel or commanding a bulldozer, nobody had more influence on the architectural career of Pete Dye.

Teeth of the Dog in the Dominican Republic led to Oak Tree in Oklahoma. The Stadium Course at TPC Sawgrass near Jacksonville, Florida, was followed by the Stadium Course at PGA West in Palm Springs, California. Then it was Blackwolf Run in Wisconsin, the Honors Course in Tennessee, the Ocean Course on Kiawah Island, Brickyard Crossing in his adopted hometown of Indianapolis, West Virginia's Pete Dye

Alice and Pete Dye

Golf Club, Whistling Straits back in Wisconsin, and dozens upon dozens of others.

The number of individuals who worked with or for the Dyes isn't quite as long as a roll call of the hundred-plus golf courses they've created, but it's close. Over their long careers, the Dyes hired, employed, mentored, and collaborated with dozens of apprentices who eventually came to architectural prominence themselves. These include Jack Nicklaus, Greg Norman, Jason McCoy, Bobby Weed, Bill Coore, Tim Liddy, Lee Schmidt, Brian Curley, Tom Doak, John Harbotte, Scott Sherman, Jeff Potts, and Rod Whitman, among others. Almost all are members of the American Society of Golf Course Architects, whose august roster also includes Pete and Alice's two sons, Perry and P.B. The brothers Dye were born into and reared in the game much like their parents. They were picking up rocks as toddlers, riding on earth-moving equipment at the same age other kids were riding their bikes. Either individually or in tandem with their parents, Perry and P.B. have created more than a hundred courses themselves. Add in Pete's brother, Roy Dye, who passed away in the mid 1990s, and Roy's children, Andy, Matt, and Cynthia, and the list of Dye designs spreads to all corners of the globe.

Pete's courses will live on for generations, challenging, in-triguing, befuddling, exasperating, and delighting golfers long after he himself is gone. But those who've known, worked with, and befriended the man throughout his career are quick to point out that Pete Dye is as unique as the courses he's produced. Forever the iconoclast, it's no wonder his resume is chock-full of innovative course designs. Consider the fact that, despite his numerous successes and worldwide fame,

his entire staff consists of two employees—Diane Darsch in Florida and Shannon Meeks in Indiana—to help manage the business. He does not do contracts. A handshake is good enough for Pete. He's not one for detailed blueprints or archi-tectural drawings. His modus operandi is to walk and walk the land, then walk some more, until a vision of a golf course, a routing plan, forms in his incredibly fertile imagination.

It was Ben Hogan who, when asked about his success, alluded to a ceaseless practice regimen. He said famously: "The secret is in the dirt." Same with Pete Dye. He'd roust his crew before the rooster crowed, using one of his favorite expressions: "You can't build a golf course from bed." He and his co-designers would take to the field before first light, preceding eighteen-, sometimes twenty-hour days, whether coaxing a green-grass playing field out of impenetrable swampland, thick forest, dense jungle, worthless scrubland, rocky hillsides, barren desert, or fallow farmland.

Arnold Palmer once remarked: "What other people may find in poetry or art museums, I find in the flight of a good drive."

If the reader agrees with Palmer's sentiment, and sees the game itself and the venues on which it's contested as an art form, then golfers everywhere owe a debt of gratitude to Pete Dye. Because this former "insurance huckster," as he was once affectionately lampooned by the grateful membership of Crooked Stick Golf Club, metamorphosed into one of the most ingenious, innovative, and visionary course designers of the modern era. Pete Dye, Alice, and the rest of their family have bequeathed us hundreds of dazzling masterpieces on which to revel in the game.

Urbana Country Club

Designed by Paul Francis "Pink" Dye, with nine holes added by P.B. Dye

It is remarkable how life so often turns on a whim, a chance encounter, a happenstance. If it was not for a timely automobile breakdown some ninety years ago, there would probably be no such thing as a Pete Dye golf course.

"My dad had never played golf before," Pete explains. "Several years before I was born, his automobile broke down on the old Federal Highway Number 40 when he was returning from Washington, D.C., to our hometown of Urbana, Ohio. The breakdown occurred in Farmington, Pennsylvania, near a historic hotel called the Summit Inn Resort. He stayed overnight while repairs were made, hit some golf balls, and played nine holes for the first time. He was hooked!"

"Pink" Dye quickly decided a course was needed in Urbana, and procured 60-odd acres from his in-laws for construction. "My mother's side was the Johnson family," Pete continues. "They had about a thousand acres, and they gave dad some hilly, difficult acreage that couldn't be cultivated as farmland." Thus began a tradition of Dye architects making do with exceedingly difficult terrain.

"My dad got a small group of investors together, sought out the great architect Donald Ross, who was working nearby in Ohio at the time for some advice, and started to work building his own course. It was six holes to begin with, and then three more were added the next year. I came into the world a few years after that, and as a boy, began working on that golf course, cutting greens, watering, and helping with routine maintenance from as far back as I can remember."

The course itself is partially wooded, surrounded by cornfields. It features some long-range views amid its moderate elevation changes, with a couple of farm ponds and a few adjacent farmhouses. There are some uphill blind shots, small greens canted from back to front, and no shortage of sidehill or uneven lies. Ohio has long been a golf-rich state, with superior venues like Scioto, Camargo, Firestone, Inverness, Muirfield Village, and the Pete Dye–designed Golf Club, to name but half a dozen. Among these bigger names, the rural qualities of the Urbana Country Club, particularly after its 1993 expansion, qualify it as one of the state's hidden gems.

"When my ninety-four-year-old grandmother told me to finish the golf course that grandfather started, that was built all those years prior on her family's land, all I could say was, "Yes ma'am, I'm ready," recalls P.B. Dye, who undertook the task some seventy years after the original course was built. Working from a course routing produced by his late uncle Roy, Pete's brother, P.B. made certain to emulate the pushed-up greens that his grandfather had originally built, though little other dirt was moved in construction. "I could live anywhere I like," P.B. continues, "but I choose to make my summer home in a log cabin next to the second tee of this golf course. That's how much it means to me."

Andy Doss, like his first cousin P.B., is a grandson of course creator Pink Dye. He is also Pete's nephew and a former president of the Urbana Country Club. "Our expansion budget was tight, so we knocked down the necessary trees, opted for single-line irrigation, required minimal drainage because there was so little earth moved, and tried to make the addition fit in seamlessly with the original course," says Doss, who runs the in-town insurance firm that was begun by his great-grandfather in 1893. He relays an anecdote that paints a clear picture of the rural sensibility of the golf course and the small town of 11,000, located midway between Dayton and Columbus in central Ohio. "When the additional nine holes were built, P.B. wanted to construct dirt greens like our grandfather did, instead of modern sand greens. We got the dirt from a local potato farmer, and when the bent grass started to come up, so did a few potato sprouts!"

"It's a pleasant Midwestern golf course, no frills," says Perry Dye. "But the fact that my grandfather insisted on building a golf course in a town that at the time only had 6,000 residents, with maybe six golfers, is really something. And now here we are, nearly a century later, with his descendants building courses all over the world."

The original and indigenous Dye design, Urbana Country Club is woven into the fabric of the community, and has been a simple and straightforward place to enjoy the game since shortly after Pink Dye turned his first shovelful of earth back in 1922. "It's where the story really begins," says Pete Dye, ostensibly referring to his fifty-year career as a course designer, but at the same time, to the celebration of his remarkable career that follows.

Opposite: 15th hole (top) and 8th hole

played downhill, and that is one of the philosophies I maintain today in my work. If you're playing downhill, you see more of the golf you are playing. Visually, it has a greater impact on the game.

Pete Dye has had a tremendous impact not only on me, but on the world of course design. He has always been very innovative and unafraid to try things in his work. He brought back from Scotland many elements that represented his interpretation of what Scotland and its old-style golf courses looked like. He then took those elements and applied them—rightly or wrongly, however you might view it in this very subjective form of art—to a piece of ground in the United States. Frankly, I like Pete's work; I like it a lot. Pete is the consummate artist, and I respect that. He is superbly talented at developing both a strategic and aesthetic vision of a golf course.

What Pete Dye has done for the game of golf is something for which we should all be thankful. He changed the way we think about golf course design, and how design works. And he did it for one simple reason: He wanted to design good golf courses, period. He did it for the love of the game, not for monetary reasons. But the irony is that because of the attention that Pete Dye–designed courses have brought to the game, there are lots of people who are now able to make a living at golf course design. Me included.

It's no easy task to chronicle the highlights of a career as widespread and successful as Pete Dye's. But Joel Zuckerman has done a wonderful job of capturing some of the nuances of not just the courses themselves, but the people, the personalities, and the locations that make up the entire story. It's also interesting to see the selection of courses in the book produced by the next generation of Dye architects: Pete and Alice's two sons, and their nephews and niece. As someone whose own family is involved in the design business, I can appreciate that aspect of the book as much as anybody.

I have to chuckle that Pete contends it was I who brought serious name recognition to the art of golf course design. He would crack that even though he adored Pinehurst Number 2, played it constantly during his military days, and that it inspired him in his future career, he wouldn't have known if it was designed by Betsy Ross or Donald Ross. The reason it's ironic is because now golfers travel near and far to play Pete's courses.

Pete's hard-running hook always provided him with impressive distance off the tee, especially because he's so slightly built. Pete Dye the man never was imposing, physically. But Pete Dye the architect? As long as the game is played, he'll be considered a giant in the field.

Harbour Town Golf Links, 17th hole

Dye's Walk

With Alice Dye

"I started at the graveyard, and I never looked back." Sounds like some kind of hokey country and western song, but it's actually how Pete Dye has occasionally described how he and Alice's architectural career commenced. The first hole of the thousands he's created is 20-odd steps from an 1800s-era burial ground—just to the right of the first tee at what was then called El Dorado, for many years thereafter known as Royal Oak, and, after new ownership took over in late 2007, as Dye's Walk.

Trial and error. Pete Dye admits as much, reminiscing about he and his wife's first endeavor as course designers. After much effort, and a little bit of advertising, Indiana's "power golf couple" were hired to do a nine-hole layout south of Indianapolis, in the town of Greenwood. The operative numbers were 1959, and thirteen. The former refers to the year that El Dorado was begun. The latter refers to the number of times golfers were required to cross a diagonally positioned creek during the nine holes. So it's safe to say that Dye's demonic nature as a course designer never had to develop—it was there from the get-go.

"There were too many creek crossings," Dye admitted years later. "I also shouldn't have had the out-of-bounds markers on the right side of so many holes, because most golfers slice more than they hook." But his self-criticism might be unduly harsh—Pete and Alice also got many things right.

The Dye holes emphasize placement more than power, and are as fun and intriguing as they were when they were first built during the Kennedy years. All those creek crossings have mostly become ponds over time, and there are far fewer crossings than there were originally. But the cleverness of the routing, the holes lying intimately in the wooded valley, the differing shot shapes required to access the greens, are all present. As is variety. The two one-shot holes are 150 yards each, but one plays downhill while the other goes straight up. Not all is petite, either. The 440-yard 15th (originally the 6th) has a blind drive and approach, while the next is a brutish par-5, 565 yards and pond-fronted besides.

Local architect Gary Kern added the second nine in the mid-1970s. The actual Royal Oak that inspired the course's first renaming has died, but still stands as a stark aiming point on Kern's doglegging second hole. The next is severely uphill, narrow and tree-lined, one of the toughest par-3s in the region. But as solid as the Kern nine may be, it's literally the opening act. Dye's Walk's cachet is as Pete and Alice Dye's first-ever nine holes, and despite its golden anniversary status and overall lack of length, it still holds up remarkably well today.

"Owning Pete Dye's first golf course is like owning a vintage car, or maybe an original painting by a great artist," offers Rich Riley, who, along with partner Brian Benham, are the new principals.

Though they are veteran property investors, neither had been in the golf business previously. "We felt like our community needed this upgrade," states Benham, a native Indianan. "We feel that this club will become the premier private facility on the south side of Indianapolis. It's on a great piece of property, and absolutely beautiful."

The widening of State Highway 135 was probably the major reason precipitating Dye's return to the property after a decades-long absence. The road abuts the downhill, dogleg par-4, which was the first hole on his résumé. The hole now turns more severely to the left to accommodate the road widening, and several other of his original holes are being modified owing to that ripple effect. Far more noticeable is the spanking-new clubhouse, built after the modest original was bulldozed into the ground. "It's our passion to make this an important golf course," states Benham. "We will be improving the infrastructure, adding irrigation, and developing a facility that will do justice to this course's historical importance. We want to make a good golf course great."

A longtime member of the professional staff recalls a comical conversation he had with Pete Dye, who was readying to pay a long-overdue visit to his original stomping ground several months before the new ownership took over. The architect had an unusual request: "When I get down there, let's take a tour. But keep me away from sharp objects. I might be inclined to hurt myself after I see what I concocted there all those years ago."

No worries, Pete. Your harsh self-assessment is amusing, but off the mark. To you it might be El Dorado, and many others think of it as Royal Oak. But a half-century after you walked downhill from that graveyard, and in so doing embarked on one of the most notable careers in the history of golf course design, all will soon know this first course as Dye's Walk, a name deserving of its creator. "There are a hundred Pete Dye designs, at the minimum," says Rich Riley. "But there is only one that was first."

Pete Dye's a genius, and Alice Dye, who has been like a second mother to me over the years, is a wonderful balance point and sounding board. Not just in golf course design, but in business and in life. Alice has been the stability for them, and keeps Pete organized—and believe me, he needs it! He has this amazing ability to visualize golf holes before they exist, and sometimes the reality of day-to-day life can interfere with his work. That's part of the reason that Alice is so key to the equation.

Carol Semple Thomson, *two-time Curtis Cup Captain; seven-time USGA champion; twelve-time Curtis Cup team member*

16th hole

Top: 13th hole
Bottom: 17th hole

Maple Creek Country Club

With Alice Dye

As the saying goes, you never forget your first.

Though they went on to design courses practically all over creation, Pete and Alice Dye's first eighteen-hole effort was an unpretentious property on the east side of Indianapolis. Christened Heather Hills at inception, the course that was renamed Maple Creek still entices today, nearly fifty years after opening. It was and remains a modest place: 80 acres to start (since expanded to 120), built quickly within the confines of an $80,000 budget, the Dyes earning one-tenth of that figure as their design fee.

By modern standards, the course is of modest dimensions, not even 6,700 yards from the tips—but gargantuan compared to opening day, when it topped out at little more than 6,000 yards. But there's more to the story, and this intriguing golf course, than the numbers on the scorecard.

Seven words sum up the difficulty: Grassy Creek, overhanging trees, single-file fairways. The first runs through the initial ten holes, sometimes fronting the green, sometimes encroaching laterally. The multitude of hardwoods necessitates all manner of bending tee shots that must curve around the tree canopies—wayward pellets will come crashing to a halt among fluttering leaves. The last scorecard indignity is a direct result of its immediate predecessor: Those trees make narrow landing zones appear skinnier still.

Legend has it that volatile coaching icon Bobby Knight, the basketball genius and possibly the most famous chair-thrower ever to come out of Indiana, pitched a fit when he couldn't pitch his ball to safety from the confines of Grassy Creek's petite but perilous 4th hole. Most golfers are more placid than the fiery coach, but innocent-looking, seemingly guileless Maple Creek will, on regular occasions, give even the most tranquil golfer something to steam about.

The inward nine, which encircles the first nine in clockwise fashion on the property's outskirts, is much longer, and thankfully much wider. The claustrophobia abates, but a firmer grip on the whipping stick is a necessity. The front side par-4s barely average 360 yards, while the half-dozen heading for home average about 400 yards each. Currently, there's almost a 500-yard disparity between the two nines, though the addition of a front-side par-5 and the substitution of a back-side par-4 with a one-shot hole will bring this inequality back into balance.

Above: 11th hole
Right: 4th hole

In many ways, Maple Creek looks and plays much older than it really is. It hearkens back to the game's so-called Golden Age of architecture, the 1920s and 1930s, when Donald Ross, A.W. Tillinghast, Alister Mackenzie, Charles Blair Macdonald, and Seth Raynor were creating some of the finest courses the game has ever known. The Dyes' first full-length effort features small tees and small greens. Both cart paths and bunkers intrude minimally, and with little lasting effect. Housing is sparse, and confined mostly to the property's eastern portion. A single descriptive might well be "intimate," and that's exactly the type of attitude owner Dave Bego is trying to retain.

Bego grew up around the game at Maple Creek. Now he's a successful area businessman who has spent time as both club president and board member. He bought the club when it was headed into the clutches of a housing developer in 2006, and is determined not only to protect fond memories of his youth,

but to protect the legacy of the first full-length Dye golf course. "It would be criminal to allow his inaugural eighteen holes to be plowed under. Pete will stand the test of time as one of the game's great designers."

The architect himself thinks the course has stood the test of time. The new owner and the old master were touring the property together by golf cart shortly after Bego's tenure began, contemplating course changes and refinements. There was a noticeable gleam in Dye's eye as he inspected his handiwork so many long years after his initial effort. "He didn't say it in so many words, but I got the feeling that Pete was pretty proud of how he began his career, before he developed his world view, before he got famous, before he started working for billionaires and building some of golf's most famous courses. Indianapolis is the heartland of America. And around here, we like to think that Maple Creek is the heartland of Indianapolis golf."

Crooked Stick Golf Club

With Alice Dye

It all depends on whether or not you are a Hoosier.

For avid PGA Tour fans outside Indiana, the name "Crooked Stick" likely conjures images of mullet-headed, mile-long John Daly laying waste to the field at the 1991 PGA Championship. Long John began the week as the ninth alternate, got the eleventh-hour call, drove all night from his Arkansas home, and, without benefit of a practice round, won the tournament and burst into the nation's golf consciousness.

However, for those golf aficionados within the state borders, Crooked Stick is one of Indiana's premier courses, one of its most prestigious private clubs and truly the course where Pete Dye began to metamorphose into PETE DYE.

Assuredly, with no disrespect to eldest son Perry, Pete and Alice refer to Crooked Stick as their firstborn—despite the fact they had built some ten other courses previously. Because it was Crooked Stick where the Dyes first did it all—located the land (a 400-acre cornfield about fifteen miles north of downtown), purchased the option on the acreage, raised the money, drew the routing, and completed construction.

The resolution printed below was presented to Pete after he relinquished the presidency of the club five years after it was formed. Its eloquence goes well beyond a description of the history of Crooked Stick. The sentiments were articulated on the last day of 1969 and are now some forty years old, but in the satirically insightful manner in which the Dye style of architecture is described, they remain timeless.

WHEREAS, there was once a time when CROOKED STICK GOLF CLUB was merely a gleam in the eye of PETE DYE, a life insurance huckster, who could do a thing or two with a crooked stick and who dreamed of becoming a golf course architect;

WHEREAS, there was another time when PETE DYE'S negotiating skills (and ability to consume mass quantities of elderberry wine) enabled him to cozen the owners of about 400 acres of Hamilton County farmland out of their fields and streams, which they let him steal from them at not more than twice what the ground was worth;

WHEREAS, there was still another time when PETE DYE'S irresistible salesmanship conned a group of assorted golf nuts, with more enthusiasm than good sense, into putting up the funds (somewhat less than what was actually needed, but somewhat more than they could actually afford) to pay for the land and build thereon a golf course;

WHEREAS, there was still another time, during a walk in the woods near the clubhouse site, when PETE DYE is reputed to have picked up a gnarled old stick which gave CROOKED STICK GOLF CLUB its name;

WHEREAS, there was still a later time (interminable, so it seemed) when flatlands became rolling hills, and creek beds became lakes, and little swales became bottomless pits, and open glades appeared on the edge of the forest, and, overlooking it all in his old rubber boots, stood its creator, PETE DYE, surveying the scene with baleful eye, like a condor on a dead limb;

WHEREAS, one season followed another, and still another, until one day the wild land, so suitable for falconry, turned green, and suddenly there was a golf course unlike any seen before or likely ever to be seen again;

WHEREAS, there were field holes without fairways; there were water holes without land; there were holes with streams so

6th hole

fiendishly criss-crossed that a ball missing the first criss would surely catch the second cross, or (if exceptionally well struck) the third criss; there were some great sand traps like the Gobi Desert, and many small ones scattered about like buckshot; there were some greens so large as to require putting with a full backswing; others so small as to leave no room for the hole; one green, requiring a wedge shot over a trap at its midpoint; some greens so contoured as to roll in two directions at once, and still other greens so buried in the woods as to be invisible from any direction;

WHEREAS, there were tees marked with sections of railroad track, which gave golfers the sensation of driving from a grade crossing with a train coming; there were banks lined with utility poles which gave golfers an electric shock as they watched their drives strike the poles and ricochet thirty feet into the water; and

there were fairways so hard to find that they were marked with piles of stones evidently stolen from the graves of lost golfers;

WHEREAS, there were shots to be played from beneath the feet and other shots from over the head and the eighth hole from the back tee could best be played by a golfer on his knees; and

WHEREAS, there has come a time at last when the man responsible for this green monster, the first Club president and a charter member of the board of directors, must step down from his throne;

NOW, THEREFORE, BE IT RESOLVED by the board of directors of CROOKED STICK GOLF CLUB, speaking for itself and for all of the members, without a dissenting vote or a dry eye, that words are inadequate to describe our gratitude to our founder, PETE DYE, who has done so much to so few with so little provocation.

18th hole

9th hole

Shortly after I became head pro at Crooked Stick in the early 1980s, Pete added a long bunker to the left of the second fairway and then removed a massive cherry tree that was in the same general area. We walked into the grill room shortly thereafter, and one of the club's original members was absolutely incensed. He snarled at Pete, "It took God 200 years to grow that tree, and you cut it down in ten minutes!" I slowly backed away, not knowing what would happen next. But Pete just said, "You're dead wrong. It took me nearly half-an-hour to cut it down. That tree was a healthy son-of-a-bitch." His decision to cut it down made sense, because without the tree as an aiming point, the hole became much tougher and the bunker became that much more of a factor.

In the mid-1980s, Pete was going to renovate a couple of bunkers on the golf course, one on the front side and one on the back. He approached the board of directors and asked them whether they preferred sand, water, or grass within the hazard. They debated the issue, and decided they wanted grass in one and sand in the other. While they were considering what to do, Pete went ahead and turned them both into water hazards. I guess that shows you what he really thinks about boards of directors. Personally, I don't care what he does to Crooked Stick—as long as it's Pete Dye himself who's making the changes.

Jim Ferriel, *longtime head professional, Crooked Stick Golf Club*

Call it progress. The federal government decided to put a freeway smack through the middle of the Des Moines Country Club in 1966, and greener pastures had to be found elsewhere. When it came time to move the club from downtown, the leadership had the prescience to purchase 475 acres some ten miles west of the city, with plenty of breathing room. They also had the foresight to hire an up-and-comer named Pete Dye, a fellow Midwesterner, to build a pair of courses. Both decisions have served the club well.

Common perception among outsiders might be that Iowa is as flat as a game board. But the bluffs that frame the Mississippi and Missouri rivers on the eastern and western borders of the state provide some prominent topographical changes. The same holds true at the Des Moines Country Club, where rolling hills, several with a hundred feet of elevation change, and, perhaps most notably, rolling, undulating greens serve as the best defense against par. The song tells us that it's Oklahoma where the wind comes sweeping down the plain. But Iowa can blow a breeze as well, and when the wind whips across the gently sloping fairways, Des Moines can be an awfully tough track.

The USGA was duly impressed with the caliber and inherent challenge of the courses, not to mention the capacious infrastructure, and rewarded the club with the 1999 U.S. Senior Open. They were rewarded in turn. That championship was one of the best-attended events in USGA history, with more than 250,000 attendees.

"Let me tell you how tough the golf course was," recalls Dave Eichelberger, whose victory at that Senior Open is the highlight of a professional résumé that included four wins on the PGA Tour and six on the Champions Tour. "I didn't break 80 in any of the practice rounds prior to the tournament. It was exceptionally hot that week, and the course played very long. The reason I won the event comes down to the fact that I managed to negotiate those roller-coaster greens without a single three-putt all week. I think I was the only player in the field who could make that claim," explains the only player in the field who came home with the trophy. "I was anticipating a typical Pete Dye design, with railroad ties, pot bunkers,

maybe an island green. But I was pleased to see a traditional, parkland-style course, albeit with extremely tough greens."

There is no housing presence at the Des Moines Country Club, though several back-nine holes on the South Course abut Route 80, one of the nation's main east-west conduits, which runs in a mostly straight line from the George Washington Bridge in New York City to the Golden Gate Bridge in San Francisco.

The USGA combined the courses for the big event, using the front nine of the south and back nine of the north for their championship test. Ironically, these were the original eighteen holes on the property. When Pete Dye came on the scene in the late 1960s, the club could only afford to have a single course built. Dye took the choicest of its land and routed the golf course close by the majority of its lakes and streams. A year or so later, the club had the financial wherewithal to pay for the second course. Dye returned, added the new nines to the north and south of his inaugural routing, and split the thirty-six holes into what are now known as the North and South Courses. Interestingly, the members play both courses to a par of 73, as there is one extra par-5 and one less par-4 on both the North and South Courses.

Whatever reputation Iowa may enjoy on the international golf stage is probably as the birthplace of giant-killers. It was little-known Jack Fleck, born and raised in Bettendorf and, ironically, a former assistant pro at the mid-century iteration of the Des Moines Country Club, who beat none other than Ben Hogan in the 1955 U.S. Open. His playoff victory over the man he idolized denied Hogan his fifth Open title. More than fifty years later, Iowa City–born Zach Johnson, at the time an up-and-coming but little-known Tour pro, denied Tiger Woods his fifth green jacket when he captured the 2007 Masters.

Fleck and Johnson may be giant-killers, but within their home state's borders it's the Des Moines Country Club that's the colossus. It reigns supreme by virtue of its thirty-six holes, USGA pedigree, and abiding popularity within the capital city. And also because of the course architect who provided them their playing fields—one of the true giants in the game.

Top: North Course, 10th hole
Right: South Course, 4th hole

Opposite, top: North Course, 14th hole
Opposite, bottom: North Course, 12th hole

South course, 1st hole

The Golf Club

With Alice Dye

A great golf course stands on its own merits, but a colorful, hard-to-forget name never hurts. Pete Dye has designed courses that were christened with some of the most memorable names in the game. Among others, there's Whistling Straits, the Honors Course, Crooked Stick, Firethorn, and perhaps the greatest name in golf-dom: Teeth of the Dog.

And sometimes a very simple name will suffice, in golf and beyond. The moniker of an under-the-radar but superb Montana ski hill has been revamped to a snazzier version, but for the first sixty years of the resort's existence, it was known merely as Big Mountain. One of the most enduring rock groups of the 1960s and 1970s was known in straightforward fashion as The Band. And what is perhaps Pete Dye's least-known great golf course, situated on nearly 500 acres of rolling farmland outside Columbus, Ohio, is known very simply as The Golf Club.

Fred Jones, who passed away in 1974, was the founder and visionary behind The Golf Club. "He was a dictator, a lovable dictator," recalls Alice Dye fondly. "But the best golf clubs in the world are run by dictators." According to longtime members of the professional staff, Jones got the impetus to build his ultraprivate retreat after being soured by the goings-on at his in-town country club. He had gone to the Columbus Country Club to play golf, only to find out the course had been taken over temporarily by an outside tournament. Making alternate plans to play some cards in the 19th hole, he was told the entire facility was off-limits to members that day. He expressed his displeasure, someone suggested that perhaps he should build his own club, and Jones replied, "That's exactly what I'm going to do."

That's why there are not only no outside tournaments at The Golf Club, but precious few inside tournaments. No club championship, superintendent's revenge, fall frolic, etc. There's a two-day member-guest and a one-day member-guest. It's the type of club where, after looking out his office window on a beautiful afternoon for golf, a member can arrive on the bucolic grounds and be assured that the course is open, available, and ready for play virtually every day of the season.

The similarities in feel between The Golf Club and Chattanooga's Honors Course—another top-notch private enclave in the Dye oeuvre—are palpable. Not so much in the era in which they were created (1960s versus 1980s) or in the making (there was very little earth moved at The Golf Club, while Dye practically moved heaven and earth, not to mention a million tons of boulders, to build the Honors in Tennessee). The clubs are similar in that both are large, beautiful, and

16th hole

unsullied tracts of land. Both offer generous driving corridors that tighten as a player moves toward the green. Perhaps most important, each offers a sense of quietude, a feeling of remove and seclusion that is generally the province of high-end private clubs deep within the confines of the countryside, untarnished by perimeter housing, with modest membership rolls and limited play. It's a series of combined factors that's hard to engineer, but when it's done properly, it affords some of the finest ambience in the game.

Opposite: 18th hole

Left: 11th hole
Below: 13th hole

Acres of tall fescue, large bunkers throughout, and the insidious presence of Blacklick Creek on four different holes are the main challenges at The Golf Club. The first two-thirds of the course is predominantly tree-lined corridors, while the final six holes widen out into a series of fields harking back to the farmland roots of the property. The designer considers the design to be "Old English" in style, with a variety of different grasses and fescues combining to offer a rugged Scottish-English appearance.

The par-3 3rd hole showcases the combination of pastoral setting and Dye's wicked genius that makes The Golf Club such an engaging test of the game. From the tee, it looks like a relatively straightforward shot, albeit one with a forced carry over a fronting pond. But behind the green are a series of five separate bunkers, shored up with railroad ties, the deepest of which is a full eight feet below the green. It's the last place a golfer wants to be, particularly with the prospect of blasting over the wall, only to have the ball carry into the greenside pond.

It's amazing to consider how avant-garde Dye's design was at its late-1960s inception. From the get-go, the course was nearly 7,300 yards long. There are a half-dozen par-4s that stretch from nearly 450 yards and well beyond. One of the four par-5s is just shy of, another well over, 600 yards in length. Taking into account what is now considered the almost primitive equipment of that bygone era, where neither agronomy nor player conditioning were of the standard set today, the foresight Dye showed is remarkable. In more than forty years of existence, the course hasn't had to be lengthened appreciably.

One bit of trivia in conclusion. At the turn, many players opt for a bag of beef jerky that is made fresh regularly by the club's longtime chef. A few bites, and one's affinity for packaged, store-bought jerky will wane. This signature snack is distinctive, of enduring quality, and hard to forget. Just like a round at The Golf Club itself.

Delray Dunes Golf & Country Club

With Alice Dye

Laurie Hammer was an All-American golfer at the University of Florida and then shortly thereafter a winner on the PGA Tour. But in the 1960s, professional purses were nickels-on-the-dollar compared to the Tiger Era, where private air travel has become the standard and making a dozen-and-a-half cuts per season is practically a seven-figure income guarantee.

So in 1969, when he was offered the inaugural head pro position at Delray Dunes in the south Florida town of Boynton Beach, Hammer opted for the stability of the club pro life. He and his wife, Marlene, built a home near the first tee and began raising their family. They live there still, Marlene working in the shop and Laurie as PGA Master Professional, the first and only director of golf the club has ever known. "The Hammers are just wonderful people," says Bob Murphy, the former U.S. Amateur champion who also amassed sixteen total victories on the PGA and Champions Tours. "We've lived next door to each other for forty-odd years, so that pretty much sums things up."

However, Laurie is still a relative newcomer, at least compared to Pete Dye, the Delray Dunes designer, who beat Laurie to town by better than thirty years.

Pete Dye attended elementary school in Delray Beach, and his education as an architect continued there decades later, when he envisioned and constructed this fine-but-not-fancy golf course. It's a case of continuing education as, even into his 80s, Dye fiddles with the design features on an annual basis, adding or removing trees and mounds, changing the contour of a green, reconfiguring a hole, putting in a bunker. Is it fair to call Delray Dunes the Dye equivalent of Donald Ross's Pinehurst #2, the magnum opus with which the legendary Scot never grew tired of tinkering? Probably not, since there are dozens of Dye designs far more famous than Delray Dunes. But while Pete Dye might never reveal which of his many courses is closest to his heart, it's an absolute fact that Delray Dunes is closest to his home in nearby Gulfstream, Florida, and that's got to count for something.

The course measures 6,600 yards from the back tees, but this par-71 is a challenge for any level of proficiency. Holes are long and short, bend left and right; greens are both elevated and at fairway level. For the less-accomplished player, there are few forced carries, and bouncing the ball onto at least one side of the putting surface is an option on every hole.

While Delray Dunes is a delight to play, with generous housing setbacks, vividly framed holes, and little encroaching water, a large part of the appeal is the club itself, a perfect complement to the playing fields.

When I first met Mr. Dye, he wanted to show me his plans for redoing the par-5 4th hole at our course. He didn't have a sketch or blueprint. Instead, he lay down sideways in the fairway bunker on the hole, and while his elbow, hip, and feet were in the sand, he started tracing the hole with his index finger. Afterward, he got up and brushed himself off. I was so amazed to see a world-famous, eighty-year-old man lie down in the sand like that, I forgot to remind him to rake the bunker once he got out. I thanked him for his time, and then raked it myself.

David Tandy, *head superintendent, Delray Dunes Golf & CountryClub*

Right: 4th hole
Below: 18th hole

8th hole

Here golf is the ultimate arbiter. The clubhouse is pleasant, but not opulent by any stretch. The membership is comprised of golf lovers, period, and the bank president is happy to play alongside the bank teller, provided all handicaps are aboveboard.

In golf-soaked Palm Beach County, where hopeful players at other private clubs need to queue up for tee times, Delray Dunes is blessed with a wholly different protocol. Members show up, pair up, and divvy up, no tee times required. A midweek afternoon shotgun is more like a popgun, so mellow is the vibe. It's a club where the love of the game is paramount.

"We're lucky to have such a close association with Pete and Alice Dye," says Laurie Hammer. "They've been very involved with the club from the beginning. The Dyes are unassuming, fun-loving people, and so are the members of Delray Dunes. I think that's one of the reasons we've all gotten along so well over the years."

The golf course is constantly evolving. It was unveiled in 1969 and redone in 1977, but those were just the major makeovers. Other changes result from Dye's evolving ideas,

the storms passing through the region that denude or remove trees, and utilitarian concerns like expanding the driving range or adding a short game area. Even second- and third-generation members admit the course not only plays differently round-to-round but is also markedly different year to year.

This is an early Dye design. There are no *Star Wars*–style humps and hollows, no railroad ties, no severe contours. It's gentle, with broad-shouldered fairways leading to medium-size greens. While many of the front-side holes offer isolated fairways, midway through the inward nine the course becomes a parkland, with numerous fairways visible at once.

"Both Alice and I have a special feeling for Delray Dunes, the first course I ever designed in Florida," says Pete. "I'm always interested in what's going on over there. I guess that's why I'm always stopping by, offering suggestions, and making improvements. I want the course to be the best it can be, and it's a labor of love for me to continue refining it."

And the affection Pete showers on the golf course is returned in kind by the members, many of whom are proud to call the famed designer their friend and neighbor.

Harbour Town Golf Links

With Alice Dye, in consultation with Jack Nicklaus

He's designed well over 2,000 golf holes in his extraordinary career, but it's safe to say that the final hole at Harbour Town Golf Links, at the southern terminus of Hilton Head Island, South Carolina, is among the two or three most recognizable in the Dye oeuvre. The choppy waters of Calibogue Sound lurk to the player's left, waving marsh grasses fronting the tee box wreak havoc with wayward drives, and the candy-striped lighthouse stands sentinel behind the green, a clear target for both drive and approach. It's an epic conclusion to one of the most beguiling courses in the modern game.

"It's one of the most innovative and revolutionary designs in the history of golf architecture," says Brad Klein of *Golfweek* magazine. "It's certainly one of the ten most important courses in terms of design, because Pete Dye built all

sorts of great contour, shape, form, and strategy into a dead-level site that was really quite boring to begin with. Instead of moving massive quantities of dirt, he massaged the earth in a subtle way, turning the holes and positioning them so the live oaks draped the entrances to the green. It created a tremendous sense of corridors, and you have to keep working the ball from left to right and right to left. It's a really ingenious design."

Always quick to deflect praise, Dye gives credit to one of his colleagues, Robert Trent Jones, for inspiring his vision. "I noticed that Mr. Jones was using big machinery to carve out long tees, huge bunkers, and massive greens at nearby Palmetto Dunes at the time," recalls Dye. "I decided to do the opposite. I figured small greens, tiny pot bunkers, and a

low-profile design would separate my identity from the other designers on the island and be something really unique."

The quartet of par-3s is one of the finest collections in the game. Two are menaced by water, one is surrounded by sand, the last requires a tee shot into the prevailing breezes with wetlands and marsh grasses close at hand. It's hard to recollect any other world-class course that has the proliferation of houses and condos that are seen at the southern end of the island's Sea Pines Plantation, so it's a testament to Dye's acumen that a round here isn't like a typical ride through a neighborhood subdivision, which is so often the case in the Southeast. The strategy required on each shot and the omnipresence of the fabulous hardwoods defining and influencing the line of play draw the attention. To find success at Harbour Town, a player must not only find the fairway, but often must land on *the proper side* of the fairway in order to reach the green safely. The housing and road crossings fade to the background as players concentrate on negotiating a golf course that's both petite (barely 7,000 yards) and flat as a Scrabble board (just four feet of elevation change).

The crescendo of the finishing holes, as a player emerges from the forest to sweeping seaside views, gets most of the attention. But it's the understated, inland hole-to-hole genius of this design, admired by and bedeviling to Tour pros and resort duffers both, that maintains Harbour Town's lofty reputation. Though one of Dye's more subtle designs, forty-odd years after inception it remains an absolute standout in the golf world.

18th hole

Opposite, top: 13th hole
Opposite, bottom: 14th hole

4th hole

One time we were using Pete's only car to drive around the job site on Hilton Head. It was this old, orange Toyota. We got it stuck in the sand, and I was behind the wheel while three other crew members were pushing us out. The driver door was open so that one of the guys could get better leverage, and when the car moved, the door got stuck in the sand and bent backward. From that point on, it needed to be wired shut. But Pete didn't care.

As long as we were working hard and building the course properly, that's all that mattered. He's just not materialistic, and really doesn't care about cars. One time he told me he had a special deal with a major rental car company. I asked what it was, and he said. "I pay full price, and when I bring the car back, they don't ask any questions."

TOM DOAK, *Golf Course architect; former associate of Pete Dye*

16th hole

Left: 15th hole
Below: 7th hole

1970s An Appreciation by Arnold Palmer

I've known Pete and Alice Dye most of my life. They have been good friends of mine practically since the day I began playing golf competitively.

I remember Alice as a golfer first, and then Pete as a golfer second. Of course, beyond that the world knows of them because they have been so successful in the field of golf course architecture. Their fame derives from the fact that they have done extremely well and have compiled a wonderful résumé of courses all over the world.

I've been fortunate enough to play golf with Pete often, but I remember Alice and her golfing prowess prior to knowing him. She was an outstanding player and a very lovely lady.

It reminds me of the old expression "Behind every great man there's a great woman." Pete's game was impressive on its own, but like other areas of his life, in my opinion it was Alice who helped him with his golf game, then supported him when he entered into the field of architecture.

As an architect myself, I've admired the unique twists Pete has added to the field of golf course design, with his innovative use of railroad ties, pot bunkers, and fescue grasses. He's produced such a wide range of courses, on varied terrain, all over the world. I kid a little bit about Alice leading the way, but there's no question in my mind that they have been an extremely formidable architectural team for nearly fifty years.

I'll always have special memories of Harbour Town, on the southern tip of Hilton Head, where I was fortunate to be the inaugural champion at what was then known as the Heritage Classic. Done in consultation with Jack Nicklaus, the course came about quite early in Pete's design career. It was one of the most interesting of his designs and one I've enjoyed very much. The course had just barely opened when we went there for the first time, Thanksgiving weekend of 1969. I recall my fellow Tour pros and I were all surprised by the unique qualities of the course, so different

from what we typically saw week to week. I wish there were more courses like Harbour Town, which has never relied on length as a deterrent to scoring. It's the narrow, twisting fairways, compact greens, and thickness of the surrounding tree line that make it such a memorable test of the game. The golf course is proof positive that one needn't use length alone to provide a competitive challenge to the world's finest players.

I have a home in the Palm Springs area, and have had the opportunity to play Pete's Stadium Course at PGA West on many occasions. In fact, one of my designs is part of the same complex. Without question, the Stadium Course is one of the most exacting golf courses in the nation, and has received tremendous worldwide attention because of its many challenges. Even though it's now more than twenty-five years old, it remains one of the toughest and most talked-about courses anywhere. The same can be said about Pete's work on the East Coast, the similarly named

Stadium Course at TPC Sawgrass, south of Jacksonville, Florida. It's the island green 17th that gets most of the attention. But the golf course as a whole is tough as nails. Posting a respectable score requires a player to combine good shots with good decisions. The requirements of strategy, execution, and patience are what make this design, like so many Pete Dye designs, exceptional.

Speaking of which, Joel Zuckerman has written an exceptional book. *Pete Dye Golf Courses: Fifty Years of Visionary Design*, in words, pictures, and anecdotes, celebrates the creations of one of the great golf course architects of the modern era, and one who I firmly believe deserves consideration as one of the best of all time. This book is an impressive achievement, much like the overall body of work put together by Pete and Alice Dye.

Oak Tree Golf Club, 17th hole

Casa de Campo   Teeth of the Dog, The Links, Dye Fore, La Romana Country Club

With Alice Dye

In the last few decades, the Caribbean has emerged from a seemingly eternal golf slumber, becoming a destination to be reckoned with. In days gone by, tropical island golf was little more than an afterthought, the few courses in existence mostly basic and threadbare. But nowadays there are big-time, high-dollar venues sprouting like so much sugarcane—in Jamaica, Puerto Rico, Barbados, St. Kitts, and Anguilla, among other locales. But for every White Witch or Green Monkey (two of the nouveau marquee venues), the Dominican Republic's Teeth of the Dog is still the most colorfully named and most memorable course in the tropics. Pete Dye's first-ever island creation remains the standard by which the others are judged. And some forty years after the resort opened, with high-end golf proliferating not just at the other islands but throughout the Dominican Republic itself, Casa de Campo continues to be the Caribbean's number one golf draw. This is due not only to the Teeth of the Dog—so named because that's what the jagged coral rocks buttressing its seaside tees look like—but also because of the additional courses Dye created in the following years. The Links was the encore. The incredible Dye Fore came after that. And, adding in La Romana Country Club, a private facility that is occasionally accessible to resort guests, the quartet of Pete Dye designs makes the resort the Caribbean capstone of great golf. At least for the time being, there is not even a close second.

Casa de Campo evolved because of the vast resources of the Gulf and Western Company. More than 300,000 tons of raw sugar were produced annually at their mill in the sleepy town of La Romana, making it the largest single producer in the world. The executive in charge of the sugar operation was a Cuban exile named Alvaro Carta, who wanted to invest some of the company's growing profits back into his adopted Dominican homeland and provide economic opportunity for the mostly impoverished citizenry. Increasing the tourist trade to the region seemed like a viable option, and it was decided that a full-service resort would be constructed, with golf as its cornerstone. The land that was eventually selected was within a 400,000-acre parcel near the mill, too dry for growing sugarcane and too sparsely vegetated for grazing cattle.

The idyllic ambience of Teeth of the Dog gives no hint of its arduous origins. Importing the heavy equipment normally used in golf course construction was far too expensive. So Pete Dye made do with ill-suited machinery whose true purpose was sugarcane cultivation, and substituted man and oxen power instead. Armed with sledgehammers, pickaxes, and chisels, 300 Dominican laborers literally pulverized the coral- and limestone-strewn property, one harsh blow at a time. Decent grass-growing soil wasn't readily available either, so Dye and his right-hand man on the project, the late Bruce Mashburn, had the crew hand-dig and load the soil a mile away, one square yard at a time, into sugarcane carts pulled by oxen. A byproduct of sugarcane called cachaza was mixed with sand and the imported dirt to form the topsoil for the golf course. Making matters even more difficult were the countless boulders peppering the proposed playing corridors. The laborers carted them to the edge of what were to become the fairways, painstakingly building a peripheral stone wall that eventually stretched two miles and contained over 20,000 tons of rock.

The 7,000 acres that encompass the Casa de Campo resort are a tropical paradise of bougainvillea and hibiscus, not to mention a wide range of charming red-roofed casitas, high-dollar waterside megamansions, and long-range ocean views. The whole facility is a color riot and a visual feast. The prettiest acreage on the property is to be found at the Teeth of the Dog.

For many years, Pete and Alice Dye made their island home in a simple thatched-roof bungalow that sat unobtrusively among the showcase homes, to the right of the par-3 7th. The Dyes' former vacation home may be low-profile, but this signature design is anything but. The course features generous fairways and swaying greens that mimic the pitch and roll of the nearby Caribbean Sea. Speaking of which, among the seven seaside beauties that rightly cement the Teeth's international reputation, the finest is arguably the 5th. This one-shot diamond is as dramatically beautiful as the 7th at Pebble Beach or the 17th at Cabo del Sol's Ocean Course on Mexico's Baja Peninsula. Both the tee box and green protrude well into the lapping waves of the sea, and while subsequent par-3s are longer and more dangerous, none are as pulse-pounding. The penultimate hole also deserves mention. Only the boldest and bravest will attack this par-4 by launching over the ocean with a big draw or hard pull, looking far down the fairway. The rank and file will admire the stunning scenery and then aim well left of "La Playa." The long iron or fairway wood approach to follow is the price that must be paid for this conservatism.

Teeth, whose inland holes wind through sugarcane fields and stands of coconut palms, royal palms, bitter orange, almond, and teak trees, is generally a second-shot golf course. Approach shots must skirt or avoid sand, water, and swales, with a heavy toll exacted for indifferent ball-striking. The one-shot holes are easily among the finest quartet in the

world—besides the aforementioned 5th, the 7th and 16th are practically in the sea itself.

Many newly constructed courses provide five or more sets of different tee markers, making the course appropriate for players of any caliber. But Teeth of the Dog truly delivers, on the waterside holes in particular. The excitement and intimidation factor, the anticipatory thrill of lofting the ball across the water, is available to all levels of golfer. At the championship level, the carry might be several hundred yards. At the most forward markers, it might be fifty. But the course is designed so that players of even modest ability are never cheated out of the pleasure (or pain, as is often the case) of launching the ball over the sea to safety.

Despite his renown, Pete Dye is a regular guy in the best sense of the word. If the architect weren't so modest, he might have consented to adding the word "To" in front of the course name Dye Fore, because the fourth course he built at the resort is another spectacular achievement.

Back in 1970, Pete asked me to accompany him to Casa de Campo in the Dominican Republic, where he was building the Teeth of the Dog. The resort was in its infancy, and there were numerous kinks that needed to be worked out. Food and beverage service was especially difficult, because the help at the time didn't know English, and there were major communication gaps.

Pete decided to get involved, as he was a hands-on guy. He decided there should be a numeral system on the menu, so a patron could order by the number. One morning we were eating, and some poor guy next to us couldn't get his food. He was waiting and waiting, and more waiters kept coming out, trying to appease him. Finally, they came out with ten plates of huevos rancheros. He had ordered one #10, but the wait-staff had interpreted it as ten orders of #1! As far as I know, that was the end of Pete's food and beverage career!

Joe Webster III, *course developer; owner of the Dye Preserve in Jupiter, Florida*

Opposite: Teeth of the Dog, 7th hole
Below: Teeth of the Dog, 5th hole

Above: Dye Fore, 16th hole
Opposite: Dye Fore, back nine

One word describes the property—GIGANTIC. Or, similarly, a popular description offered by longtime members of the professional staff: Huge fairways, huge bunkers, huge greens, huge numbers on the scorecard.

Located well above the resort proper near the European replica village of Altos de Chavon, Dye Fore is one of the largest golf parcels imaginable. As seen from the open-air 19th hole, the fairways of just the par-5 10th and especially the enormous, tumbling 18th, another true three-shot hole, seemingly feature the same volume of turf that would comprise a full nine holes at a normal-size course. Perched on the bluffs overlooking the winding Chavon River and stretching more than 7,700 yards from the back tees, Dye Fore is a mountainous and arduous trek. Tee shots must skirt imposing ravines, the occasional blind approach shots are launched at greens often surrounded by steep drops, and there's an overall capaciousness, an up-and-down sensibility that makes the facility memorable. Gilles Gagnon has been the resort's director of golf since 1980 and offers this assessment: "When you finish playing The Links, you usually have some energy left. When you walk off Teeth, you're tired. But at the end of a round on Dye Fore, you're exhausted, the tank is empty."

Words hardly do it justice and photographs tell only half the story. The only way to appreciate the majesty of Dye Fore is to walk its massively tilting fairways and send lofted irons skyward to its precipitous greens.

The dominating visual feature is the Chavon River, some 200 feet below the fairway, which winds between sheer granite cliffs before spilling into the Caribbean. The inward journey features dramatic river views with virtually no housing. The outward half showcases not only the river, the marina, the sea, and the mountains, but some of the most brazenly opulent vacation homes in the hemisphere. Who's to say what's more impressive? Is it the incredible 4th and 5th holes, back-to-back downhill dogleg par-4s? Both are bracketed by a ravine above the river leading to the sea, and both the tee shot and approach must be steered gingerly away from the precipice. Or is it the eye-popping mansions lording it on the periphery of these dual fairways, several rumored to contain nearly as many bathrooms as there are holes on the course? Neither is a sight that's seen with any regularity. But while the manor homes are off limits, golfers are welcome to test their courage on one of the Caribbean's most daunting golf challenges.

The Links, 13th hole

Though The Links was Casa de Campo's second course, dating from the mid-1970s, it has been sublimated over the years and demoted to a third, or afternoon option, by Dye's seaside and riverside creations. The course is inland a bit, away from the ocean, winding above the resort's polo field and adjacent to some horseback riding trails. It has more of a typical resort feel and, despite some lengthening, is several hundred yards shorter than the others. But the course is far from a pushover—the greens are small, offset, heavily contoured, and often elevated. It's more demanding from the tee than the other courses, as wayward drives will nestle and often vanish in thick Guinea grass or become stymied among thickets of trees. Water features dominate the inward journey. The difference here is that lost pellets won't disappear heroically, plunging into ravines as at Dye Fore, or into the Caribbean as they do at Teeth. But they will disappear nonetheless.

The course's true mettle is found midway through the inward nine, as the fairways wind around, over, and through a series of water features that give The Links its imprimatur. The 12th is a wonderful Cape hole, where daring players will attempt to carry more of the right-side water hazard than will their conservative companions. The 13th and 16th are challenging par-3s over water, while in between are two estimable par-4s with lagoons menacing the left side of the landing area.

When it was built in 1990, La Romana Country Club was the biggest and broadest course in the area. That was prior to the advent of Dye Fore, and before the architect toughened up and appreciably lengthened Teeth of the Dog in 2005—turning it, in the memorable words of veteran travel writer Brian McCallen, from Pete's pet Spaniel into a pit bull. This private club is worth a visit, assuming it can be arranged through either the resort concierge or one's hometown professional.

There is very little water in play, and little in the way of water views, either. The fairways at La Romana Country Club are ultra wide, and both the rippling greens and the par-3 holes are colossal (from the blue tees at 6,660, they average just less than 200 yards each. From the tips at 7,200 they are almost 220). Though the course is lined with homes, the setbacks are generous enough so a golfer never feels he is aiming down a cement alley.

In the mid-1970s, I represented the United States in the World Team Amateur Championships at Casa de Campo. We were playing the Teeth of the Dog, one of Pete Dye's best-known designs. My teammates were George Burns, Jerry Pate, and Curtis Strange. We would all go on to turn pro and win a combined thirty-five times on the PGA Tour, but back then, we probably weren't as good as we thought we were.

Anyway, Pete was watching us for a few holes in a practice round, and at the long oceanside par-3 16th we all hit terrible shots. Pete immediately got all over us and said, "Is that the best you guys can do?" We challenged him to do better. He grabbed a four-wood out of my bag, took a practice swing or two, and with his first and only shot of the day, knocked it into the center of the green. At that point, I think we all bowed down to him. He's a great designer, and was a heck of a player as well.

Gary Koch, *former PGA Tour pro; NBC broadcaster*

The Links, 16th hole

La Romana Country Club, 17th hole

I've been friendly with Pete and Alice Dye for many years, ever since I was about twenty-one. I had won the Amateur a few months earlier, then was fortunate to win the individual title and help our team win the overall title at the World Team Amateur Championship, which was the first big tournament ever contested at Teeth of the Dog. Anyway, more than thirty years later, I was down with my two sons spending Thanksgiving at Casa de Campo in 2005. Teeth of the Dog was under renovation at the time, so we were enjoying the other courses on the property. Pete knew how much it would mean to me to play the course where we had won that team championship. He arranged for the course to be opened just for us. They cut holes, put in flagsticks, and Pete, my two boys, and I played as a foursome. Afterward they took the flagsticks out, and the course didn't officially reopen for several weeks. I've had some great moments on Dye-designed courses, including winning the first Players Championship (then known as the Tournament Players Championship) at TPC Sawgrass in 1982. But that round with Pete and my boys on Teeth of the Dog was as sweet as any of them.

Jerry Pate, *former U.S. Amateur and U.S. Open champion*

The country club is also something of a haven for a Who's Who of Dominican major leaguers. A visiting golfer might end up playing behind Sammy Sosa, Manny Ramirez, Albert Pujols, or any number of homegrown baseball stars, be they members or guests, relaxing away from the diamond and the resort proper.

There are expansions in the works throughout the resort and its immediate environs. The private country club has added an additional nine holes, and Dye Fore will eventually be bifurcated, then melded together with two more nines yet to be built, morphing into a thirty-six-hole facility. But despite the ongoing golf growth at Casa de Campo, Teeth will always be top dog. "It doesn't matter how long it takes you to get here, or how many problems you might have encountered traveling," says Gilles Gagnon, who has never been lured away from his island paradise despite dozens of different job offers he's received over the decades. "Once you stand on the 5th tee box, the Caribbean Sea just a few steps away, all your worries melt away." Asked why Casa de Campo benefits from so many repeat visitors, some of whom return annually for decades on end, the French Canadian professional concludes succinctly, "I think it's because golfers remain hopeful that they can bite the Dog before the Dog bites them. But, just like in life, it is much more likely that the Dog is going to bite first."

La Romana Country Club, 15th hole

Fowler's Mill

With Roy Dye

"You can't get there from here." This satirical expression, probably originating in Maine, refers to the difficulty in getting from one out-of-the-way spot to another.

It's likely been heard a time or two by golfers in northern Ohio inquiring as to the whereabouts of a worthwhile public-access facility known as Fowler's Mill, in the microscopic burg of Chesterland. Here's the fact: Though it's undoubtedly countrified, in the best way possible, this early 1970s Pete Dye beauty is but thirty minutes from the heavily populated eastern suburbs of Cleveland. A longtime member of the professional staff explains wistfully, "Some people think we're in Egypt." If only Egypt were so inviting.

Cleveland-based TRW Corporation, wanting a corporate golf amenity such as other regional business giants like NCR and Firestone had, originally planned a fifty-four-hole facility on this whopping 1,500-acre property. Instead, they scaled back plans for their employee-customer-family retreat, opting to only build twenty-seven holes. The remainder of the land was donated to the Geauga Park District, assuring a huge buffer zone and a natural environment.

The facility was sold to American Golf Corporation some fifteen years later, and opened to the public in 1986. "It thrills me when one of my great designs is opened up to all golfers," said Pete Dye, who worked on the property with his brother Roy. It's also a thrill for the golfers on course.

Fowler's Mill, renamed in honor of an early area settler and gristmill owner named Milo Fowler, is a wonderful walk through the woods. It's the first Audubon-certified course in Ohio, filled with birdlife and meadow creatures. There are almost no parallel fairways. Each gently doglegging hole is in its own isolated corridor, with little interference from—or even awareness of—other golfers on the course. The Chagrin River winds throughout the property, an intimidating influence on several holes. There are some split-fairway options, steeply banked par-3 holes requiring dramatic carries, fields of fescue grasses, native vegetation areas, a fifty-acre lake that makes the hairpin 4th hole one of the scariest in the region, and a host of other reasons why the course is considered among the top five public-access facilities in Ohio.

Perhaps the most succinct way to characterize the typically truncated golf season at Fowler's Mill—which often begins in late spring and ends in mid-autumn, just like this chapter—short and sweet.

Left: 4th hole
Opposite: 7th hole

Amelia Island Plantation Oak Marsh Golf Course

The Stadium Course at TPC Sawgrass is undoubtedly the most famous Pete Dye creation in north Florida. But eight years earlier and some fifty miles north of his Ponte Vedra Beach masterpiece, Dye produced a fine members' course at Amelia Island Plantation.

Back in 1973, Dye created three separate nine-hole tracks, called Oak Marsh, Oyster Bay, and Oceanside. More than twenty-five years later, his longtime design associate Bobby Weed added nine more holes, and then modified the existing oceanside nine into a separate eighteen-hole track called Ocean Links. But Dye's original eighteen holes, now known as Oak Marsh, still exist and offer a staunch but enjoyable challenge to members and resort guests.

Veteran staff members report that visitors head to Ocean Links straightaway, lured by the prospect of five surfside holes. But once they've completed their initial rounds, the third round, or "tie-breaker," usually goes to Dye's Oak Marsh. It's not hard to understand why.

Oak Marsh is of modest length, not even 6,600 yards from the tips, but with potential trouble in most every direction. Fairways twist and turn as at Harbour Town (created just a few years prior), waste bunkers lurk, and shaping the tee shot is paramount. Aiming right or left is one thing, but the required tee ball on the 15th brings this sensibility to the extreme. From the back tees, a golfer is confronted with a natural tunnel dead ahead, made of the intertwining branches of dual hardwoods fifty yards forward. The ball must stay above the water hazard but be zipped beneath the branches with a low line drive of a tee ball. Not a shot you'll encounter every day.

The seesaw greens have tremendous pitch and roll, with the types of severe inclines that are rarely built in the modern era. If the sophisticated mowing equipment of today had been available during the Nixon years when Oak Marsh was created, allowing for the buzz-cut conditions that have since become common, the greens would be nigh unplayable.

Though developed as a real-estate course, the housing presence on Oak Marsh seems incidental. It's not the lack of houses, but more the encroachment of the flora and fauna, a junglelike buffer zone between the playing corridors and the homes themselves, that mutes the effect considerably. "It's really a nice balance," comments Perry Dye, who worked as a laborer during initial construction. "The homeowner wants a golf course view. The players want a golf environment, unsullied by housing. This course serves both interests, and works better than most."

While lacking the spectacle of the ocean itself, the waving marsh grasses on the western edge of the property aren't exactly an eyesore. The closing stretch in particular is hard by the marshland, and the concluding trio of holes, with their long, low-country vistas and scoring difficulty, are both gorgeous and dangerous concurrently. It's a stellar conclusion to a real sleeper of a golf course.

Oak Marsh Golf Course, 3rd hole

Right: Oak Marsh Golf Course, 8th hole
Below: Oak Marsh Golf Course, 14th hole

Oak Marsh Golf Course, 7th hole

Top: Oak Marsh Golf Course, 9th hole
Bottom: Oak Marsh Golf Course, 16th hole

The Cardinal Golf Club

Renovated in 2007

It's no surprise that Pete Dye has produced more than forty courses in Indiana and Florida—they are the two states where he's spent most of his adult life. But North Carolina also had a profound effect on Dye's career, though he has only worked there sporadically through the years. He became enamored of Pinehurst Number 2 when stationed at Fort Bragg during his military days, playing and studying the course repeatedly—at one point saying the Donald Ross masterpiece "impressed me more than any other course I had seen."

Dye has since impressed many a North Carolinian golfer himself, with his work some seventy-five miles due north of Pinehurst, in the town of Greensboro. When he first built the course in 1975, The Cardinal quickly took its place among the best venues in the state. At the time, the course was situated on 140 rolling acres in the middle of nowhere, the quiet countryside of the Piedmont region an ideal location for golf.

The heavily wooded, broad-shouldered routing, with its lakes and the ubiquitous Brushy Creek winding through the property, has hosted some of the region's finest players. With some form of water encroaching on nearly every hole, this par-70, 7,000-yard parkland beauty has been the site of both the Men's and Women's North Carolina Open and the North Carolina Amateur Championship. It is also home to the prestigious Cardinal Amateur, which has been contested on the grounds since the 1970s.

Despite its stellar reputation, financial difficulties plagued the club consistently. Ownership changed hands, the members eventually acquiring the facility themselves, but both course conditions and the membership rolls continued to deteriorate; some thirty years after its debut, the course was practically on life support. The irrigation system was antiquated, the greens were in bad shape, members were jumping ship, and the entire operation, bleeding Cardinal-red ink, needed a serious financial jumpstart.

Fortunately, John McConnell took notice. The healthcare entrepreneur netted millions when he sold his Raleigh-based

18th hole

company, Medic Computer Systems, in 1997, and added greatly to the fortune almost a decade later after buying, running, and then selling A4 Health Systems. In his youth, McConnell competed intensely with his older brothers on their homemade golf course back on the Virginia family farm, so it's no surprise he has since turned his attention to the golf business.

He paid $1.7 million for the cash-strapped Cardinal and poured nearly $5 million in renovations into the clubhouse and golf course, most notably hiring Dye to return and fully restore his original design. "The Cardinal was practically at rock bottom when I bought it," recalls McConnell. "The golf course was worn out, many of the members had left, and the clubhouse was very dated. There had not been any real investment in that facility in several years. But thanks to Pete Dye's renovation, it is now once again one of the toughest, but fairest, courses in the state."

"I wouldn't call it dilapidated, but like any course that reaches a certain age, it needed updating," explains Dye. "I was elated to go back there and work on it, just as I've done at Harbour Town, the Ocean Course, Crooked Stick, TPC Sawgrass, and many others over the years."

The work began in the summer of 2006 and continued for more than a year. Dye, in his never-ending quest to thwart technology, added bunkers and repositioned existing ones much farther down the fairways. He refashioned greens that had become slow, bumpy, and two-dimensional, making them heavily contoured and slick. Thanks to the state-of-the-art irrigation system that was installed, conditions are once again lush.

The daunting nature of the redesign is readily apparent at the par-3 12th, which originally measured 160 yards across a lake. Dye moved the tee box around the lake and stretched the hole to 220 yards, with water in play the entire length of the hole and behind the narrow green. The redo earns high praise from the man who designed the treacherous island green 17th at the Stadium Course at TPC Sawgrass and at least a hundred other one-shot holes that make golfers shiver in their soft-spikes.

"I really think the Cardinal's 12th is my hardest par-3 ever," concludes Dye. "You can't ignore the water. It's everywhere you look. The course was well known to begin with, and I really think we've made it much better than it was. It really jumps out of the ground now; it's as good as we could do."

Oak Tree Golf Club

Once upon a time, in any type of all-star, club-versus-club competition, Oklahoma's Oak Tree Golf Club would have been a prohibitive favorite against pretty much any other private golf club in the world. But that was before PGA Tour pros began descending en masse to Orlando, congregating at posh enclaves like Isleworth and Lake Nona. A look at the all-star lineups paying dues at either high-dollar development is to see the modern essence of golf glitterati—Tiger Woods, Mark O'Meara, and Stuart Appleby among other marquee names at the former, luminaries like Ernie Els, Retief Goosen, and Justin Rose in residence at the latter.

But these are mostly a bunch of Johnny-come-lately types, lured to the peninsular state by the agreeable weather and tax advantages. The Oak Tree gang may not boast the same golf résumé—Tiger's more than sixty-and-counting Tour wins alone are nearly the equal of the professional victories garnered by Gil Morgan, Mark Hayes, David Edwards, Doug Tewell, Willie Wood, Bob Tway, and Scott Verplank combined. But the Oklahomans have two things that these faux-Floridians do not. The first is authenticity. These are real-deal Sooners, or Cowboys, as the case may be, either by birth, or by osmosis owing to their collegiate ties to Oklahoma State. Second and more important is their day-to-day access to one

of the finest championship tests in the world—venerable Oak Tree Golf Club.

"When I first came here I hated the place," admits Scott Verplank, who was an All-American at Oklahoma State and won the 1984 U.S. Amateur Championship at Oak Tree before embarking on a stellar professional career. "We'd come down here, and it was unbelievably difficult. As an aspiring professional, I had certain expectations about my game. But back in those days, breaking par wasn't even a consideration. That's how hard it was. But over time I grew to really love the course, and respect the fact that while it's very tough, it isn't unfair. At one time, there were lots of wild, native areas that would really punish an offline shot. But even though that vegetation is gone, it's still a very tough golf course."

It's not surprising that so many hardened Tour pros call Oak Tree home, considering the course was conceived and brought to fruition by a couple of their peers from an earlier era. Joe Walser, once the Oklahoma Amateur champion, partnered with his childhood buddy Ernie Vossler, a former Texas Amateur champion, and decided that a world-class course was needed in Oklahoma City. Both men had spent significant time on the PGA Tour after their amateur days, and felt that Tulsa's famed Southern Hills shouldn't have a monopoly

Opposite: 4th hole
Below: 16th hole

Above: 12th hole
Right: 13th hole

16th hole

on any Major championships that might come Oklahoma's way. "Build us a championship course," said Walser to Pete Dye. "One with no compromise."

The championship nature of Dye's creation is revealed immediately, as the opening tee shot must thread its way through a series of oak trees—lined up like dominoes—hopefully coming to rest on what can only be described as a single-file fairway. The slightly uphill approach must carry an expansive water hazard, the first of ten holes with a watery mien.

At 7,400 yards from the tips and with a par of 71, the course can bludgeon with its sheer length. But it's also a test of delicacy, as the heavily contoured greens will often repel any approach shot lacking exactitude. Short irons to the par-5 3rd or par-4 6th might look luscious in the air. But come up a foot or two short of these elevated greens and the ball will rebound off closely mown collars, careening down the fairway to a waiting collection area and leaving a hit-and-pray recovery shot.

In other instances, gnarly, sink-to-the-bottom Bermuda rough awaits an inaccurate approach. Too dainty with the chip and the ball remains in the tangle. Too bold, and it's a 30- or even 50-footer left for par, up and over contours on a slippery, multilevel green. And no self-respecting discussion of Oklahoma golf is complete without mention of the wind, which comes sweeping down the fairway often enough, making a hard task harder.

"When I first showed up around here as a college freshman, it was really fun, coming to this men's-only club in the middle of nowhere. It was a boom time, and you would occasionally see helicopters next to the driving range, that's how some of the members would get out here," says Verplank. "The place had a real mystique. Members would bet their guests that they couldn't break a hundred, and most of the time they'd collect."

The club has since evolved into a different entity, much to the Ryder Cup and President's Cup stalwart's satisfaction, as he now visits the club with his wife and children in tow. The neighborhood has also evolved, growing up around the club. It's no longer in the middle of nowhere, and helicopters have long since stopped buzzing the grounds. However, the golf course remains a first-rate, championship test and one of the finest, most challenging in the nation's midsection. The mystique of Oak Tree remains intact.

Oak Tree Country Club East and West

When you've designed as many courses as Pete Dye, the occasional case of mistaken identity is practically a given. For example, there's understandable confusion regarding his dual Stadium Courses, even though his yeoman's efforts on the north Florida coast at the TPC and in the California desert at PGA West are more than 2,300 miles apart. Oklahoma's Oak Tree Golf Club and its thirty-six-hole counterpart, Oak Tree Country Club, are even more of a muddle, as they are only separated by the width of a two-lane road.

Upon its mid-1970s inception, the Golf Club was earmarked for men only, and stayed that way for decades. Even in the modern era, it's unabashedly male-dominated. But the Oak Tree Country Club came into existence in the early 1980s to fill an entirely different need. The Oklahoma City suburb of Edmond is full of well-to-do families, and there was a great demand for a full-service country club. It was an easy decision for original owners Joe Walser and Ernie Vossler to bring back Pete Dye and allow him to replicate the success he had already enjoyed in the neighborhood.

The two country club courses, both playing to a par of 70, with just one par-5 per side, intermingle with some consistency. For example, the 3rd tee on the West and the 9th tee on the East are separated only by a narrow strip of rough perhaps a dozen steps wide. But the East is the championship test, far more exacting in its demands than the roomier West course. The watery final stretch—the half-dozen holes heading toward the clubhouse—showcases the ferocity of the course. So it's no wonder that for more than two decades the East has served as host venue for the highly regarded Oklahoma Open, traditionally one of the most sought-after state titles in the land. Stalwarts like Bob Tway, Gil Morgan, David Edwards, Todd Hamilton, and Lucas Glover are among the champions who have been crowned.

"The easiest holes on the East course are less demanding than the few easy ones across the street at the Golf Club," offers golf course architect Mark Hayes, an Oklahoma native and former Ryder Cup player with three PGA Tour victories on his résumé. "But I think the toughest holes on the East are just as tough as the hardest holes at the Golf Club. They are just about all you want. Even during the Oklahoma Open, they almost never use the way-back tees. It would be too difficult."

The East course is a tough slog from the outset. Forget the tips at nearly 7,100 yards; even from the 6,400-yard middle markers, the half-dozen front-side par-4s average 410 yards. The housing presence diminishes appreciably midway

through the outward journey, as the course abuts the wide-open property line to the south and east. It's a bunker-strewn landscape, humps and hollows wreaking havoc with shots drifting from the short grass. It's a stiff enough challenge, but merely a preamble to the watery finish. Four of the final six, including a pair of distinctive par-3s, are completely menaced by water.

This isn't to imply the neighboring West course is a push-over. With the exception of a couple of tree-lined par-4s early on the inward nine, the driving corridors are generous. But just like its immediate neighbor, it has a multitude of bunkering throughout, and Dye has made liberal use of periphery greenside mounding, so offline approaches will lead to awkward stances and angles toward the pin. The best illustration

of such is the par-5 7th, where the final fifty yards is a sand-strewn loop-de-loop. Water is less of a presence than on the East course, but there are several shots sure to intimidate those with aquaphobia, the tee shot on the par-3 14th being the most notable. Several of the greens have some serious contour, the par-4 12th and 17th being prime examples.

The housing presence is more palpable on the West course than it is on many other real estate–driven Dye designs, owing to several factors. This Plains terrain is more wide open, and these mostly brick homes are stately, not the low-slung, wood-paneled abodes often seen in the Southeast. Also, the tree cover is relatively sparse and doesn't serve as camouflage in the leafy, broad-branch way it does in other, lusher areas.

East, 17th hole

West, 3rd hole

East, 8th hole

Despite being longer and at least a couple of shots tougher, the East course gets more play, and not only because the membership likes a challenge, but also because of the clubhouse return. The West course loops out from the central area completely, and doesn't loop back to the clubhouse until round's end.

In a neighborhood bursting with imposing homes, none is more impressive than the fairway-view fortress belonging to Tour veteran and former PGA Champion Bob Tway. For all his success, Tway never captured a USGA event, unlike his son Kevin, who won the 2005 U.S. Junior Amateur Championship. But later that same summer, the newly crowned national champ could only manage the bronze medal at his home course, in the Oak Tree Country Club Junior Championship. This surprising result paints a powerful picture, showing that the Oklahoma golf pipeline is still full to bursting, and that the Oak Tree Gang–Generation Next is readying to make their mark.

La Quinta, PGA West
The Mountain Course, The Dunes Course, The Stadium Course, The Citrus Course
With Alice Dye

Developers Ernie Vossler and Joe Walser told Pete they wanted "the hardest damn golf course in the world. We want a golf course so hard that people in Japan, who have never been here, will complain about how hard it is." The architect took them at their word, and made it his business to deliver. His creation was known as The Stadium Course at PGA West. Well over two decades after it first opened in the mid 1980s, it continues to beguile and bedevil all golfers who attempt to meet its ferocious challenges.

"The worst piece of land I ever started with was this featureless, barren acreage," recalls Dye. He managed to work his magic on the terrain in the usual fashion, and the swaths of green grass peppered with rock-walled lakes, railroad ties, berms, mounds, sand caverns, and thousands of tree plantings (including numerous magnificently gnarled mesquite trees)—all surrounded by the majestic Santa Rosa Mountains—make The Stadium Course a real beauty. The only things truly ugly on the property are the predicaments that the resort players find themselves in, their mood as the round progresses, and their scorecard.

Every trick in the book. That's what Pete pulled to make the Stadium so stupefying and harsh. Bunkers dug halfway to China. Tough fairway angles and offset greens. Water hazards expansive enough for sailboats. The putting surfaces are large and rolling, but most players probably won't notice their inherent difficulty. They're breathless from the arduous journey from tee to green. Jim Murray, the Pulitzer Prize–winning *Los Angeles Times* sportswriter who spent nearly forty years at his post, summed up The Stadium Course in his succinctly humorous style: "You need a camel, a canoe, a priest, and a tourniquet to get through it."

Most of the mayhem was done on purpose. But as has often been the case in his remarkable career, what has become one of the most memorable junctures on the course came about by accident. "I had envisioned a greenside bunker of medium depth on the par-5 16th," explains Dye. "I told the bulldozer operator to dig until he hit water, but that didn't happen until the pit was more than twenty feet deep." The developers were dubious about the penal nature of the hazard, but Dye extricated a golf ball onto the putting surface on his very first attempt, so they let it stand.

Of course, Pete Dye was skillful enough to play in the U.S. Amateur, British Amateur, and U.S. Open. The overwhelming majority of golfers stuck within this cavern of doom most

assuredly are not. So the twenty-foot-high wall of grass that must be carried to reach the putting surface is as imposing as the Berlin Wall and inspires more praying than the Wailing Wall. Dye once remarked, "No one can describe the jubilation of hitting a shot over the twenty-foot-steep bank of that bunker." Perhaps he meant that literally. No one can describe it because virtually no one can do it.

The 16th is merely a stage-setter for the dazzling 17th, known as Alcatraz. This is an island green par-3, but played downhill and surrounded by rocks—a much prettier shot than its East Coast cousin, the island green 17th at TPC Sawgrass. The hole is a little longer, the green a little larger. But the intimidation factor? The heart-and-pulse pounding as a player begins to take the club back? It's identical. The only difference is the time zone.

If The Stadium Course is the Michael Jordan of PGA West, iconic, awe-inspiring, world-renowned, and intimidating to all who attempt to tangle, then The Mountain Course is Scottie Pippen, a versatile and brilliant "second banana," or supporting player with few equals. It predates The Stadium Course by some four years. Built in the early 1980s, its location is at the La Quinta Resort, perhaps five miles from the PGA West complex, which in addition to the marquee Stadium Course is also home to a panoply of resort and private courses designed by superstar-players-turned-designers named Nicklaus, Norman, Palmer, and Weiskopf.

There are very few public-access or resort facilities in the golf-rich region of the California desert that are carved so close to the slopes of the lower Santa Rosas. Several tee boxes at The Mountain Course are notched into the mountain itself, and the middle portion of the opening nine is shadowed by the imposing peaks looming directly to a golfer's left. They are so close to the playing surface proper, a pulled or quick-hooked shot might literally rebound off the rock facing back to safety. The greens are a puzzle, despite the prevailing wisdom that putts have a tendency to break away from the mountain. It isn't cut-and-dried. Subtle breaks on each putting surface can wreak havoc with such a simplified point of view.

The Mountain Course is the perceived favorite of both members and regular visitors to this multicourse complex. The Stadium might be the "must play," but the Mountain is the repeat play. Although it has many of the distinctive Dye features, like forced water carries, pot bunkers, elevated

The Stadium Course, 9th hole

greens, and railroad ties, its demands in the playing are slightly less intense. It also has the flexibility in design that allows a scratch player to be challenged from the tips while a less-skilled or occasional player can negotiate the property from the forward markers in comfortable fashion. This is in direct contrast to the Stadium, which plays either long and brutal or short and brutal.

The Dunes is adjacent to The Mountain Course at the La Quinta Resort. Among other reasons, its fame derives from the par-3 6th hole, facetiously known as the "shortest par-5 in the desert." At 185 yards and ringed by deep bunkers, any of-fline tee shot will likely result in a five on the card.

This course is more utilitarian in nature than the other Dye designs. There's a bit of an industrial motif, as a round includes traversing a cement wash, a broad canal used to funnel the occasional deluge away from the housing neighborhoods. There are a few power lines in sight, and some tees abut busy roadways. But while not as scenic as the other area

Dye courses as a whole, a survey of its parts reveals a wide variety of ultra-challenging golf holes, particularly around the turn. When playing from the tips—not overly long at 6,700 yards—one must keep a good hold on the driver, lest it slip from the grasp and helicopter into a waiting lake. That's how close the water lurks to the teeing grounds at the daunting par-3 8th, the reachable par-5 9th, and the demanding par-4 10th. The Dunes is characterized by a host of elevated greens, so mid- and short-iron accuracy are imperative. Missing side-to-side will make for a long day with the sand and gap wedges, which should always be close at hand. One can't compare the difficulty factor of the Dunes with other Dye creations in the area, the Stadium and Mountain courses in particular. That said, the finishing trio, while not as staunch as The Stadium, are as demanding as anything else he's done in and around Palm Springs. In fact, the penultimate hole is an absolute bear. Nearly 440 yards in length, with a horseshoe-shaped lake guarding the green, a bogey five is an acceptable score for most any player on the course.

When Pete was speaking at the Grand Opening of PGA West, he kept referring to me as "Joe Webster," which is another developer he's worked with extensively. Afterward I said "Dammit, Pete, you spent $30 million of my money and you don't even know my name!"

Joe Walser, Jr., *principal, Landmark Development Corporation*

Opposite: The Stadium Course, 17th hole
Below: The Mountain Course, 16th hole

The Citrus Course is well named, sitting as it does in a former grapefruit grove. At the right time of year, players can maintain their energy by picking a grapefruit, orange, or tangelo off the myriad trees that provide this mellower Dye design with incredible beauty, ambience, and fragrance. Any player contracting scurvy during the course of the round has no one but himself to blame.

Of the quartet of Dye courses in the PGA West–La Quinta megalopolis, Citrus in the only private enclave. Those lucky members have a real gem. There are hundreds of palo verde trees, full-canopied mesquites, and yellow-bloomed acacias dotting the property. With the hanging fruit, soaring palms surrounding the greens, and colorful plantings adorning the landscape, it might be easy for a cynic to dismiss the course as nothing more than eye candy. But it can be a punisher despite the pretty packaging.

Citrus was constructed in the same general timeframe as the nearby Stadium, but this effort is Dye as Dr. Jekyll, not as Mr. Hyde. It's flatter, calmer, and gentler. There's water abounding, though some of it is incidental or ornamental. But some is decidedly not.

The fear-inducing 3rd is a lengthy 200-plus-yard par-3 where any ball leaking right will never be struck again. Same scenario on the 13th, albeit from shorter range. The final hole is considered one of the staunchest in the desert, 450-odd yards with a ball-eating bunker in the landing zone and a lake guarding the green.

One of the great things about Citrus is the fact that good shots aren't going to bounce into bad places, as in some of Dye's more contentious designs. A solid shot will be rewarded. And only shots poorly struck will come to real grief.

The Coachella Valley might as well be renamed Golf City, with PGA West and La Quinta Resort far and away the single largest entity. There are a grand total of nine courses available under a single class of membership. And of the nine, nearly half were designed by Pete Dye, including the two that are the most popular and renowned. A handful of other designs are scattered throughout the region as well. If the sum total of this body of work doesn't make Dye the mayor of Golf City, one can make a good argument for calling him the sheriff.

The Citrus Course, 18th hole

I was doing routing work for the Dyes prior to construction at PGA West. Alice and I debated at length as to how the closing holes should be configured. We were trying to strike a delicate balance between the housing presence, sight lines for viewers, and traffic flow during large tournaments—all the while keeping the golf holes from being repetitive. I eventually made my points very clear, and Alice came to agree with my perspective. The Dyes were leaving, and Pete U-turned back into the office for a final word. "You are now one-out-of-two in arguments with Alice. That's a world-record percentage, and if I were you, I'd retire from competition right now." I took his advice, and never argued with Alice again.

Tom Doak, *golf course architect; former associate of Pete Dye*

Westin Mission Hills
Pete Dye Course

How classic is the Palm Springs setting at the Westin Mission Hills Resort and Spa? Depending on one's starting point, the drive might include a turn off Frank Sinatra onto Bob Hope Drive, through the intersection at Gerald Ford, before a final detour onto Dinah Shore Drive.

There are two courses available to guests at this sprawling full-service resort complex. The Dye course debuted in 1987, the Gary Player several years later. The concentration of championship courses in the neighborhood rivals anything in the desert region. Besides the duo at the Westin, there are three other courses right next door at Mission Hills Country Club.

Considering the various Houses of Horrors he's authored elsewhere in this desert, courses like PGA West Stadium and Mountain, and the adjacent Challenge Course at Mission Hills Country Club, calling this Pete Dye's most benign effort in the Coachella Valley isn't saying a whole lot. But the fact is that this course, designed primarily for casual resort players, lets a golfer breathe easy. At least between tee and green.

Players need to choose their tees carefully. They should not automatically step to the back of the box, regardless of the fact that the ultimate yardage is basically the same distance as most courses' blue markers. First, it's a par-70, with only one par-5 per side. So its 6,700 yards plays more like 7,000 yards on a regulation par-72 track. Second, there are some tremendous disparities in the length of the par-4 holes. The black markers, often located on the far side of the road, can be as much as 60 yards longer than the gold markers, which play around 6,150. This is apparent on the opening nine especially, with a trio of par-4s that average more than 450 yards from the tips. Most players will have a far more relaxing round taking that giant step forward to the penultimate markers.

Elevated greens, occasional false fronts, and sizeable mounding surrounding the putting surface give this course its teeth. The fairways are mostly wide, and while water becomes a dramatic factor every so often, more than two-thirds of the course has none whatever. Missing the green left or right requires a deft touch with a sand iron if the lie is shaggy, but if it's a shaved bank, which is occasionally the case, there are myriad recovery options.

When water does come into play, it gets one's attention quickly. The par-5 5th necessitates a well-struck tee shot over a lake, as does the one-shot 8th. The 14th will give pause, as two separate water bodies intrude on the playing field, one left of the fairway and another right of the green. The final hole has water encroaching on the entire left side. But mostly there

Pete Dye Course, 18th hole

are wide corridors with containment mounding that serves to help keep a ball in play and gives the surrounding housing an elevated look at the fairways. Considering the two courses see more than 80,000 rounds annually, the conditioning is remarkable. Part of the reason is attention to detail by the staff. Another is the natural drainage and sandy soil base that facilitate ideal growing conditions in the area.

Pete Dye, who so often makes golfers quake in their spikes from the tee box, offers "intimidation lite" at the Westin Mission Hills. For higher handicappers especially, it's a good introduction to the man's style, but with the punishment meted out in small doses.

Can we *ever* call Pete a pushover? Dare we call him Easy Pete? At Westin Mission Hills, the answer is a qualified "yes."

Long Cove Club

With Alice Dye

Harbour Town Golf Links is the most famous course on Hilton Head Island, and rightfully so. Many of the game's finest players do battle there every April at what's currently known as the Verizon Heritage, one of the preeminent invitational tournaments on the PGA Tour. But even though it's the course that helped put Hilton Head on the map some forty years ago, there is a contingent that feels Harbour Town isn't the best course on the island. And others believe that it's not even the best Pete Dye–designed course on Hilton Head. Some think that honor goes to Long Cove Club—nearly 700 prime acres located less than five miles from the candy-striped lighthouse that gives Harbour Town its imprimatur.

Noted architect Tom Doak was part of Long Cove's construction crew back in 1980. South Carolinian Bobby Weed was the construction supervisor, and P.B. Dye manned a bulldozer, creating "some of the finest shaping I've ever seen," according to his proud father. They were the nucleus of a crew comprised mostly of golf purists, many of whom were very good players and several of whom went on to achieve architectural prominence in their own right. Their affection for and innate understanding of the game was instrumental in producing a course that remains a timeless classic.

"I thought from the beginning it would be one of Pete's best, and I love the result," says Doak, who spent three years working for the Dyes, and once remarked, "I owe whatever I have achieved in the business to Pete and Alice Dye." Doak's brilliant minimalist style has made his best courses, much like Pete Dye's, fixtures on various Top 100 lists.

Long Cove's day-to-day appeal for the membership has much to do with the diversity of the on-site topography. The early holes wind through a portion of the extensive lagoon system, then several duneland-style holes with prominent love grasses come into play, followed by the waterside holes early in the back nine, with sweeping views of Broad Creek.

Coming back to Hilton Head more than a dozen years after designing Harbour Town, Dye knew the comparisons were inevitable. So while that original effort was notable for slender, serpentine fairways and pint-sized greens, Long Cove has neither. Like many Dye-designed courses, tee shots look scarier than they actually are, because the fairways are roomier than they appear. Peripheral containment mounding will often kick an offline approach shot back toward greens that are medium size or larger, some with as many as three distinct levels.

Much of the desirability of Long Cove stems from the holes being routed so sensibly and naturally on the land. Golf writer Charles Price summed it up well, saying, "The course has a

In the mid-1980s, Pete was just finishing up Long Cove Club on Hilton Head Island, which was a project of mine. I came down with an extremely serious spinal infection and was in intensive care in the hospital. My wife, Mary, was sitting with me; the phone rang—and it was Pete. She was so touched that Pete called me, especially when he insisted she pass the phone into the oxygen tent.

I weakly put the phone to my ear, and Pete said, "Don't you dare die, you sonofabitch! You're the only person alive that knows you owe me $350,000! A guy who owed me a ton of dough died just last week, and I can't afford to get stiffed again!" I said, "If I survive this thing, I'm gonna kill you." Mary could tell by the expression on my face it wasn't the sympathy call she had thought it was.

Joe Webster III, *course developer; owner of the Dye Preserve in Jupiter, Florida*

18th hole

13th hole

timeless transparency, and is beautiful just for golf's sake. It fits the land that's there. Nobody could intelligently pick the noblest courses without having played Long Cove."

Another reason the course turned out so wonderfully is the attention to detail the architect provided. Pete and Alice spent several months in a rented condominium just across the highway from the building site, directing construction and overseeing the work personally every day. It's a far cry from the process of typical modern architects, who fly in for the day a few times during the construction process.

Jim Stuart won the first USGA event ever held at Long Cove, the 1991 U.S. Mid-Amateur Championship. He remembers his triumphant week fondly. "Competitive golfers are sometimes leery of Pete Dye courses—you never know what type of scary, over-the-top stuff he might have up his sleeve. But Long Cove was right there in front of you, very

straightforward, and a really wonderful job with the land. It's certainly one of his best."

The club members and homeowners are avid players, so their course gets plenty of play, some 30,000 rounds annually. But conditioning remains meticulous. Long Cove also benefits from an abnormally high percentage of walking golfers. Roughly half of all member play is conducted on foot, a statistic as remarkable as it is delightful in the land of "cart-ball." Divots and unattended ball marks are few, underscoring a commitment to excellence by an involved membership.

P.B. Dye said it best when he remarked that Long Cove was built by "people who love golf." The same can be said about the proud members of this first-class facility. Their affection for the game is totally understandable, because it's in direct correlation to the exquisite playground in their collective backyard.

Our whole crew, Pete included, would be down in the dirt for twelve and fourteen hours, shaping green complexes by hand or with small tools. You'd need a fire hose to get the grime off us by day's end. Alice would come by in the late afternoon to inspect our work, all prim and proper, her clothing spotless. We'd hold our breath waiting for her approval. If she suggested a revision—a tweak or a wholesale change that would improve the design or make it more user-friendly—Pete was quick to agree, and the changes would be made. It didn't matter if it took an hour or another whole day. None of us minded, because it was the Dyes' dogged pursuit of perfection, making the course as good as it could possibly be, that drove us. We thought every change we made would improve the golf course, and it was always a sad day when the course was grassed, because then the changes were permanent. I never saw Alice pick up a shovel or drive a bulldozer. But she had tremendous influence on most every course Pete ever built.

Bobby Weed, *golf course architect; long-time design associate of Pete Dye*

8th hole

TPC Sawgrass Stadium Course, Dye's Valley Course
Stadium Course with Alice Dye
Dye's Valley Course with Bobby Weed and Jerry Pate

Deane Beman was the first Hall of Famer to swat a ball at what was to become the Stadium Course at TPC Sawgrass in Ponte Vedra Beach, just south of Jacksonville. On February 12, 1978, the then-PGA Tour commissioner hit a ceremonial drive into 415 acres of wooded wetlands and swamps filled with creatures both snuffling and slithering. It was part ceremonial, part celebratory—the Tour had just purchased the morass for a single dollar bill.

In the ensuing decades, practically every contemporary Hall of Fame member and modern golf star has followed Beman onto the property. This puts the Stadium Course on an extremely short list of public access facilities, in company with the Old Course at St. Andrews and Pebble Beach.

Pete Dye was given two directives at project's inception. The course name was derived from the fact that Beman and the Tour brass wanted large, spectator-friendly mounding throughout the facility, so that golf fans would have numerous vantage points from which to watch the game's best battle for the tournament title. And, according to upper management, the Stadium Course was to be "the most democratic course in the world," testing all aspects of one's game. It was to have short and long par-3s and par-4s, reachable and unreachable par-5s, holes bending both left and right, and no two consecutive holes heading in the same direction, so that a prevailing wind would always make holes play differently.

"Democratic" might have been the idea. "Demonic" was the end result. How tough was Pete Dye's initial effort? The Tournament Players Championship was first conducted on the grounds in 1982, and featured names like Nicklaus, Palmer, Trevino, Miller, Wadkins, and Sutton—thirty-five Majors won among them. They all missed the cut.

The pros' initial reaction was pure outrage mixed with sarcasm. "I've never been very good at stopping a 5-iron on the hood of a car," said Jack Nicklaus. "Where are the windmills and the animals?" questioned Fuzzy Zoeller. "It's 90 percent horse manure and 10 percent luck," offered J.C. Snead. At the insistence of the disgruntled Tour elite, Pete Dye quickly smoothed, widened, buffed, and softened some of the Stadium Course's rough edges. Leveled with so much criticism, he also leveled the heavily contoured greens. Over time, the course became more popular, with the pros convening annually for what is now known as The Players Championship. This so-called "Fifth Major" attracts the strongest field of the year, with nearly all of the world's top echelon in attendance. So while the Stadium Course has an incredible legacy, it's the layout itself that keeps the tee sheet filled in perpetuity, and

Above: Stadium Course, 4th hole
Opposite: Stadium Course, 1st hole

the course firmly ensconced in the worldwide top 100. It has always been phenomenally trendy with the pay-to-play crowd, eager to calm their butterflies as they try to hold on to the short iron, then hold the island green 17th. Keep it on terra firma all the way down the final fairway. Resort guests and vacationers enjoy this eighteen-hole thrill ride from opening tee shot to final putt. And a large part of the appeal, from the get-go, is that sink-or-swim little tee shot near round's end, lurking in every player's mind.

It should be noted that Alice Dye, co-architect on so many of her husband's legendary creations, was the impetus behind his single most notorious construction. The island green 17th was originally planned as a simple par-3 with a small adjacent lake. But the fine quality of sand next to the green site kept the crew digging, using the fill on other fairways. The sand-cavity was eventually so deep and wide that the Dyes, in tandem, decided to go for broke and completely encircle the green with water.

Pete Dye was called in to make some significant changes in 2006, the impetus for the alteration being drainage. The PGA Tour noted that during The Players Championship, the course played five shots harder during dry years than soggy ones. Water, wastelands, and ungainly mounding may abound, but when the fairways are sodden it's still a dartboard for the game's best. So during an eight-month, $60 million renovation, the fairways were scalped and a six-inch layer of fresh sand, the equivalent of sixteen football fields per fairway, was installed beneath the grass, the better to percolate and dry quickly after downpours. Now it's a firmer, faster golf course, where off-line shots bound more quickly toward thick rough, uneven lies, encroaching water, and other unpleasantness.

A new irrigation system was also installed, greenside bunkers were deepened, and 120 supplemental yards were judiciously added to the course, to bring back the same shot values that existed back in the early 1980s. The par-3 8th hole was a long iron back in the day, but as equipment and fitness

Stadium Course, 11th hole

levels improved, it became a mid-iron. Now, at an expanded 230-plus yards, it's a long iron or hybrid club once again. The watery 18th, daunting to begin with, is now a gargantuan 480-yard finisher.

When the course reopened after the 2006 renovation, forecaddies became mandatory. And the real deal, walking caddies, also became available for the first time. This much-welcomed addition now means that a resort guest not only can play this much-admired Tour venue, but can enjoy the walking experience in the same manner the Tour pros do. But posting scores like the Tour elite? Sorry, two out of three will have to do.

The truth of the matter is that the "other" eighteen at TPC Sawgrass, the far-less-in-demand Dye's Valley Course, is an outstanding test of the game. Though the Valley is considered among Florida's top twenty layouts itself, no faint praise in a golf-saturated state with a thousand-something courses, it can't help but wither in the tremendous shadow of the iconic Stadium Course. It's the green-grass iteration of a Billy Ripken, Jim Belushi, or Charlotta Sorenstam, doomed by comparison to its Hall-of-Fame sibling.

In the interest of full disclosure, there are a couple of general raps on the Valley that keep it from its full due: houses and power lines. There are homes throughout, and some slightly tarnished sightlines due to the power line presence. For that matter, there are several road crossings and some traffic noise, besides. But none of these potential distractions can alter the fact that Dye's Valley Course is a solid layout. It's full of testing tee shots, beautifully framed fairways, and difficult pin placements. It's a quality course, and if it existed as a stand-alone facility elsewhere in the state, or in Alabama or Georgia, people would flock to play it.

"It wasn't an easy course to build," recalls Bobby Weed, Dye's design associate on the project, "but Pete had really done the heavy lifting a few years prior on the Stadium Course, in terms of drainage issues, irrigation, and the like. We were able to tie into their infrastructure, so the construction demands weren't quite as tough." Not as tough to build, and not as tough to play.

Besides his status as a PGA master professional, Billy Detlaff has been a top-level executive of PGA Tour golf course properties for more than twenty years. "Once in a while, we'll have a resort guest claim that they enjoy Dye's Valley Course more than the Stadium. Many people feel it's one of the best resort courses in the nation. The shots around the green still demand imagination, but aren't nearly as penal as what the newly revamped Stadium Course demands."

My most memorable story about Pete Dye occurred years ago, and Pete wasn't even present. It was very early in my Tour career. I was still really green, and considered myself lucky to be sitting alongside my boyhood idol, Jack Nicklaus, and then–PGA Tour commissioner Deane Beman at the TPC Sawgrass in Jacksonville. Jack had just finished a frustrating round and was pretty disgruntled. His preferred ball flight was a fade from left to right. He was annoyed that a couple of the par-5s, number 2 and number 16, were set up for a right-to-left-player, someone who plays a hook. Distance-wise, they should have been reachable, but apparently he couldn't get his ball in the proper position on the fairway to attack the green.

He complained, "Have you ever seen Pete Dye play golf? When he hooks it, he hits a 40-yard hook. When he fades it, he hits a 20-yard hook. Even his wife, Alice, hooks the ball!"

I thought it was pretty funny at the time. But overall, I consider Pete to be a pioneer. He really broke the mold in regards to modern golf architecture, and he's someone I've long admired.

Brad Faxon, *PGA Tour winner*

Stadium Course, 13th hole

On the subject of revamped, even well into his eighties, Dye isn't slowing. He's been hired to do some revamping of the Valley Course also, rightfully so since it now bears his name. And with the infusion of dollars and the commitment to further improvements by the PGA Tour, Dye's Valley Course, understudy though it may be, will continue to be a high-caliber golf experience.

The nines have recently been reversed, mitigating what was formerly a harsh wakeup call at round's inception. The lagoons lurking to the slicing side of the first two holes are now found as the back nine begins. An equal number of golf balls will undoubtedly filter to lagoon's bottom, but at least players can't complain they weren't warmed up. Another oddity has been erased due to the flip-flop. In its former iteration there wasn't a par-5 until the 7th, which began a stretch of three par-5s in four holes.

There are no yawners on the course, but the middle of what's now the opening nine, the 3rd though the 7th, is the most interesting sequence. There are two potentially drivable par-4s for bazooka-types, and a "poor man's island green par-3," with water to the right and long, and all sorts of shaggy mounding and bunkers waiting to the left. Perhaps the most solid hole on the course—the no-nonsense 6th—is a long par-4 stretching more than 460 yards from the tips, 425 for blue tee players. A massive lagoon dominates the right side, with an equally sizeable waste bunker in the ideal landing zone.

The much-maligned power lines come into play on the short par-4 7th. If the drive is yanked left, there's no way to see the flagstick, hidden by massive mounding. But one can line up the approach regardless, thanks to the stanchion in the distance. Talk about turning a negative into a positive.

Stadium Course, 18th hole

Some serious hillsides encroach on several back nine fairways. At certain points, one would be hard-pressed to remember that this is mostly flat Florida. Though caddies are now available, Dye's Valley is no walker's gem, with some longish hauls between greens and tees.

Management tells the story of a certain group of repeat visitors to TPC Sawgrass. For more than fifteen years, this foursome insisted on going round and round the Stadium Course exclusively. Finally, one year they deigned to attempt the Valley Course and were immediately smitten with the slightly gentler layout. "They were kicking themselves that they had never checked it out," recalls Detlaff. "They really felt like they had been missing the boat."

Learn from the mistakes of others. Visit Dye's Valley Course early on. When visiting TPC Sawgrass, be sure to give "little brother" its rightful due.

Pete and I shared a condo on Hilton Head for quite a while when we were working on Long Cove. He was also taking regular trips down to Jacksonville, checking on the progress of the Stadium Course. Pete would interrupt my sleep, tromping up the stairs in his boots at one, sometimes two o'clock in the morning. The next thing I knew, he'd be pounding on my door at 5 a.m., saying "You can't build a golf course from bed!" I couldn't believe how much energy the man had, keeping on the move twenty-odd hours a day. But when you have so much passion for what you're doing, it drives you relentlessly. With the challenges that these various projects entailed, his energy never seemed to flag.

Bobby Weed, *golf course architect; long-time design associate of Pete Dye*

TPC River Highlands

Nine-hole renovation by Pete Dye
Total renovation by Bobby Weed in 1991

It's not easy being a sports fan in Connecticut. The state is home to more than 3.5 million residents, crammed into the third-smallest land mass in the nation (only Delaware and neighboring Rhode Island are tinier). The demarcation line of the Red Sox–Yankees divide is generally New Haven, but since the demise of the NHL's Hartford Whalers, which left the state's capital city in 1997, there's no true hometown rooting interest, at least on the professional level, for state residents. That's one of the main reasons the PGA Tour event contested at the TPC River Highlands every summer is one of the best-attended tournaments in the nation.

"I remember Pete went up to look at an existing golf course called Edgewood in Cromwell, Connecticut, while we were building Long Cove on Hilton Head in the early 1980s," recalls Bobby Weed. "He came back and told me it was one of the most amazing things he'd seen. It came down in buckets while he was visiting, more than four inches in one storm. But when he finally got on the property, there was no standing water at all."

The old sand and gravel quarry was an exceptional site, with wonderful soil quality and the potential for inherent drama, though the original course was considered ho hum. Dye redid the back nine entirely, intensifying the risk/reward elements of the water-laden final stretch and adding the spectator mounding that would prove to be pivotal when what was then called the Greater Hartford Open moved from nearby Wethersfield Country Club in 1984. In the three decades prior to the move to Cromwell, located some ten miles south, the Hartford Tour stop benefited from a roster of popular champions like Arnold Palmer, Lee Trevino, Billy Casper, Ken Venturi, and Sam Snead. Peter Jacobsen, as popular as any modern golfer, won the inaugural event at the new site. What wasn't as popular was the juxtaposition between the traditional front nine and Dye's radical back.

"Players described it as a Jekyll and Hyde experience. The two nines were so different," says Weed, who was named the PGA Tour's in-house architect in the mid-1980s and was then called upon to redo the course entirely in 1991. "Pete was brought in to change the back nine, add drama, and add an amphitheater effect to the finish," Weed explains. "By the time Pete was done, it seems you could put half the state's population on the hillside overlooking the finish, but there wasn't enough money at the time to redo the front nine. When I was directed to overhaul the project, it had been repurposed into something of a housing development, with a nearby subdivision, and the purchase of additional acreage allowed us to make significant changes. That's what allowed us the wherewithal to redo the course again, in its entirety."

The inward nine plays downhill almost the entire way, with several early holes routed above a ridgeline seventy feet above the Connecticut River (hence the River Highlands moniker). The most notable stretch is what's referred to as the "Golden Triangle," the 15th through 17th holes, which play around a four-acre lake. Adding the tough par-4 finisher into the equation, you get opinions like, "four of the most exciting finishing holes in a group anywhere in the world." This from Stewart Cink, veteran Ryder Cupper and consistent performer, whose inaugural PGA Tour win came at Hartford in 1997.

The finishing segment, including the drivable but dangerous par-4 15th, with water lurking to the left, the over-water par-3 16th, and the fishhook-shaped par-4 penultimate hole with a tight driving area and water short and right of the green, make for three of the most dangerous consecutive holes on the Tour. "No lead is really safe on that closing stretch," adds Weed. "Even though the course is just 6,800 yards and one of the shortest on Tour, as a par-70 it still has plenty of bite."

Though it's now wholly his design, the architect gives credit to his mentor. "Pete was working here just a short while after he pioneered the concept of stadium golf, at TPC Sawgrass. He identified the drama potential that existed around the lake, and added the amphitheater effect so the perilous conclusion would be in full view of huge throngs of fans every year when the Tour came to town. It's that reason, as much as any other, that explains why the Hartford stop is, year in and year out, one of the best-attended tournaments in professional golf."

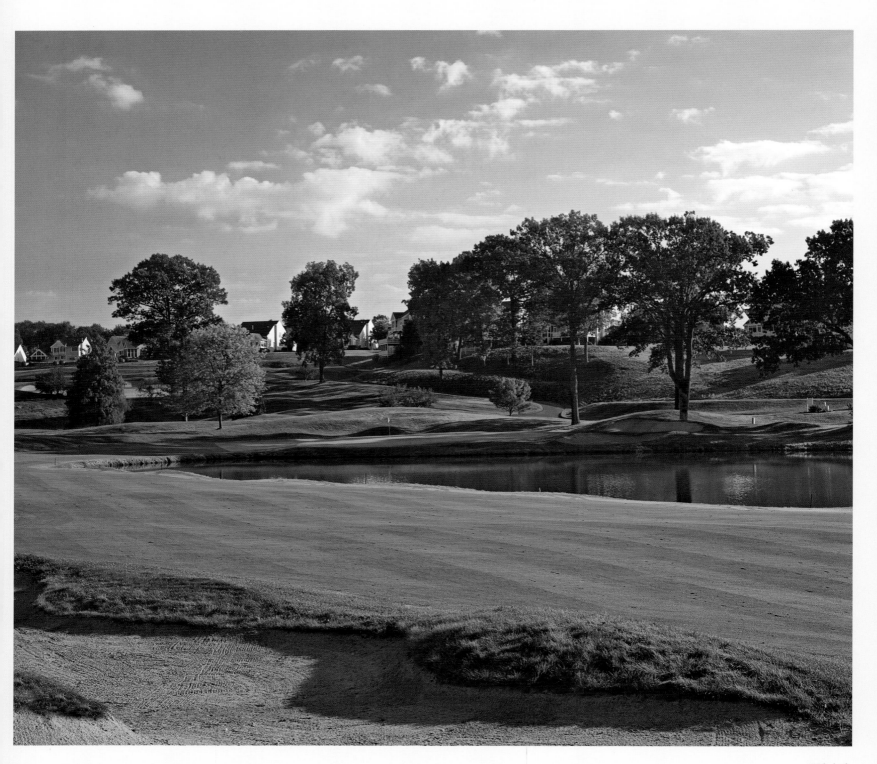

17th hole

The Honors Course
With P.B. Dye

In more than fifty years as a course designer, in steady demand all over the hemisphere and beyond, Pete Dye has worked on, inspected, and examined untold hundreds of land parcels. But it's doubtful he ever encountered a more inviting piece of raw property than the 460-acre wooded valley that eventually became The Honors Course.

Building it was a burden. (More on that in a moment.) But playing The Honors is beatific, one of the most tranquilly enjoyable experiences the game offers. The location is the rural southeastern Tennessee village of Ooltewah, some 10 miles from Chattanooga. Ringed by nearby White Oak Mountain, peppered with dogwoods, hickory trees, and other native hardwoods, covered in bluegrass and native fescues, home to dozens of bird species including wild turkeys, this is as natural and unspoiled a setting for golf as one can ever hope for.

"Rarely does one get to work with virtually untouched land, creating a course devoid of the distractions of land development and commercialism," marveled Pete Dye. Speaking of founder Jack Lupton, Dye continued: "He'll settle for nothing less than the best. He understands the traditions of the game, the difference between a golf club and a country club. He won't tolerate mediocrity. He demands excellence."

But Lupton's demands likely paled in comparison to the demands of the terrain. Fleets of bulldozers relocated hundreds of tons of dirt. Dynamite blasts roared in the valley, dislodging stumps and imbedded limestone. Felled trees with massive canopies were buried in gaping chasms. Lakes were dug, filling with the rain that never seemed to abate. Viscous Tennessee red clay and a sedimentary rock called chert—which became a four-letter word to Pete—caused more trouble. But when the trials and travails of building were finally done, the end result was one of the most spectacular yet serene creations in the voluminous Dye oeuvre.

Each hole is an entity unto itself. Despite the earth-moving, fairways seem to run with the natural contours of the land. They dip and cant just enough to cause the occasional uneven lie. Two manmade lakes, totaling nearly thirty acres, provide a threefold advantage: They're a water source, a different visual perspective from the heretofore rolling meadow sensibility, and add a healthy measure of angst on several tee shots and approaches.

All eighteen holes are real yeoman's work, but the apex of the round comes early through the inward nine. These highlights include the robust, downhill par-5 11th, the petite dogleg par-4 12th, the left-sweeping par-4 13th with its canted green, and the short 14th, a simple one-shot hole over acres of gnarly,

18th hole

waving fescue grass. This hole, perhaps more than any other, distills The Honors down to its organic essence. So it's ironic that Pete Dye originally designed the hole with a massive waste bunker from tee to green, before the autocratic Lupton ordered it changed. He reprimanded Dye, saying, "This isn't a Florida golf course," and the sand was quickly replaced with an intimidating field of native grasses.

Speaking of grasses, though there are many varieties on the property, including the different fescues and native broomsedge, the most essential is the resilient Zoysia of the fairways, which helps make the course so enjoyable. It's springy underfoot, props the ball up, and is resistant to the temperature extremes of the area. Nurturing the conditions is Superintendent-in-Perpetuity David Stone, hired at the outset,

whom Pete Dye has called "probably the best thing that ever happened to The Honors Course. David understands grass, and grass is what makes a golf course great."

In the playing, the heavy-duty fans circulating air on the greens are the only modern-day intrusion. In many ways the course is a delightful anachronism, a step back in time, with winding earthen footpaths to the fairway cut among hip-high fescue, rustic wooden bridges over water, and rough-hewn stonework surrounding the lakes and elevating several teeing grounds.

No golf course can really be described with efficacy, but The Honors Course renders in sharp relief the ongoing futility of this profession. How can one begin to convey the serene ambience, the quietude of this rolling, wooded meadow? The

8th hole

only sounds on this glorious acreage come from the *thwack* of the golf ball, the occasional exultance after a great shot, the melodious birdsong, and the plaintive cry of (please forgive, as I can't resist) the Chattanooga Choo Choo rolling to the south.

In closing, a brief word about one of the most distinctive course names in golf. Founder and visionary Jack Lupton, a Coca-Cola bottling magnate, was a longtime member of Augusta National, and a close friend and ardent admirer of Bobby Jones, golf's consummate amateur. Lupton had Dye build his hometown course to honor the amateur golfer and amateur game. The club has been honored in turn, playing host to major events such as the U.S. Amateur, Mid-Amateur, Curtis Cup, and NCAA Championship. But Lupton offered an additional rationale for the name. "The golfer should feel that regardless of how they're playing, it simply is an honor to be there." Truer words are rarely spoken, but one thought in addition: Those who really love the game and admire its essential beauty must chart a course to Chattanooga. Because a round in this quiet Ooltewah valley is both an honor and a privilege.

The Ogeechee Golf Club at the Ford Plantation

With P.B. Dye

Three major elements combine to make this course exceptional. The first thing a visitor notes is the absolute dearth of play. There have never been as many as 10,000 rounds played annually, and there likely never will. Considering that the region's temperate climate makes golf a year-round pursuit, the course averages fewer than twenty players a day.

The second notable factor is the dissimilarity between the front and back nine, practically bipolar in their difference. The outward nine holes are a straightforward journey through forests of pine, oak, and palmettos. With expansive waste areas festooned with ball-eating love grass, and smallish greens averaging 4,000 square feet, shot-making is at a premium.

However, Dye forsook traditionalism and constructed the inward nine holes in the midst of the plantation's antebellum rice fields, which Henry Ford had turned into lettuce fields back in the 1930s. This nine might be described as a low-country links, bereft of trees, with incidental water intruding on just a few occasions. The designer moved more than two million cubic yards of earth during construction to achieve the desired result.

The 13th hole in particular is an attention-getter, and certainly one of the most demanding two-shot holes in Pete Dye's oeuvre. Players tee off just steps from Lake Clara, named for Ford's wife. Hard by the lakeside, with all sorts of fish, fowl, and reptiles close at hand, the setting is pristine and slightly primeval. It's an absolutely striking golf hole. And at 450 yards from the tips, into the prevailing wind and with the lake menacing both drive and approach, a player must strike the ball with absolute precision to have any hope of success.

Pete Dye once called the Ogeechee Golf Club "arguably my finest southern design." A strong sentiment, considering that world-renowned classics like Harbour Town, the Ocean Course, and the Stadium Course at TPC Sawgrass are within a few hours' drive. It's a slight overstatement, but his thoughtful work at the low-profile, low-density Ford Plantation still deserves serious attention.

Opposite: 12th hole
Below: 17th and 18th hole

Firethorn Golf Club

With Perry Dye

Without knowing the background, one would be hard-pressed to draw a parallel between soft-spoken Midwesterner Mark Wible and the late, self-aggrandizing entrepreneur Victor Kiam. The former was born, raised, and lives low-profile in his beloved Lincoln, Nebraska. The latter, an early iteration of businessman-turned-celebrity, who at one time owned the NFL's New England Patriots, used to trumpet his corporate triumphs in television commercials that aired worldwide.

However, they do have one thing in common. In his first and most memorable commercial for Remington shavers, Kiam crowed, "I liked it so much, I bought the company." Wible, a longtime member and now owner of his hometown Firethorn Golf Club, eventually did the very same thing.

Wible was an executive at Nebraska's National Bank of Commerce when he joined Firethorn in 1989, three years after the course debuted. When the bank was purchased by Wells Fargo in 2000, Wible decided to leave, joining forces with his largest customer, Landscapes Unlimited, one of the world's largest golf course construction companies. "I cut my teeth in the golf business during a five-year stint there, where I was basically an in-house investment banker, helping them to arrange financing for their various projects."

Dick Youngscap, the original driving force and managing partner at Firethorn, knew Wible as a longtime member and fellow golf-businessman. He approached him to become the club's general manager in 2005. Wible accepted only after negotiating partial ownership, and several years later, bought the entire operation outright. Youngscap's notoriety in the golf world grew exponentially a decade after Firethorn opened. He was the visionary behind the highly acclaimed Sand Hills Golf Club, in the sparsely populated north-central plains of central Nebraska, "There's a fine line between persistence and stupidity," explains the entrepreneur. "Neither golf course project seemed to make any sense at inception. But fortunately they've both turned out nicely."

Pete Dye's architectural acumen and decision to bring target golf to the plains eventually led to the success of Firethorn. And, some years later, Youngscap's association with Dye enhanced his credibility as the Sand Hills project came to fruition in the mid-1990s.

12th hole

14th hole

For the uninitiated, Sand Hills, a Ben Crenshaw–Bill Coore design, is widely considered among the top ten or fifteen courses in the world. The official address is Mullen, Nebraska. Population 500-or-so. But as Cat Stevens used to sing, it's "miles from nowhere."

By comparison, Lincoln is a metropolis of nearly a quarter-million souls, with the fortunate few occupying 140-odd home sites at the Firethorn residential complex. Many of the homes are well removed from the playing fields, occupying higher ground on the periphery, with the prairie-style golf course routed lower, on gently rolling terrain in the property's center. "Dick is a naturalist, and wanted the golf course to occur as naturally as possible, with little earth moved," explains Wible.

Pete Dye agreed with the philosophy, and the course lies in low profile on the former cornfield from which it sprang.

"When Pete first walked the land with me, he said, 'If I don't help you with this, I think you'll make a mess of it.'" So recounts Youngscap, like Wible a Lincoln native. Dye recognized that the ridgeline bisecting the acreage was a natural divide for the nines, the more open terrain to the north, a heavily wooded parcel to the south.

Though the original course plan called for a roomy 200 acres, Dye lobbied for an additional 40-acre parcel toward the southeast, containing a conservation pond. The land was purchased, and Dye rewarded the developer's generosity by routing the finishing holes around the water hazard, adding

4th hole

even more challenge, beauty, and distinctiveness to a course that was soon to be one of the most talked-about in the state. Some fifteen years after opening, a former protégé of Pete's named Rod Whitman, a talented but little-known Canadian, added an additional nine, bringing Firethorn to twenty-seven holes in the late 1990s. "Before Pete came along, every course in Nebraska was wall-to-wall bluegrass," explains Youngscap. "Firethorn was the first target-style course in the plains, and caused quite a stir."

The buzz was good, but membership sales weren't. In the mid-1980s, the economy was in a rut, interest rates were high, and the agriculture climate in the doldrums. "Our biggest problem was the folks that could afford the membership couldn't play the course. It was too tough. And those that *could* play the course, the talented 'flat-bellies,' couldn't afford to join," recounts Youngscap.

Perry Dye, Pete's firstborn son and Firethorn's co-architect, suggested that to jumpstart cash flow the club should lease

memberships to those who couldn't afford the mid-four-figure initiation. "They paid a one-time $1,000 fee to lease a membership," recalls Youngscap. "Then they were responsible for full annual dues. Many lessees were regular patrons of our pro shop, restaurant, and bar, adding greatly to the bottom line. It wasn't long before we had a full complement of 300 members."

Firethorn's current owner began his association as a full member, not as a lessee. "I was about thirty years old when I joined, and it was a real stretch for me at that time. I really had no good reason to join a private golf club. It was a financial overextension, to say the least," relates Wible, who still couches things in banking terms. "But I never regretted it. I loved the whole atmosphere, it was great on a personal level, and a great means to do business."

What was once simply a business tool has now become his entire business. "It's not without its challenges," concludes the owner, "but Firethorn is definitely a labor of love."

Old Marsh Golf Club

There are nearly a hundred golf courses in Palm Beach County, Florida. In this region the game is as unavoidable as an annual hurricane threat, and the town of Palm Beach Gardens might well be the eye of the storm. Stand-alone facilities like Old Palm and Frenchman's Reserve, and multi-course developments like BallenIsles, PGA National, Mirasol, Eastpointe, and Frenchman's Creek are all within the city limits, and available to those with the dollars and the desire.

Old Marsh has an edge on the rest—mainly because the edge of the 460-acre property sits farther west than any of the competing communities. It's surrounded to the north, south, and west by untold acres of marsh, in addition to the 200-odd acres of wetlands within its own boundaries. The name Old Marsh has a distinctive ring. But All Marsh might be closer to the truth.

The fact is this: There is plenty of room to maneuver the golf ball amidst the 75 acres of dedicated turf on 7,000-plus yards of golf course. But the wide playing corridors are dwarfed by a zillion acres of unplayable lies that encircle them, and therein lie the psychological demands of Old Marsh.

"You have to go to coastal Carolina to find a private course enveloped in so much open space," said Pete Dye, as he embarked on a two-year permitting process to begin work on the course in the mid-1980s. "My first glance at the proposed site made me wonder whether a roaring lion might appear from deep within the high grass, since the marshland's rich vegetation and abundant wildlife reminded me of Africa."

There are no lions to be found, but exotic birds—forty species in all—call Old Marsh home. Anhinga, ibis, sand hill cranes, blue heron, the shrimp-spearing roseate spoonbill,

wood stork, and dozens of others make Old Marsh not only a friend to the Audubon Society, but an ornithologist's reverie.

Golfers will be shaken from their reverie quickly, though, as one forced carry after another lies in wait. Dye initially envisioned a course even harder than the one he ultimately produced. The rugged par-4 4th was initially conceived with a more daunting carry over wetlands than what currently exists. But when the head pro and his assistants, all former Tour players, couldn't find dry land, Dye relented. He moved the back box forward, grumbling that now he understood why they were *ex* Tour players.

The routing is clockwise on the outward journey, with all the trouble to the right, and then counterclockwise on the return, where the marsh is on the opposite side of the fairway. So, depending on a player's particular swing flaw, there will always be a more manageable nine. Slicers will be sweating things till they can breathe a bit easier on the 10th tee, while the pull-hook crowd will live in dread anticipation of the waving-grass challenges that await them on the long march home.

Most golfers only see the course from a playing perspective: the sweep of the fairway, the shape of a bunker, the tilt of the green. But Pete Dye put as much emphasis on the subsurface as he did on the playing field proper. At Old Marsh he designed a unique drainage system that inhibits irrigated water from leaving the property and sullying the environmentally pure marshland beyond its borders. Instead, all water on the course is drained into canals or retention ponds. And while golfers have occasionally been known to curse at Pete, the animals and birdlife are fortunate to have him.

12th hole

Above and opposite: 5th hole

Walking is encouraged, and a fine caddie program is in place. About one-quarter of the 20,000 or so annual rounds played are conducted in ambulatory fashion. But Old Marsh isn't quite a traditional walk in the park. This expansive routing necessitates a couple of cart-shuttle points on property, notably from the 9th green to the 10th tee, that are used to keep things moving on the course.

The southern end of the property borders Mirasol, for several years the home of the PGA Tour's Honda Classic. This is a more traditional Palm Beach County golf development, with the requisite flowerbeds and fountains. But there's a large wetland buffer zone between the two communities, as different in style and philosophy as salt and pepper. Old Marsh is low profile, and not just because the property is countertop flat, with fairways morphing seamlessly into putting surfaces in traditional Scottish style. It's also an understated membership. There's not much nighttime lighting or signage to be seen. It's mellow and low-key, a well-kept (in every sense of the word) secret.

Members tell of golf-loving visitors who come down to Old Marsh for the indelible playing experience and then branch out a bit to see some of Florida's other attractions. They might head north to Orlando for family-oriented theme park action, or south to the Everglades to get back to nature. Invariably, those who come back from the fan-boat tour through Florida's famed swampland primeval sound a variation on a theme. They tell their hosts it was great, but they spied just as many flying, swimming, or crawling critters on or around the fairways of Old Marsh as they did in the Glades.

Which leads to a five-word summation of this inspiring and memorable site: Wildlife, wild course, wonderful experience.

Pete was reconstructing a hole on our home course in south Florida. There was a huge pile of dirt where he was going to relocate a lake. A disgruntled homeowner came out of his villa and demanded to know why his view of the golf course and green were now obstructed. Pete looked at him and then says dryly, "I'm building a marina here." The confused homeowner replies, "This isn't a marina, it's a golf course!" Pete says, "Oh yeah, you're right," and walks away. The guy just looked at me, dumbfounded. He didn't understand that Pete doesn't like to be bothered with questions about what he's doing. Since he usually doesn't work with plans, he improvises as he gets a feel for what's needed on a project. Looking at his incredible design legacy, you have to say he's been right far more often than he's been wrong.

Bob Murphy, *PGA Tour and Champions Tour winner; NBC golf analyst*

Atlanta National Golf Club

With P.B. Dye

Milton, Georgia, well north of Atlanta and far from its traffic-laden suburban sprawl, is home to a wonderful yet little-known collaboration between Pete and P.B. Dye. In a city that boasts legendary venues such as East Lake and Peachtree, prestigious clubs like Cherokee Town & Country, Atlanta Athletic Club, and Piedmont Driving Club, the Atlanta National Golf Club flies a bit below the radar. But this former dairy farm, with silos in view on several holes and just fifteen homes on the property, is one of the metro region's better tests of the game.

Jack Damico is one of the original founding partners of Atlanta National Golf Club. "We interviewed a number of architects, but there were those who wanted to make the project bigger and more elaborate than what we were comfortable with. We weren't interested in subdivisions with swimming pools and tennis courts. We just wanted a top-notch golf course. Pete Dye realized we weren't a bunch of business titans but an enthusiastic group of working professionals who wanted to convene in a golf-only environment. He was happy to accommodate our desires."

And he must have been ecstatic to find out he'd have almost 250 acres on which to implement his vision—nearly twice the normal acreage devoted to eighteen holes—and free from infrastructure constraints. But the kicker is that it's a delightful course to walk, with minimal distance between greens and tees. Nearly three-quarters of rounds played are ambulatory, with just fifty carts on-site to service a membership approaching 400. Only once or twice is the commute more than a minute to the next tee box, but wide playing corridors containing wetlands, grasslands, groves of trees, lakes, and creeks make Atlanta National a bountiful experience.

The Dyes fashioned an internal loop encircled by an external loop to take best advantage of the property. The opening nine is tightly routed in clockwise fashion, while the second nine runs counterclockwise on the perimeter. The professional staff comments, "It's a real Dye sample platter," as there's a bit of everything on display. There are wetlands to contend with, expansive waste bunkers, some with islands of grass within, others shored up with railroad ties. There are short par-4s, reachable par-5s, daunting over-water par-3s, rock-walled streams, scattershot bunkering, and the lurking presence of what's known as Chicken Creek winding throughout.

Greens are large, none larger than the medium-length par-3 2nd. The putting surface is more than fifty yards long,

11th hole

and players approach from a runway-style tee box. This rare combination provides a hole that can literally play a hundred yards different from day to day, depending on where the superintendent puts the tee markers and the flag.

The 12th is another potential card-spoiler, a 200-yard par-3 completely over water, played into the prevailing breeze. The silos in the background that remain from what was once the Little River Dairy Farm make for a pastoral setting. But there's nothing tranquil about white-knuckling a long iron or fairway wood on the tee box with the wind blowing into the player's face. While Dye is the acknowledged master of the strategic short par-4, the risk/reward nature of the tiny 16th isn't owing to architectural acumen but to the fact that permission couldn't be secured to build a green on the far side of the creek—resulting in a truncated hole of under 300 yards.

At the project's outset, all the elements were falling into place. The founders had a great piece of rolling property,

a great designer, and a great group of founders. However, tradition was lacking. "We approached Gene Sarazen," recalls Damico. "We asked him if we could commission a statue of him in his Master's putting stance. He readily agreed, and this life-size metal statue of 'The Squire' sits proudly in the club's Garden of Golf, and became our logo." So Atlanta National is covered—they have a playing legend out front and the artistry of a designing legend behind.

In a way it's curious that Pete Dye has worked so infrequently in Georgia. It's one of the largest states east of the Mississippi River, and has a deeply rooted golf tradition. Furthermore, neighboring states like Florida and South Carolina are Dye hotbeds, with well over three dozen courses between them. But his work at Atlanta National, taken in concert with his other Georgia effort at the Ford Plantation, south of Savannah on the eastern coast, proves one thing. Quality trumps quantity every single time.

Mission Hills Country Club Pete Dye Challenge Course

With Alice Dye

Mission Hills Country Club is probably best known for hosting an LPGA major—the Kraft Nabisco Championship. The Tour has been coming to Mission Hills since Desmond Muirhead designed the club's first golf course in 1972, and the tournament was given major championship status in 1983. And though it's no longer officially referred to as the Dinah Shore (her name came off the event in 2000), it is contested on what has been renamed the Dinah Shore Tournament Course. One of the LPGA's most distinctive annual rituals is when the victor leaps into the pond adjacent to the 18th green after the final putt has fallen.

However, if the event were held at the Pete Dye Challenge Course, located on the northern portion of the property, the leaping options would be many. Two out of every three holes on the Dye design have a significant water presence, making it (no surprise here) the most demanding of the three courses on the property.

The names have changed, but the quality remains. When Pete and Alice Dye debuted the third and final course at Mission Hills in 1988, it was known as the Dinah Shore Course. But when the celebrity singer, a golf lover and long-time supporter of the LPGA, passed away in 1994, it was decided that her name would grace the tournament course. So, as has happened on several occasions over the decades, a course was renamed in Pete's honor. (Two examples come to mind: The Valley Course at TPC Sawgrass is now known as Dye's Valley, and in south Florida, what was previously known as Cypress Links was revamped and renamed The Dye Preserve. Of course, the ultimate honor is in Bridgeport, West Virginia, which from inception has been called Pete Dye Golf Club.)

Though it's a marvelous golf challenge, it is said that the Dye effort attracts less play than the tournament and Arnold Palmer courses, mainly owing to the intimidation factor caused by its many lakes and ponds. That's hard to understand. First, of the dozen water holes on property, only two have water right. So the majority of players, the faders and slicers of the world, have a much easier time of it than the hookers. Second, there is a great deal of foot-high netting separating the fairway from the hazards. It has no bearing on a shot that soars into the water, but a ball that's bouncing and jouncing toward the drink will be repelled back to the playing field. Last, one would think that at a high-end club of this caliber, amid some of the priciest real estate in the West, the financial burden of golf ball purchases would be well down the list of ongoing expenditures.

Though the abounding water presence gives the course its imprimatur, the "dry" holes are wonderful and strategic. The most dedicated set is midway through the opening nine, and they are among the best on the course. The par-4 5th is highlighted by a cavernous waste bunker that runs the entire right side of the landing area on this 400-plus-yard hole, forcing golfers to fly the hazard perpendicularly from the angled tee box to have any reasonable hope of reaching the green. The next is a simple par-3, dry as the surrounding desert. But it's an anxious shot regardless, as the target is a dramatic plateau green. The 8th is a petite par-4, but the tee shot is surrounded by chaparral bushes, there's a gnarly bunker complex encroaching on the landing zone, and the elevated green can be an elusive target.

Throughout the course there are deep, shaggy trenches that preclude views of flagsticks and high mounding bracketing the fairways, serving a double purpose. Since the homes are located well above the fairways, their views are more imperial. And stray drives will result in all manner of ungainly, uneven lies, complicating the approach shot.

In the decades since the club was established in the 1970s there have been numerous glitzy, extremely high-dollar golf-and-real-estate developments brought to fruition from one end of the desert to the other. But regardless of this proliferation, Mission Hills, ringed by marvelous long-range views of the San Jacinto, Santa Rosa, and Little San Bernardino Mountains, remains one of the most prestigious and well-thought-of clubs in the region. The presence of the Pete Dye Challenge Course goes a long way in explaining why.

Opposite, top: 7th hole
Opposite, bottom: 13th hole

Destination Kohler
River and Meadow Valleys at Blackwolf Run, Straits and Irish at Whistling Straits

The question to ask is not: "How did Pete Dye and Herb Kohler collaborate repeatedly over a dozen-odd years, building a series of superb courses that now comprise one of the most desirable golf and resort destinations in the United States?" Rather, the question is: "How did they collaborate at all?"

These are two fiercely independent, nose-to-the-grindstone, no-nonsense sons of the Midwest. Each is wildly successful, widely admired, and somewhat controversial. Both men are used to getting what they want. Kohler is the head of one of the nation's largest and most prosperous private companies, best known for plumbing fixtures but highly diversified, with something along the order of $6 billion in annual sales and approximately 30,000 associates. Pete Dye, who seemingly never met a board of governors he didn't prefer to ignore or an executive committee whose counsel he would rather not seek, might sum up his self-assuredness with a subtle twist on an old expression: "It's the Dye way or the highway."

"My initial impression was that he was an odd duck," recalls Kohler. "He was completely straightforward, had no pretenses. But I hired him because I liked him. He is the consummate artist and golf psychologist, doesn't own a computer, is always pressing forward on the leading edge of agronomic issues. He made me laugh, then and now. He's a great liar, a constant storyteller, but there is no one I respect more." The architect counters, "Herb is very competitive, very intense. He knows what he wants and goes after it."

Dye came into the picture as the business titan continued to add amenities to what was becoming, in piecemeal fashion, an unlikely resort complex in the factory town of Kohler, Wisconsin, near Sheboygan, an hour north of Milwaukee. The genesis of the project was Kohler's renovation of The American Club, an out-of-use European immigrant workers' dormitory located across from the company factories. Though outside consultants did not endorse his decision, Kohler opted for a comprehensive renovation rather than raze the historic 1918 structure, which was in virtual disrepair. Three years later, in 1981, the former dorm had been reborn as a luxury inn. "The hospitality business was built with zero vision," offers Kohler. "We had one little success built on another little success, and suddenly the combination of those successes and the demand for golf became synergistic."

The initial course was named Blackwolf Run, after a prominent Winnebago Indian chief from the 1800s. Shortly after the course opened for play in the summer of 1988, there were lines outside the pro shop door. Golf-loving Wisconsinites and guests of The American Club, who for the first several years were shuttled to a public course here or a private course there, had never before had nearby access to such a beguiling venue, with its rolling terrain, woodlands, wetlands, abounding river, and streams. But despite the setting left by glacial runoff, with native grasses, unusual mounding—some of it Indian burials—and a color palette of natural flowers, it was the strategic element of the routing, the go-for-broke mentality that golfers found irresistible, making the course an instant hit. "I don't know if I could ever design a course hard enough to keep dedicated golfers on the sidelines," Dye says. "They love to dig in, fight me tooth and nail, and though they curse, scream, and call me names, that *one* memorable shot will always bring them back for more." At Blackwolf Run, there are dozens of memorable shots. So it's not hard to envision Herb Kohler, dismayed at the sight of a perpetually filled tee sheet, summoning Dye: "We need another nine. A five-diamond resort cannot tolerate a three-month lead time for a tee time."

The third nine opened in the summer of 1989, and a fourth nine—when the lead time still did not diminish—the summer after that, bringing the total to thirty-six holes.

Opposite, top: The clubhouse at Whistling Straits
Below: Meadow Valleys, 7th hole

Meadow Valleys, 15th hole

Meadow Valleys was created utilizing the original Valley's nine at Blackwolf Run and nine of the new holes. This second eighteen-hole course is considered the most playable of what eventually became four courses at Destination Kohler. It looks and feels more like a traditional Wisconsin golf course than do the other venues, with its rolling, farmland feel and the silos in the distance.

The River is an absolute stunner. It features the daunting Sheboygan River on twelve holes and is an extremely scenic parkland experience, wooded and with abundant wildlife. It's a bit more target oriented, with accuracy more of an imperative in comparison to its adjacent neighbor. In autumn, golfers get more to remember than just the changing colors of the trees. There's a salmon run in the Sheboygan River, and anglers vie for prime position on its banks with the same sense of urgency as do the avid golfers lining up for tee times.

The original Blackwolf Run is holes 1 through 4, and 14 through 18 on the River, and what's now known as the back nine of the Meadow Valleys. The fourth nine that Dye added after the fact—now known as the River's 5th through 13th in particular—are nothing short of spectacular. Major elevation changes, mostly downhill off the tee, swooping doglegs, and the constant risk/reward presence that tempts golfers to bite off as much as they dare, make this "second act" first-rate in every respect. As Dye once memorably commented, "Even the most stringent right-wing conservative may be a gambling maniac when it comes to golf. I want to make sure risky shots are presented as often as possible."

His second effort is analogous to film director Francis Ford Coppola, like Dye another highly acclaimed artist, following up his epic film *The Godfather* with a sequel that received equal critical acclaim. His artful integration of the new holes is somewhat overlooked, owing to his headline-grabbing creation several years later—the otherworldly Whistling Straits. But for significant championships, most notably the 1998 U.S. Women's Open (scheduled again for 2012), the original course, now routed among the thirty-six existing holes, is played in a composite fashion. This is much like Boston's twenty-seven-hole Country Club being played as a composite for numerous U.S. Opens, or as it was in the 1999 Ryder Cup. Speaking of which, the 2020 Ryder Cup has been awarded to Whistling Straits, the second Dye design to achieve this rare accolade (Kiawah Island's Ocean Course served as the host venue in 1991).

Above: The Straits, 13th hole
Opposite: The Straits, 7th hole

With his thirty-six-hole complex doing brisk business close by The American Club, Kohler decided to expand his horizons and his burgeoning golf empire concurrently. He found 560 lakeside acres about ten miles northeast of the resort itself. The land was a former army airport base that had operated as an anti-aircraft weapons firing range during World War II. Though the property was an ecological ruin filled with toxic waste, concrete bunkers, and fuel storage tanks, it also featured a plateau rising seventy feet above the waters of Lake Michigan.

Though he didn't take up the game until he got into the golf business himself, Kohler quickly developed an affinity for links golf, whose roots are in the seaside courses of the United Kingdom. "I want this course to look raw, big and wild, a throwback with sand, native fescue, and extensive dunes," is what he requested of Pete. "With a twinkle, he agreed."

By the time Dye was done conjuring the flat landscape, employing forty years of cunning and experience, an armada of earth movers, and 1,300 truckloads of sand imported from an area farm, the wondrous creation was still hard by the shores of Lake Michigan—but it looked as if it were sitting on top of the Irish Sea. To heighten the Eire mystique, Kohler imported a flock of blackface sheep that roam the golf grounds along the

lakeshore unencumbered, adding a uniquely appealing touch. He also decreed the course would be walking only—carts would be about as welcome on property as waterfalls, spurting fountains, and lovingly tended flowerbeds. This was meant to be the antithesis of a typically cushy resort course. "He told me he wanted a walking course, and I thought he was crazy," says Dye. "I enjoy walking, and thought I'd be the only one who ever played this course, but I was wrong. He set a trend."

The course got its name when Kohler, walking the lakeside landscape in ultrablustery conditions during construction, noted that the wind was whistling, with whitecaps breaking on the rocky shoreline of the lake. Hence the name Whistling Straits.

The entire venue, but the shoreline holes especially, is subject to the vagaries of the weather. Locals swear the temperature can drop 20 degrees in a matter of minutes, and that the gale-force winds rumbling along the two-mile stretch of lakeshore can sound like a midnight train. Shell-shocked golfers will be more concerned with the bogey train. Troubles, like the wind, come quickly and from all directions, not least from a dizzying and virtually uncountable series of bunkers in all shapes, sizes, and depths—as many as there are dimples

Above: The Straits, 12th hole
Opposite: The Straits, 17th hole

on a golf ball. Noted architecture critic Ron Whitten painted the picture vividly when he commented that the bunkers are "scattered about like laundry in the aftermath of a tornado."

Veteran Ryder Cupper Lee Westwood exhibited his dry wit prior to the 2004 PGA Championship: "I've been told there are ten difficult holes and eight that are impossible," offered the Englishman. "I'm still trying to work out which the ten difficult holes are."

Though the sheer number of sand blowouts are nigh uncountable, at least those pock-marking the fairway play as waste bunkers. Grounding the club, removing loose impediments, and taking practice swings are all within the letter of the law, and thank goodness for small mercies. One other mini blessing is that 10 or even 15 percent of the bunkers are strictly mental hazards—there's virtually no way on God's green earth they could be accessed. But then again, put a twice-a-year golfer on one of Pete Dye's pain paragons, and anything can happen. And because the fescue grasses are generally wispy and thin, offline tee shots are usually found (by the competent, and mandatory, caddy) and easily advanced. Another advantage is the sand-based fairways, which drain more quickly and efficiently. The Straits and the neighboring Irish have been known to be open, playing firm and fast, while the original, inland courses at Blackwolf Run have been occasionally bogged down by spring floods.

The Irish is the baby of the bunch, dating from the summer of 2000. It lies directly west of the Straits and differs from its Lake Michigan–hugging neighbor in one major respect. Put it this way: Early on, the Creeks Course was the name taken under serious consideration. There's more calculation involved playing the Irish, as a cerebral golfer must continually decide whether to go up and over or lay safely back from the numerous creeks bifurcating the fairways. Seven Mile Creek and three others come into play on seven holes and, in concert with assorted ponds, give the course a watery mien.

Despite the constant views of Lake Michigan from the Straits, it is the quartet of incredible par-3s where the water lurks most prominently. An egregiously sliced or hooked tee shot on any of these one-shot gauntlets (depending on whether the golfer is heading north or south, or is right-handed or a southpaw) will come to an ignominious end on lake's bottom.

While most of the sculpting on the Straits is toward the periphery, the Irish presents its elevation changes front and center, with numerous tee shots and approaches playing both up and down the centerline, particularly early in the inward nine. Looking west from some of the tee box pinnacles toward the flat Wisconsin farmland beyond the property line shows the prestidigitation the designer employed, conjuring the soaring, fescue-covered dunes out of a landscape that was previously a flattish and uninspiring wasteland whose chief redeeming feature was proximity to the lake.

The owner and architect have managed to stick together through thick and thin, even when the tension was thick and the patience worn thin. "He's demanding," says Pete Dye,

Pete and I went to the very fancy five-star restaurant at Whistling Straits in Wisconsin. He walks in with his dog, Sixty. (Sixty got his name because he cost Pete $60, by the way.) Nobody but Pete Dye could walk into a restaurant like this with an unleashed dog, but that's another story.

Anyway, Pete orders a plate of roast beef for Sixty. It was an enormous platter, so Pete took some for himself, and put the rest on the ground for his dog. The dog couldn't finish all the meat, and Pete started wrapping the leftovers. I said, "Are you saving the rest for Sixty?" He replied, "Hell, no. I'll eat it myself."

Sam Puglia, *owner of the Dye Course at Barefoot Resort in North Myrtle Beach, South Carolina*

The Irish, 11th hole

speaking of Herb Kohler. "He pays close attention, is a tree hugger, and he's a bulldog. Once in a while he gets his nose in a little too far, and I don't listen." It was just such an incident that nearly precipitated the demise of their relationship in the early stages, as Kohler explains.

"One day Pete said to me, 'I've planted seventeen holes, but there is one that hasn't even been roughed in. We need to finish this golf course, today.' I told him I'd try to meet him at noon, and we'd locate the final par-3 on Blackwolf Run, which was our first course. My schedule that day was hectic. Midday came and went. I found him on a hard line and told him I'd come down to the site around 5:00 P.M. and he said 'Fine, but we need to make a decision today, and it would be worth your while to help me figure out where we're going to locate this hole.'

"I finally freed myself just past 6:00 P.M., went down there, and saw four large piles of smoldering logs, each perhaps twenty-five feet tall. Then I saw that the nearby grove of seventy-foot-tall American elm trees, some of the last remaining species in Wisconsin, which had been ravaged by Dutch elm disease, was gone. And behind the 16th green, I was shocked to see a brand-new tee box that must have been eighty yards long, an adjacent four-acre lake that appeared twenty feet deep, and above it a roughed-out green exactly where the grove of elms had been."

While the owner had been lobbying to have the green nestled by a series of river rapids preserving the elms, the architect knew that the ensuing 150-yard walk to the 18th tee was untenable for championship play.

"There was nobody around," recalls Kohler. "I found a security guard who told me that at the 5 o'clock bell there was a crew of nearly twenty men running bulldozers, chopping trees, and hauling logs. Then he told me Pete had left for the airport and cleared out of town.

"I reached him that evening in Indianapolis. I told him we needed to come to a real understanding of how we were going to communicate and build a golf course. And if we couldn't do so quickly, then someone else was going to finish the job, and that person would be credited for the design. Pete was back within twenty-four hours, we had a long discussion, and it hasn't been an issue since," continues Kohler.

Kohler admits that the par-3 17th hole Dye freelanced is wonderful, and despite his own desire to save the trees and have the green hard by the river, it was somewhat impractical. "We would never have hosted the U.S. Women's Open if I had gotten my way," he admits.

With the quartet of courses long complete and the tumultuous times behind them, these dual (and often dueling) iconoclasts are now part of a mutual admiration society. "Pete has a marvelous knack of usually getting his way, no matter what the circumstance," says Herb Kohler, about whom the very same thing could be said. "He'll find a way to get it done how he wants to, whether he's dealing with a demanding owner, the Department of Natural Resources, or the Army

Top: The Irish, 11th hole
Bottom: The Irish, 15th hole

The Straits, 1st hole

Corps of Engineers. And invariably, his way turns out to be better than all the rest. I've never had the honor and pleasure of being associated with a human being who possesses the raw talent of Pete Dye."

And Dye says: "Herb is crazy to work with. He had no knowledge of golf when we got started, and he would still fight me on so many things. I couldn't believe it, given his lack of experience and background. But he was right so much of the time."

The Kohler and Dye story is not unlike other creative duos who put aside a difference in philosophy or a tempestuous patch or two to make a lasting impact—think of Simon and Garfunkle or Lennon and McCartney. The plumbing magnate and the old dirt devil worked through the occasional friction, and together made the unlikely address of Kohler, Wisconsin, one of the most sought-after destinations in golf. Much like

the legendary performers noted above, Kohler and Dye, differences aside, managed to work together in great harmony.

The reader might be curious as to the modest beginnings of the Kohler Company, before it became internationally synonymous with state-of-the-art plumbing fixtures, and, far later, known as one of the gold standards in the resort world. The business was founded by John Michael Kohler in 1873. The Austrian immigrant, who was making farm equipment in his foundry and machine shop, figured out a way to apply enamel to a horse trough and then sell it with four legs as a glossy bathtub. More than 135 years after its humble start, it's clear that his grandson Herb's decision to branch into the hospitality business, using these four Dye-designed golf gems as lynchpins of The American Club experience and Destination Kohler, has proven equally innovative, and just as slick.

I once spent nearly a week with the Dyes in Indianapolis, writing a cover story for a major golf publication. One night we were having dinner in their home, and the phone rang incessantly. First it was Ray Floyd calling, then Greg Norman, then others, luminaries in the golf world all. They were asking Pete's advice, wanting his opinion on various matters, telling him stories, and vice versa. The next day, after golf at Crooked Stick, we were having dinner at the club. Pete was clearly in his element here, with every member there coming up to say "hello,"

including former Vice President Dan Quayle. The next day Herb Kohler sent his private jet to get us—Pete, his dog, Sixty, and me—and we flew to Sheboygan, Wisconsin, to tour Pete's newest pride: Whistling Straits. Herb couldn't wait to give Pete a big bear hug when he saw us having lunch. He let everyone in the room know Pete Dye was his special guest. His courses may engender controversy, but the man himself? I don't think I've ever met anyone in golf so universally liked and admired.

George Fuller, *veteran golf writer*

Harbour Ridge Golf Club River Ridge Course
With P.B. Dye

From the back veranda of the Harbour Ridge clubhouse, the St. Lucie River dominates the landscape. From this vantage point it looks to be as broad as the mighty Mississippi, wider than Lake Michigan. Access to the St. Lucie River is one of the primary attractions of this club and real estate enclave in Stuart, Florida. The deep-water dockage allows boat owners to get to the Atlantic Ocean quite expeditiously, via the river and intercoastal waterway. The Gulf of Mexico is also accessible, by heading south and then west across Lake Okeechobee.

It's not only the boaters who have options, but the golfers as well. They can choose from a mellower Joe Lee design, Golden Marsh, or a very demanding Pete and P.B. Dye design, River Ridge.

And even within the Dye design, options abound. The course is a pocket-size puzzle, and there is a wide range of ways to proceed safely from tee box to green. River Ridge isn't even 6,700 yards from the tips, but the slope rating is a sky-high 148. The blue markers tip the scales at a seemingly anemic 6,200-and-change, but are sloped at an ultra-formidable 142. The white tees are pegged at a distance normally associated with senior tees—less than 5,600 yards, yet with a 129 slope. And bear in mind there's not a shot or two missing off the scorecard—it's a regulation par-72 course. It's picture-book proof that the concepts of tiny and taxing aren't mutually exclusive.

The river views are limited to the par-4 3rd, a no-nonsense 420-yarder where only the most egregiously sliced tee shot or approach will end up in the riverbed. But even as the course moves west, away from the water, the interest level remains high. The subtle fairway ridges and undulations ensure that shots from the same general area will play very differently from day to day. The awkward lies and stances aren't limited to full shots. They are even more prevalent around the greens, where humps, hollows, and bunkers of all shapes and depths lurk just steps from the putting surface, requiring both imagination and a deft touch with a high-lofted club.

While the panoramic river view is fleeting, wetlands encroaching on the fairways are an enduring fact on River Ridge—it's a ball-eating track of the first order. Not only are there numerous marshlands peppering the grounds, but many are environmentally protected areas, so hunting amidst the long grass for a wayward pellet is strictly verboten.

The membership doesn't seem to mind. Harbour Ridge is a "green" community, eco-friendly in nature, and inveterate ball hawks stomping amidst the native habitats in a bullheaded search for a misplaced Pinnacle are about as welcome as a faux waterfall or garish fountain on the property.

Speaking of bullheaded, playing with a "danger-be-damned" attitude on this perilous course will make for a long day of scorecard suffering. The P.B. Dye influence is apparent as the round moves into its middle stages. The younger of Pete and Alice's two sons is known for building very demanding tracks. This course isn't terrifying, but it is intimidating. There's a discomfort level in some of the approach shots over water, a tee ball that must sail over an extensive wetland, a well-placed bunker that gobbles up a seemingly ideal tee shot. Are the members a gang of masochists? Seemingly not. Though Pete Dye's winter home in Delray Beach is in relative proximity, he's almost never been called in for the tweaks and renovations, both minor and major, that he performs with regularity at other courses. Apparently the members' mindset is: If it ain't broke, leave it be.

The way to succeed on River Ridge: steady and cerebral off the tee, using the fairway woods or even the long irons liberally. Play away from trouble, and short of bunkers and lagoons. Play for bogey from out-of-position, and practice damage control. Don't get impetuous and rack up a row of doubles and triples. Remember that the course is actually easier, wider in many places, than it first appears. Case in point: From the back tees the par-3 12th is 206 yards over a seemingly endless lagoon. The visual trickery of the water and encircling vegetation makes it look closer to 266. But the actual carry to safety is only 160–170 yards. The reality is that this is a hole on which a thinking, not easily ruffled golfer will card bogey or better without undue anxiety. It's the 18th handicap hole for a reason, though at first blush it appears as though it might take a half-dozen blows to negotiate from tee to cup's bottom.

Management calls the Dyes' River Ridge course "relentlessly subtle." It's a clever description. While not as nuanced, another accurate depiction might be to call it a course-management laboratory. If one can play disciplined, station-to-station golf at the Dyes' effort here in Stuart, one can manage one's game efficiently most anywhere.

Opposite, top: 14th hole
Opposite, bottom: 18th hole

Kearney Hills Golf Links

With P.B. Dye

What do Pete Dye's best-known public-access courses have in common with caviar? Both entities are expensive, indulgent, and for the common man anyway, a bit hard to stomach.

Many of Pete Dye's legendary courses are part of the public sector—Harbour Town, Whistling Straits, Teeth of the Dog, the Ocean Course, and the Stadium Course at TPC Sawgrass among them. All players are welcome, but the privilege doesn't come cheap—green fees generally run a couple hundred bucks. Now compare these marquee names to Kearney Hills Golf Links, a bluegrass beauty in Lexington, Kentucky. Granted, there's no ocean, signature lighthouse, or infamous island green. But there's also no bridge loan needed to access the first tee. Value is the watchword, and this municipal masterpiece is undoubtedly one of the best deals in the game. When the course opened in 1989, walkers paid a dollar per hole. But inflation being what it is, those days are long gone. The same privilege has crept up about two bits a year over two decades, and now costs nearly $25. When management attempted to raise the green fee for the legions of out-of-county residents who flock to the facility by literally two whole dollars, they were practically run out of town.

There are thousands of affordable golf courses, but what sets this facility apart, and has raised its profile, is the unique challenges of the layout. Kearney Hills is fun for any player, but can test the likes of Gary Player if need be. The course has hosted both the men's and women's Public Links Championships, and besides its USGA pedigree, also served as a longtime host of the Champions Tour. With the greens shaved down and the rough grown high, especially if the wind is funneling through this mostly treeless expanse, Kearney Hills can present a formidable challenge for top-tier players.

The term "links" is bandied about far too often, considering that less than one percent of the world's golf courses are actually constructed on links-land. This certainly holds true at Kearney Hills, some 600 miles from the seashore, whose rolling terrain was previously in use as a motocross track. But there are at least two characteristics in place here that replicate a links experience to a slight degree. The first is that both Kearney Hills and a true seaside links depend on the wind as defense against scoring. When the wind abates, the course becomes docile, though short grass accuracy is imperative. And while there's no fescue to be found off the fairway, the rough in the form of Kentucky bluegrass is more like glue-grass—a sticky thatch of greenery that impedes the club-head, making it difficult to advance the ball with either power or precision toward the intended target.

Above: 17th hole
Opposite: 12th hole

2nd hole

At one time Kearney Hills Links was more popular in Japan, of all places, than anywhere domestically, and the only U.S. golf course logo more coveted than theirs was Pebble Beach. The opening of a Toyota plant in nearby Georgetown, Kentucky, coincided with the golf course's debut, precipitating this odd union. For years, hundreds of Japanese automotive executives were flying in and out of Lexington to monitor the plant's early progress. On any given weekend, fully half the golfers attempting to meet the challenges of Kearney Hills were Japanese, and were such a regular presence that signage on the course and throughout the clubhouse was in Japanese as well as English. The furor reached its apex when Isao Aoki won a Champions Tour event there in 1994, and management could barely keep soft goods in the pro shop, so quickly were they being scooped up by Aoki's proud countrymen.

Now that the Toyota plant is running smoothly, the flow of visiting executives has been diminished. But despite the course's waning popularity in Asia, spoiled Kentucky golfers who love both the challenge and the affordability will keep Kearney Hills immensely popular for the foreseeable future.

This despite the fact that during construction, "Indiana Dye," no doubt egged on by his fun-loving son P.B., purposely ruffled a few feathers across the Kentucky state line at the only golf course he ever built in the state.

It was a University of Kentucky football coach who discovered Pete's on-course blasphemy from above. The approach path to the Lexington airport is close by the golf course. From the airplane's window seat, the coach was shocked and dismayed to see a fairway bunker to the right side of the par-4 13th hole carved into an exact replica of the University of Indiana's logo. These neighboring states are natural basketball rivals anyway, but in the late 1980s their border war was at its peak. The coach first approached the course manager and, after being rebuffed, eventually the city's mayor, attempting to have the offending U.I. sand pit removed. The controversy finally died down, and the one-of-a-kind hazard remains to this day, proving one thing. Kentuckians love their Wildcats, certainly. But apparently they also respect the artistry, acumen, and, let's face it, the mischievous side of Pete Dye.

16th hole

1990s An Appreciation by Greg Norman

I have had the pleasure of knowing Pete Dye for more than twenty years, and have long since come to the conclusion that he is a true genius. There are numerous reasons why I say this, but the single most amazing thing I have witnessed about Pete is his ability to create a golf course without a set of plans. He loves to see his courses evolve as the construction progresses, which allows his genius to resonate across the entire property.

While several of the leading architects from golf's "Golden Age" in the 1920s and 1930s never used plans or blueprints, they had, much like Pete, an uncommon feel for the lay of the land and what was required for a well-balanced, strategic golf course. Pete will tell you that he has a rough conceptual idea for the layout of a course in his head, and that's it.

From that point on, it's as if he's painting a masterpiece without having any directions to follow. He sketched the original routing for the Stadium Course at TPC Sawgrass on the back of a place mat, and he hasn't changed much since we started collaborating many years later.

The first Pete Dye course I ever played was Harbour Town Golf Links on Hilton Head Island. It is a fascinating and beautiful course that tests the skills of the professionals who compete in the Heritage Classic every year. It was a groundbreaking design in 1969, and, despite advances in technology, it was equally testing nearly twenty years later when I was fortunate enough to win the tournament. Now, an additional twenty years have passed, and even with the influx of technological innovations to clubs and balls, it remains one of the finest courses on the PGA Tour.

It has been my pleasure to play many other courses showcased in this book, including Crooked Stick, Oak Tree, the Stadium Courses at the TPC and PGA West, Old Marsh, The Golf Club, Brickyard Crossing, and the Mountain Course at La Quinta among them.

Pete's designs don't let players just hit to point A and

then to point B. Instead, golfers must carefully position shots so they can manipulate the ball onto what are almost always well-defended greens. He requires golfers not only to execute demanding shots but also to think their way around his courses.

I first respected Pete from the viewpoint of a professional golfer and have now developed a great admiration for him as a fellow designer. We've worked together several times in Florida, including at Medalist Golf Club in Hobe Sound, and more recently, at Tuscany Reserve in Naples.

Pete has enlightened me about design principles that will surely influence the courses I build in the future. And, despite his vast experience and many accolades, Pete gives ample credit to those who have influenced him and collaborated with him. He genuinely welcomes input, and I have seen firsthand how that works. Contrary to what many might think, Pete listens.

I would also be remiss not mentioning his work ethic.

He'll work day after day until sundown with men thirty, forty, and fifty years younger than he. It is a sight that must be seen to be believed.

In my opinion, Pete is one of the true visionaries of our time. During the award ceremonies at the Brickyard Crossing Invitational in Indianapolis in the spring of 1994, I called him a great ambassador for the game of golf. His dedication to make the game better is unparalleled.

Pete and his wife, Alice, also a talented designer, are true bellwethers of the golf course design profession. I am honored that I was asked to write a tribute for a book that showcases his many architectural triumphs through an unforgettable fifty-year career. Most important, I am proud to call Pete Dye a dear friend.

Avalon Golf and Country Club, 14th hole

The Ocean Course

With Alice Dye

For the visiting golfer, Charleston, South Carolina's, reputation rests on Kiawah Island. And Kiawah's golf reputation goes no further than the seminal Ocean Course, wild and windswept, a harrowing ground on the island's easternmost end.

It was the first time ever that the Ryder Cup had been awarded to a course that didn't exist. The powers-that-be decided that the matches needed to be moved from California to the East Coast, so that the European television audience could watch the drama unfold live. As a result, Pete and Alice, hired in the late 1980s, had only two years to build a seaside masterpiece, one that would not only challenge the world's most talented professionals in the autumn of 1991, but would be enjoyable for generations of golfers to follow. They succeeded magnificently.

"When I first walked the land, I fell in love with the site," recalls Dye. "This narrow, two-and-a-half-mile beachfront had beautiful ocean views on one side and vast saltwater marshes on the other. I would have bent down on my knees and begged for the opportunity to build there."

The Dyes worked eighteen-hour days, come hell or high water. And they dealt with both. Hurricane Hugo battered Charleston mercilessly in 1989, flattening the landscape and toppling trees like dominoes. But the indefatigable architect worked on nonetheless. Though the roads were closed for weeks, he took a boat to the island, and he and his crew built the leveled dunes back up with bulldozers. They quickly recreated the stunning routing that had just begun to take shape prior to the monster storm.

The course was ready just in time, and the 1991 Ryder Cup was the most grippingly contentious international golf match ever played. It was a down-to-the-wire affair, draining for players and spectators alike. Victory for the host team was only assured when European stalwart Bernhard Langer narrowly missed a six-foot putt on the final green of the weekend's final match. Had the putt fallen, the visitors would have captured the Cup.

What makes the Ocean Course so mesmerizing, so memorable? It's the once-in-a-lifetime location. It's the dazzling views and the omnipresent ocean winds, which seem to come from everywhere at once, buffeting both player and ball, then dying away in an instant. It's the prospect of disaster lurking on virtually every shot—a favorite saying among staffers is: "We don't sell golf balls, we rent them." The minimal housing presence adds to the wild and wooly landscape. The dedicated turf on the course is just fifty-five acres, but the vistas, seascape, wetlands, sand, and ball-eating vegetation occupy an area six or eight times that size. Brawny as the golf course appears, with generous fairways, oversized greens, and cavernous bunkers, it's dwarfed by the majestic natural panorama: the sea, sky, and sand that surround it. The course will have an encore in the international spotlight, hosting the 2012 PGA Championship, the first of golf's professional Majors to be contested in South Carolina.

The Ocean Course, brutally difficult and beautiful, is indisputably one of Dye's very best. It's one of the most thoroughly invigorating psychological and physical battles a player will ever find in this great game.

Opposite: 10th and 17th holes
Below: 13th hole

It was my first visit to Kiawah Island's Ocean Course. It was the first day of my first (and only) Ryder Cup. I was on the first green in my first match and left my first putt pathetically short and well right of the target. I was quivering like an anemic palmetto in a tropical storm, and my partner, Sam Torrance, my best friend in the world, walked up to me and provided words of encouragement I'll take with me to the grave. "Pull yourself together or I'll play with the Americans, and it'll be three against one."

The Ocean Course was brand-new when we played it, and tougher than nuclear physics. But it's been tweaked and improved over the years by the great Pete Dye, and is better and more spectacular than it was at the beginning. That's one bit of good news. The other? Sam and I are still speaking.

David Feherty, *European Ryder Cup Team member; CBS golf analyst*

Left: 8th hole
Below: 13th hole

Above: 15th hole
Right: 5th hole

Brickyard Crossing Golf Club

Renovation

If he can build them in swamps, on the sides of mountains, on scorched earth, or in arid desert, why shouldn't Pete Dye be able to rebuild a golf course on and around the world's most famous racetrack?

More then thirty years prior to this renovation, when his architectural career was still in its infancy, Pete Dye served as the general chairman of the Indianapolis 500 Festival Invitational Tournament, a PGA Tour event. At that time, the course was still in its original 1928 iteration, as conceived by Bill Diddel. Diddel was a five-time Indiana State Amateur champion who designed more than 100 courses in his career and served as an Eisenhower-era mentor to an up-and-coming architect named Dye. Diddel routed half the course inside the oval itself, and the other half outside the fence. In the mid-1960s, an additional nine was added beyond the fence, bringing the total to twenty-seven. When Dye was hired to renovate, the decision was made to eliminate nine holes and increase the overall spaciousness of the golf experience, in part to make room for a Racing Hall of Fame Museum within the track itself. When Dye was done, there were four holes inside the track, numbers 7 through 10, with the remaining fourteen winding their way around the spacious grounds outside the fence line.

The now-sterling golf course and the iconic racetrack intertwine very naturally, even beyond the symbolic fact that Dye used sections of the track's old retaining wall to bolster the sides of Little Eagle Creek. Players enter the Speedway through an underground tunnel, and exit the same way four holes later. But because the property is so massive and the use of trees and mounding so clever, even from within the oval it's sometimes easy to forget about the one-of-a-kind location. The irony is that the proximity to the grandstand is never closer than it is *outside* the oval, on the property's northeast corner. An errant approach to the long par-5 12th or a pulled tee shot on the tough par-3 13th could potentially clatter into the stanchions supporting the stadium-style bench seating on the infamous third turn. Making birdie on this hole, with railroad ties left and the always lurking Little Eagle Creek to the right, is high excitement. But it's a mere trifle, say veteran race patrons, compared to the thrill of some three dozen supercharged race cars roaring down the mile-long straightaway at nearly 200 mph, prior to the turn.

Opposite, top: 12th hole
Opposite, bottom: 10th hole

11th hole

4th hole

Later in the back nine, the course moves completely away from the Speedway. Other than encroaching power lines, the setting becomes completely pastoral. It's reminiscent of the 1800s dairy farm it once was, prior to becoming America's racing shrine. The farm's old white barn, perhaps the best-known symbol of the golf course itself, still remains and is the perfect aiming point from the 18th tee.

Though it's not quite the unreal bargain it was in the LBJ-Nixon era, when green fees were a buck during the week and twice that on weekends or holidays, Brickyard Crossing remains an excellent value for the modern daily fee player. It goes beyond the unheard-of setting within the oval and winding through the Speedway. Put this hazard-laden, rolling, dipping property anywhere—in a cornfield in Keokuk, a pasture in Paducah—and it would still be eminently worthwhile. It's the enticing mixture of long and short par-4s, the kill-or-be-killed tee shots that must bend right or left to avoid the creek or waste bunkers. It's the stout quartet of one-shot holes, including Dye's version of the Redan Hole—the scary 7th, within the confines of the track itself. That's why the tee sheet remains filled in perpetuity, but especially during Race Week. The far end of the driving range doubles as a helipad, shuttling VIPs and racers to and from the property. The Saturday and Monday surrounding the Indianapolis 500 are among the busiest days of the year, though the course is closed on Sunday, race day. Asked why, the professional staff provides a logical answer. It's nigh impossible to play through 400,000 people.

10th hole

Luana Hills Country Club

With Perry Dye

"It's a jungle out there."

Perry Dye isn't referring to the increasingly competitive golf course design market, but to the unbelievably lush Luana Hills Country Club, one of the Dyes' only Hawaiian efforts. Not even twenty minutes from the Honolulu Airport, it's an eon, a light-year away from the hustle and flow of the freeways, tunnels, and traffic leading out of the nearby metropolis.

Pete Dye has often built courses on spectacular terrain. And the luxuriant Maunawili Valley, located through a gap in the Pali Cliffs on the windward side of Oahu, with its waterfalls, deep ravines, dazzling flowers, and incredible canopies of green, is, in its own unique way, as memorable as any seaside or mountaintop he's worked on previously.

It's a bantam track, weighing in at less than 6,600 yards from the tips, with most play conducted at 6,200. But it's a quirky and breathtaking ride just the same. Plateau greens featuring the only bent grass on the island of Oahu, frighteningly steep drop-offs into the vegetation, waste bunkers off the fairway, and humpy, roiling landing areas where a level lie is solely a matter of chance—all combine to make Luana Hills a difficult and intimidating round.

Common understanding in the pro shop is that a first-timer will likely lose as many balls as his or her handicap. So the typical eighteen-handicapper should be prepared to offer up six sleeves of ammo to both the golf and mountain gods who doubtless populate this incredibly beautiful valley.

The topography that makes the course so memorable also serves to provide a different type of golf challenge than most players are used to. The course necessitates quite a bit of bunny-hopping from one limited-landing zone to the next. "Keep your ego in check and play plenty of irons," offers Perry Dye, referring to any number of back nine holes, but the par-5 13th in particular—a 400-yard curio.

For all but the most robust golfers, there's not even a faint hope of clearing the deeply vegetated ravine that bisects the fairway nearly 300 yards from the tee. So one must dink a fairway wood or hybrid, bunt a short iron into the narrow landing area beneath the green, and then loft a wedge onto a hard-to-hold putting surface that looms above the fairway like a volcano. Grip-it-and-rip-it golf it's not.

The opening nine has the longer views and the more majestic tee-ball carries. Miss the fairway, and the ball will disappear into impenetrable foliage on one side or plunge into a subterranean waste bunker on the other. The inward nine, routed lower in a tropical valley, has more blind shots and the aforementioned station-to-station imperative. In the

original thirty-six-hole plan for the facility that never came to fruition, these were planned as the opening nines of separate golf courses. They tie together well regardless, but the subtle differences in the topography and strategy make for an out-of-the-ordinary round.

Never mind the topography. There's also a distinct difference in precipitation. The opening nine is shadowed by majestic, often cloud-shrouded Mount Olamana and receives far more rainfall than the lower terrain that's nearly adjacent.

Luana Hills is far from a household name in Hawaiian golf, lacking the glitz, history, and PGA Tour pedigree of venues like Princeville, Kapalua, and Poipu Bay, to name but three. But this Pete and Perry Dye collaboration, practically the picture-book definition of a hidden gem, is filled with royal palms, koa trees, birds of paradise, and all manner of exotically beautiful flora and fauna. The course is exhilarating, mystifying, and excruciating concurrently. It's well beyond jungle golf. Call it Jurassic Park golf instead.

Opposite: 3rd hole
Below: 7th hole

Pete Dye Golf Club

A two-word descriptive adorns West Virginia license plates. It refers to the natural beauty of the landscape, but is equally applicable to the finest golf course in the state. Because, just like West Virginia itself, the Pete Dye Golf Club is also Wild, Wonderful.

A typical golf course can be built in a couple of years' time, but it took a full sixteen years—longer than it took to build the Brooklyn Bridge and about the time it took to construct the Taj Mahal—to complete the Pete Dye Golf Club. But this fabulous, mining-themed course is completely atypical—an apt description also of the owners, the father-son team of James D. and Jimmy LaRosa.

"If I had left Pete to his own devices, I'm sure the course would have been finished much sooner," explains James D., who was involved in the strip mining business for thirty-five years and owns all the heavy-duty earth-moving equipment needed to build a golf course. "But I was very involved in trying to assist Pete, right or wrong. And when I said I wanted a unique, unmatchable golf course, I meant it. Committing the time and resources necessary to achieve this objective was never an issue."

The course sprawls over 275-plus acres on a 1,200-acre property that was originally unreclaimed mine land. For those unfamiliar with the mining business, it's hard to fathom how ghastly the property was before Dye and the LaRosas began the restoration process. Picture Dante's Nine Circles of Hell, but in this case the circles were gob piles (smoldering slag heaps of coal); a strip mine pit (now a sparkling four-acre lake at the club's entrance); coal waste; sulfur balls; carbonaceous matter; abandoned equipment; scattered mine posts; scraggly weeds; and withered vegetation. The successful turnaround from earthen abscess to dazzling golf course, this incredible refurbishment of abandoned mine land, is probably the main reason why the Pete Dye Golf Club is one of the master's "must-see" creations, and truly one of his greatest achievements.

"I've seen many of Pete's great courses," says James D., who surprisingly has never had more than a passing interest in playing golf. "And I can't imagine that any of them have changed as dramatically from start to finish, or have gone from what was as bad as we had here to something that's as beautiful as what we have now."

7th hole

15th hole

Drama abounds throughout the acreage. There are waterways snaking through the property, plenty of elevation changes, split-level fairways, ravines, and expansive waste bunkering. Though generous from the tee box, it's an exacting course from an approach-shot perspective and exciting at every turn. The greens at the Pete Dye Golf Club mimic the drama of the surrounding landforms. They tilt and pitch in every direction, much like the fairways. This sensibility is at its peak on the dizzying 17th. Standard adjectives for undulation don't suffice, so perhaps the best descriptive is "warped." Which, come to think of it, is a word that's often been used by frustrated golfers to describe the architect's sense of humor.

Jimmy LaRosa, who in contrast to his father is an avid player, was the original impetus for the project. "Because of the spectacular terrain in the heart of coal country, the time we needed to make the course a reality, and the fact that we were able to call it the Pete Dye Golf Club, we've become known as such a special place," explains Jimmy. "But it shouldn't be that hard to understand. Our family has always given back to both our community and the state. Not only because of what West Virginia's resources have given us, but because of our family roots, which date back to my immigrant grandfather, who lived in a coal camp adjacent to where the course is built. Pete Dye relished the chance to turn this property into something wonderful. Add in the fact that we are not only owners, but also accomplished earth-movers who assisted Pete in his efforts, and you can see how all of the circumstances came together to make this club so unique."

"From when we first met Pete until the time the course was finally completed, he built some of his most renowned courses, including the Stadium Course at TPC Sawgrass, the Ocean Course at Kiawah Island, and Blackwolf Run, among

During one of Pete's many visits to our construction site, he had an appointment to meet Mr. Joe Hardy, who wanted him to look at some land at his Nemacolin Woodlands Resort in Pennsylvania, about a ninety-minute drive from our club. He asked me if I minded driving him up there, which I was happy to do.

Pete came right out of the field that day. He was muddy, dusty, he carried his battered overnight valise, which was open, with all kinds of stuff sticking out of the top. I was dressed in my normal casual fashion, but was a bit more cleaned up than Pete. Anyway, we get up there, walk into the hotel lobby, and Joe Hardy, who had never met either of us previously, walks right up to me, and says, "Mr. Dye, it's great to meet you." I laugh, and tell him Pete is the other guy. I guess Mr. Hardy assumed he was the laborer who was given the assignment of bringing the famous architect up to meet him.

James D. LaRosa, *founder, Pete Dye Golf Club*

Left: 18th hole
Below: 9th hole

Right: 18th hole (foreground) and 10th hole
Below: Mine shaft and 7th hole

others," he continues. "We were privileged to witness and benefit from the evolution of Pete Dye, and it's no surprise that our course is so highly acclaimed in its own right."

Cynical observers may have thought the prospects of ever completing the project to be as tenuous as those of a canary in a coal mine. But they didn't know James D. LaRosa, who lives by the tenet that the mark of a man is what he finishes, not what he starts. "He was the toughest, most tenacious, never-give-up son of a gun I ever worked for," Dye says. "When we discussed calling it the Pete Dye Golf Club, I told him, you can call it any damn thing you like, if we can just get it finished! But I will say that it's eighteen of the most exciting and memorable holes that I have ever built on one course."

The coal car at the club's entrance gate sets the tone, but there are other reminders of the property's origins at every turn. A rotary car tipple and multiple attached coal cars stand adjacent to the tenth fairway. A pair of 1,000-foot-high smoke-stacks are used as a distant aiming point off the fifth tee, and there's a gargantuan ventilation return near the first green. But the most distinctive manmade feature is the honest-to-goodness mine tunnel that connects the sixth green and seventh tee. Players move through a dank channel, a gloomy reminder of the hardship and harsh reality of a miner's life. Transitioning from bright sunlight into dim shadow, the temperature plummets noticeably while making the 100-yard walk beneath the mountain. It's just one of the reasons why this stark homage to the coal industry, perfectly juxtaposed between stunning golf holes, is one of the coolest accoutrements in golf.

Las Vegas Paiute Golf Resort Snow Mountain, Sun Mountain, The Wolf

With Perry Dye

If a first-timer were blindfolded and airlifted to any of the fifty-four different tee boxes at the sprawling Las Vegas Paiute Golf Resort, they would have a hard time believing they were in the same area code as Celine Dion, Wayne Newton, Danny Gans, or any other superstar stalwart charged with entertaining the hordes of eager tourists regularly descending on Sin City. It's only twenty miles due northwest from the glitz of the Strip to this majestic desert panorama, where mountain views extend in every direction and the only notable sounds are the percussion of club hitting ball, but it seems more like 200.

The original Paiute reservation remains a ten-acre parcel in what later became downtown Las Vegas, bequeathed to the tribe by a Mormon rancher early in the twentieth century. Some seventy-five years later, in 1983, Congress granted a 3,000-acre parcel to the tribe, which promised to use it as a means of economic development. Golf seemed a natural avenue to pursue, and Pete Dye was given the plum assignment, having been chosen over a number of other accomplished architects. The tribal council in power at the time was impressed with both his innovative course routings and his willingness to work only with plants, trees, and vegetation that were indigenous to the area, keeping the courses as close to a natural state as possible.

Nearly 700 of the 3,000 acres are dedicated to the golf property, including the three courses, two full-service practice facilities, and an expansive clubhouse. The original Snow Mountain debuted in 1995 on the easternmost point of the property, followed by Sun Mountain in 1997 to the north and then the marquee Wolf Course, to the south, in 2001. There were discussions about a fourth course—an amalgam of Pete Dye's best holes, a tribute course as such—but those plans have been abandoned.

The overall feeling at the Paiute Resort is one of quietude, with sweeping desert views contained within a hushed environment. The Sheep Mountain Range is the dominant viewing feature to the east, some 10 miles from the low-slung, 50,000-square-foot clubhouse that is at the nexus of all three courses. The Spring Mountains are in the middle distance, as is 12,000-foot Mt. Charleston. Red and orange mission poppies, yuccas, and Joshua trees dot the on-course landscape, as does a variety of wildlife. There's not a real wolf on the Wolf Course, or on the Snow Mountain or Sun Mountain courses, either. But there are coyotes, roadrunners, bobcats, and the occasional badger, among dozens of other creatures making their home on the property.

Snow Mountain, 18th hole

There's scant water to be found on these desert courses, only about 15 percent of the holes having any type of lake or pond. Not surprising, considering only about four inches of rain fall annually. But what little water exists is a brilliant shade of blue, fresh well water that comes from an aquifer beneath the property. This liquid's so clear that management claims it's just as clean as the tap water flowing from the faucets of the mega-hotels down on the Strip.

The ball-striking demands throughout the property are staunch enough on their own. But consider just one view—the slightly elevated tee box of Snow Mountain's 10th hole. It's an unforgettable juxtaposition of lush green fairway and aquamarine lake, totally enveloped by ocher-colored desert wash leading to the surrounding mountain ranges. Views like this repeat themselves throughout the trio of courses, and it's reasonable to assume that the power of concentration of even a Tiger Woods or Ben Hogan would be tested by such a mesmerizing landscape.

Snow Mountain and Sun Mountain have similar design characteristics, though the former plays to a draw and the latter to a fade. Both are less daunting than the championship-caliber Wolf Course. Though the fairways are generally wider on the Wolf, the course is more troublesome in its

One time I was traveling with Pete by private jet, going off to one of his construction sites. He was paging though a recent golf publication, which featured a "Best of" list of golf courses. He looked at me with a small smile, and said, "How many of my courses do you think are on this list?" I guessed twenty. He said, "Ha! One more than that," and tossed me the magazine. I was paging through the story, and then he said, "How many courses do you think the guy in second place has on this list?" I told him I had no clue. He told me it was thirteen. He had a gleam in his eye when he said so, and you could tell he was very pleased to be such a commanding frontrunner. As a coach, I'm very competitive, and it was very interesting to see this competitive side of Pete, if only for a few minutes.

Devon Brouse, *head golf coach, Purdue University*

The Wolf, 17th hole

The Wolf, 15th hole

entirety—tougher greens and rolling, dipping fairways rife with hazards—some with stadium-style mounding. The Wolf's putting surfaces are encircled by shaved banks that offer a variety of recovery options, including putting, pitching, or chipping the wayward orb onto speedy but not overly tricky greens. Fortunately, all the courses play a bit easier with a local rule dictating that any ball lost in the desert can be played as a lateral hazard, so the misery of a stroke-and-distance penalty is mitigated by half, to a stroke penalty alone.

The Wolf may one day host a high-profile, perhaps even a professional, event. Speaking of which, LPGA Hall-of-Famers Karrie Webb and Annika Sorenstam helped debut the Wolf with a bang, competing as they did in a Shell's Wonderful World of Golf episode filmed on property. But it was a PGA Tour star, a Major champion with a double-digit win total, playing far from the camera lens, who illustrated how difficult the Pauite's signature course can be. He began his round from the tips, at 7,600 yards, the longest course in Nevada. After several holes he took a few giant steps forward to the penultimate markers, seeing no need to bloody himself with no money or title at stake.

The most notable of the fifty-four holes is undoubtedly the 15th on Wolf. Golfers assume this is Pete Dye's paean to his best-known creation, the island green 17th at TPC Sawgrass near Jacksonville, Florida. But this hole has more in common with its West Coast cousin, called Alcatraz, located at the brutally tough Stadium Course at PGA West in the California desert. Both the Paiute and the Palm Springs holes are much longer carries from the tee, with larger, rock-walled greens. The fact that the Nevada iteration has three separate tiers makes it probably the toughest of this island trio.

Regarding wind: It's no secret that the gusts can blow mightily on this rock-strewn desert floor, with nothing to impede its progress as it funnels between the surrounding mountain ranges. But the two breeziest months are also the busiest—March and October. So, while the Paiute trio is sometimes thought of as a wind tunnel, its reputation far exceeds the reality through much of the year.

Besides giving the Paiute people more visibility and an economic engine to increased prosperity, the playing fields of their wonderfully conditioned golf resort afford any member of the Tribe who's so inclined the chance to learn the game. It's surprising there isn't more interest among them, as their access to the courses is complimentary. Not so for the rest of us, but, as nearly 100,000 annual rounds conclusively attest, the prospect of paying green fees is no barrier to those who want to enjoy some of the finest golf in all of Nevada, in a setting nothing short of spectacular.

You wouldn't think a guy with fifty years of design experience and more than 100 courses under his belt would be insecure about his future job prospects. But Pete Dye is nothing if not confounding. "I know I'll always be employed in this country," he's been known to say, "as long as I can keep three billionaires happy."

The titans to whom he refers are Wisconsin plumbing magnate Herb Kohler; Bill Goodwin, who owns both the Kiawah Island and Sea Pines Resorts in South Carolina; and Joe Hardy. Pete kept Hardy happy by consenting to build the lumber baron's marquee golf course at Pennsylvania's Nemacolin Woodlands on a rock-and-boulder-strewn parcel, as opposed to the softer, more malleable property he would have preferred to work with some twenty minutes from the burgeoning resort. "I'll build it on one condition," warned the architect, knowing full well the effort needed to negotiate the sandstone, limestone, and thick tree cover that were the hallmarks of the property. "Don't ask me what it's going to cost."

Fortunately, the 84 Lumber Company founder has plenty of resources, and isn't afraid to use them. When he bought a nucleus of 400 acres in the Pennsylvania village of Farmington back in 1987, he had a simple goal—to give his then twenty-one-year-old daughter, Maggie, a nice place to go fishing. "People see what we've done here, and think I have all this vision," says the gregarious octogenarian laughingly. "That's a bunch of bullshit! We bought the camp, which had a basic golf course and thirty-five rooms. We figured we needed to upgrade the golf. Pittsburgh was a real corporate headquarters town in those days, so we figured a conference center would make sense. And my wife and girls always loved spa treatments when we went on vacation, so I thought a spa would be a good addition. Those were the three basic facilities of the resort, but I never envisioned all this."

"All this" is a cornucopia of amenities, a wide range of offerings for every member of the family and to suit most any taste. Among them are an off-road driving school, an on-site exotic menagerie, a classic car display, paintball, croquet, mountain biking, fly fishing, shooting, gymnastics, archery, tennis, horseback riding, cooking classes, and at least a dozen other activities, indoor and outdoor, stirring or sedate.

Southwestern Pennsylvania is real blue-collar country— one might even describe it as true blue—particularly in the border region adjacent to hardscrabble West Virginia. At a glance it seems like a curious place to locate an ultraplush, multifaceted, and architecturally significant megaresort complex. But Joe Hardy methodically constructed this field of dreams by operating with the mantra from the movie of the same name: "If you build it, they will come."

And come they do to Nemacolin Woodlands. From Pittsburgh, seventy miles west. From Washington, D.C., and Baltimore, Cleveland, and Akron, all of which are within a 200-mile drive. Even 300 miles—from Philadelphia—or

18th hole

Above: 1st hole
Left: 3rd hole

4th hole

New York City, beyond that. The resort has been an economic godsend to a region where good work is hard to find. When the resort initiated a caddie program in 2006, there were ten applicants for each of the jobs available. All told, more than 1,000 citizens of the greater Uniontown-Morgantown area have found gainful employment at the resort. So did Pete Dye.

His creation is called Mystic Rock, and the premier course on the property features broad driving boulevards, blindingly white bunkering, and large, often elevated greens with mostly soft contours. It's a plush resort course full of niceties—larger-than-life statues of Vijay Singh, Gene Sarazen, and John Daly dot the property. There are fountains, even an eye-pleasing waterfall. The full-service, state-of-the-art halfway house with wraparound deck is both larger and nicer than many club-houses in the golf universe. It's a true pampering experience, with lots of polish.

There are lots of solid holes, but the par-5 holes on the inward nine are the most eye-catching. The 11th is a sweeping downhill dogleg with an expansive lake menacing the entire right side. The tee shot on 16 must be launched over a boulder field the size of a small quarry, with water pinching the green. Visitors are often blissfully unaware of the original nature of the terrain. "I've often been asked how much it cost to truck in all the boulders," says Joe Hardy, shaking his head gleefully. "They barely believe me when I tell them that to build the golf course we buried 90 percent of the rocks that were here when we started!" All in all, Mystic Rock is a handsome, solid test, PGA Tour–worthy, even, as evidenced by its former status as the home of the 84 Lumber Classic.

Despite the challenges of running an upscale resort busi-ness in a down-market economy, Nemacolin Woodlands continues to gain both prominence and visitors. Joe Hardy explains how in his usual irreverent fashion: "We've added amenity after amenity after amenity. At this point, all we're missing is the ocean, but we're working on that, too!" There are some things money can't buy. But, because they have come so far so fast, one can only surmise there still might be sea changes ahead.

When you're with Pete, you usually get upper-floor, deluxe suites at hotels. One time we were working at Nemacolin Woodlands Resort in Pennsylvania, and our rooms supposedly had floor-to-ceiling mountain views. I never saw them, because we checked in long after dark and were out of there before first light. The only hotel employee we usually have contact with is the night clerk. That's who's on duty when we arrive, and they're still on the job when we check out. That's life with Pete.

Tim Liddy, *golf course architect; long-time associate of Pete Dye*

Left: 16th hole
Below: 12th hole

The Fort Golf Course

With Tim Liddy

What does a dollar buy? A bag of chips, a pack of gum, a quart of gas. And, if you're lucky, the architectural services of Pete Dye.

The Fort easily rates among the most memorable and challenging golf experiences in the state of Indiana. It's located within an hour's drive of a million citizens in greater Indianapolis, but is an isolated entity unto itself—not a roadway crossing anywhere, not a home on the property or even on the periphery. Fort Benjamin Harrison was a military installation dating from World War I on Indianapolis's northeast side. It closed in 1996. The state of Indiana purchased the property from the federal government—2,000-acre Fort Benjamin Harrison State Park—and the military-only golf course contained therein. Pete Dye was called upon to renovate the existing course, which was slated to open to the general public. He magnanimously charged the city fathers of his adopted hometown a single dollar, not even the price of a Big Gulp soda.

Big gulp. That's what most golfers will be taking, after a couple of easier warm-up holes, when they stand on the tee of the swooping par-4 4th, nearly 480 yards from the tips, a full 440 from the penultimate markers, narrow and tree-lined. It's a wakeup call, for The Fort is as rugged and hardy as the military personnel it once served. The golf course is almost 240 acres in size, nearly double the acreage of an average course—but then, The Fort is anything but average. "The damnedest piece of property I ever saw," says Pete, who's seen more than his fair share. Central Indiana is generally flat as a card table, but this heavily wooded, heaving and rolling parcel, rife with wetlands, gullies, and ravines teeming with wildlife, is a geographical aberration.

The elevation changes were already in place. The state of Indiana is most fortunate that Dye didn't have to manufacture the landscape. It would have taken untold millions and countless man-hours to replicate what occurs naturally on the site.

Dye has so often been typecast as a designing sadist—the Marquis de Sod is one of the cleverer nicknames he's been called. But at The Fort, he and Tim Liddy toned down what must have been a ferocious experience. They removed more than a thousand trees, leveled greens, and excised fairway crowning that sent tee shots skittering toward the rough.

"During construction, we were digging up all sorts of ordinance—mortars and shells—because we were tearing up a portion of the property that was once a firing range," recalls Tim Liddy. "It could get pretty scary."

5th hole

Even in its somewhat softened reincarnation, The Fort can still be scary in the playing, and reminiscent of the military installation it once was. Difficulty is the watchword, and the intimidation factor is real. Those who cannot consistently get the golf ball airborne, neophytes who are cowed by fescue and forced carries, will need to seek shelter from the storm. Thankfully, there's a brief respite from the course's viselike grip on the seventh tee. After six holes of corridor-style golf, the property plateaus, offering a roomier sensibility as the outward nine concludes.

Golfers dive back into the woods, literally, on the 10th, a short, severely downhill par-4 where placement is paramount. Precision gives way to power by round's end, with the final four holes the most demanding on the course. The 15th is nearly 450 yards, followed by a true three-shot par-5 of 560 yards that sets the stage for a more than 230-yard par-3. The final hole plays uphill—more than 425 yards, unless play is being conducted from the tips, in which case the yardage swells to some 475. It's safe to assume that many a good-looking scorecard has been defaced in the final hour.

The words "golf resort" and "Indianapolis" don't seem a natural fit, but there are twenty-five well-appointed rooms at The Fort, and a popular restaurant besides. It's not a traditional resort, certainly not in the spas-and-waterslides way. But if logic dictates that a golf resort should first and foremost contain a first-class golf course, then The Fort qualifies with ease.

10th hole

18th hole

Purdue University The Kampen Course

Golf-loving students, faculty, alumni, and friends of Purdue University give credit to Pete Dye for the creation of the campus's signature Kampen Course, considered one of the best college golf facilities in the nation. Pete himself gives at least partial credit to radio announcer Paul Harvey.

"I heard him on the radio one time, talking about how golf courses weren't environmentally friendly," explains the architect, who learned much about turf grass, chemicals, and agronomy by taking seminars at Purdue in the 1950s. "It gave me the idea to redo their golf course in an environmentally friendly way, work with the school's agronomy students during construction, and show them that golf and the environment can coexist. And it didn't hurt that the school is in Lafayette, just fifty-odd miles from Indianapolis."

While Dye was willing to donate his design fee, the funds required for a comprehensive renovation of the existing course weren't in the school's budget. Pete decided to assist with the fundraising, and attended a dinner with some potential donors set up by Purdue's president. Pete didn't recall having ever previously met a well-heeled matron named Mrs. Kampen, who was present at the fundraiser. But she was asking after Alice, reminiscing about a New Year's affair she attended with the Dyes in the Dominican Republic, and commenting on how much her late husband had enjoyed playing golf with Pete on Teeth of the Dog. He winged the encounter, and much to his surprise and delight, their dinner conversation quickly resulted in a major donation, a princely sum that kick-started the project financially. Other major donations followed, and Pete then leaned on his contacts and suppliers in the golf industry to donate funds and equipment for construction. "A sand supplier I know in Indianapolis agreed to provide the sand we needed for the project," recalls Dye. "He called me up later, though, commenting that he didn't realize we were rebuilding the Sahara Desert!"

At first meeting, Pete wasn't thrilled about the long hair, scruffy beards, ponytails, and earrings that seemed standard issue on his hastily assembled construction crew—made up entirely of the university students studying agronomy, forestry, entomology, etc. Pete told the project manager he wasn't working with those guys, and the manager retorted that if that was the case, he wouldn't be working with anybody. But ultimately Pete was impressed with his crew's work ethic, desire, and natural affinity for the task at hand. "They were wonderful, haircut or no haircut. The project turned out beautifully."

18th hole

Much of this heavily bunkered, fescue-laden course is routed around a natural marsh known as the celery bog, to the right of the brutally long par-5 6th hole. The greenish bog is home to all sorts of birdlife, and thanks to the sophisticated filtration and recycling system Dye devised, the course's water runoff goes through several stages of cleaning before entering the bog.

The place is a living, green grass laboratory. Just off the 8th tee, a tough par-4 with waste bunkering down the entire right-hand side, is a sign for the Turfgrass Research and Diagnostic Center, which is housed in a building just a long iron from the hole itself. It showcases the symbiotic relationship between the course and the students who take care of it and study it on an ongoing basis.

"It used to just be a farmer's course," explains Devon Brouse, the school's head golf coach and director of golf operations, who was a Purdue agronomy student before embarking on his golf career. "It was long, flat, back-and-forth, with almost no features whatsoever. What's transpired

Top: 7th hole
Bottom: 9th hole

here is amazing." Brouse, who spent twenty years coaching the golf team at the University of North Carolina, came back to Purdue in 1998, shortly after the course reopened. "It's a great course regardless, very challenging and full of contour. It's very special. But the fact it was done so inexpensively, so quickly, and using student labor with no prior golf course construction experience makes the end result almost hard to believe. It's all a credit to Mr. Dye and Tim Liddy, and shows you what can happen when a designer is on site every day, for months at a time."

Kari Bennett is an Indianapolis-area golf professional who achieved All-America status as a Purdue golfer. She feels fortunate to have honed her skills on the Dye redesign. "Playing that course on a regular basis was instrumental in my development as a golfer. The natural beauty, and particularly the

challenge of the course, made me a much finer player. The 17th is a wicked par-3 over water, 180 or 190 yards for women, often into the wind. The last is an exhausting par-4, a driver and then a 3-wood, where you're just hoping to reach in regulation. When other teams came to play our course, we had a major advantage."

Major advantage, perhaps major asset, is the operative expression. For the elite players who compete on it. For the average golfers who attempt to meet its many challenges. For the agronomy students who built it, and those who now maintain it. For the university community at large, who take great pride in this sterling amenity. All thanks to the foresight and generosity of Pete Dye, who learned much of his trade in seminars on the campus and, decades later, decided to give back to the school the best way he knew how.

16th hole

Bulle Rock Golf Club

The hint is the horseshoes. Bulle Rock Golf Club is so magnificent in scope, pleasing to the eye, and engaging in the actual playing, it's quite easy to overlook the understated but elegant tee markers—blue, white, red, etc., delineating the teeing grounds. But the fact is, the markers are actual equine footwear, that proverbial good luck charm. And their importance goes beyond the fact that it's fortunate golfers indeed enjoying this former horse farm–turned destination golf course on a sweeping, 1,000-acre property.

The club's distinctive name stems from the fact that Cassandra Sappington and several other members of her family were buried in a small cemetery on the property generations ago. Cassandra's grandfather James Samuel Patton is believed to be the first man to transport a Thoroughbred horse to North America, back in 1730. That horse was Bulle Rock. And to honor her grandfather's memory and keep the tradition alive, this was also the name Cassandra chose for her own horse many years later, a horse that was part of her wedding dowry.

Bulle Rock Golf Club is the brainchild of a forward-thinking construction magnate named Ed Able, who made his fortune and then made a commitment to golf in middle age. His network of contacts afforded him access to many of the nation's most highly regarded private clubs, including Seminole and Pine Valley. But he eventually tired of waiting for invitations to these bastions of the game, and he decided to build an upscale, public-access course of his own. He found appealing acreage in the Maryland foothills not far from the Chesapeake Bay, and made it accessible to anyone who might want to venture forth.

"What's impressive to me is this area's history, the fact that they can track the title of this land all the way back to King George," Pete Dye says. "The history was as interesting as anything to me, so I felt like I had to build something extra special to go with it." He did.

Everything about Bulle Rock is on a grand scale—the head-tilting elevation changes, width of fairways, height of trees, size of greens. Hole highlights are many, but the 550-yard par-5 2nd, with its rock-strewn stream menacing either a daring approach shot or a cautious lay-up, is an early indicator that the course is both bold and beautiful. It's a terrific blend of talent and terrain, Dye's artistry showcased on a phenomenal canvas.

The course snakes up, over, around, and through a fescue-laden forest. The look, direction, and elevation of holes constantly vary. The uphill slog on the dogleg par-4 5th, a brute at 450 yards, is followed by a dizzying drop on the 6th, another par-4 where a player is tempted to yell "Geronimo" upon making solid contact from the tee. The 11th is a downhill par-5—and needs to be—at 665 yards from the tips. The 14th is downhill also, but swinging from the heels isn't recommended, as the tee ball needs to be fitted precisely on the fairway of this 330-yard par-4.

When asked about the little-expense-spared theme of his facility, including a comprehensive practice area, richly appointed locker rooms, and well-merchandised pro shop, Able wryly noted, "I spent $18 million on the golf course. But at least a quarter million of that was on jet fuel flying Pete back and forth from various other projects he was doing."

Eventually the money ran out for the additional eighteen holes planned for the property, though the Dyes had most of those roughed out. But financing the addition was slower than expected, and with the tragedy of September 11, 2001,

Opposite, top: 13th hole
Opposite, bottom: 11th hole

Below: 9th hole

it ground to a complete halt. The end result of the project's interruption is a championship course and a practice facility that is remarkably capacious in width and breadth. An ownership change means that eventually there will be a significant housing presence, with some 2,000 dwellings including stand-alone houses, townhouses, and condominiums. But the majority of these will be located in clusters away from the golf course proper, with only a small percentage bordering the playing corridors themselves.

The LPGA Championship moved to Bulle Rock in 2005 after a long run at nearby DuPont Country Club. The venue change was immediately validated when Hall-of-Fame members Annika Sorenstam and Se Ri Pak captured the first two titles, with fellow Hall of Famer Karrie Webb in the runner-up position in both 2006 and 2007. "There are plenty of great holes out there," offers Beth Daniel, yet another member of the LPGA Hall of Fame and former LPGA Championship winner. "I think it's a course that favors a long hitter, but you can't argue with the caliber of champion that has been produced at Bulle Rock over the first several years."

Original owner and course visionary Ed Able once remarked that "plenty of people *say* they want to build a world-class golf course, but for whatever reason, it doesn't happen. I'm very glad to note we not only said it, but did it, thanks to the hard work and expertise of Pete Dye." Though Able is no longer involved, there can be no disputing that Bulle Rock Golf Club, just like the prize-winning stakes horse for which it was named, remains a true Thoroughbred.

Colleton River Plantation Club Pete Dye Course

Almost three decades after creating Harbour Town Golf Links, their initial and most famous collaboration, Pete Dye and Jack Nicklaus returned to the Carolina Lowcountry and worked together again. Sort of.

Colleton River Plantation Club is both the premiere and premier high-dollar development located west of the Hilton Head Island Bridge, in the gateway town of Bluffton, South Carolina. It was deemed folly in the early 1990s when plans were announced for a big time golf-and-real-estate enclave that was to be constructed away from the marquee island itself, on the mainland. But Colleton set the standard, and subsequent real estate endeavors have pushed farther and farther west on the US 278 corridor, which is the only access road to Hilton Head Island. Nicklaus was on site first, delivering a traditional routing with a slam-bang riverside finish in 1992. Dye delivered his vision half-a-dozen years later. Each golf course stands on its own merits, but in tandem, they make up arguably the finest two-course complex in coastal Carolina. Colleton River's nearby neighbors to the west are also high-end thirty-six-hole golf-and-real-estate facilities, but are monochromatic in nature, the golf courses created by a single architect. The Colleton courses, truly chocolate and vanilla, are the main reason why this wonderful development is the area's finest.

The 1,500-acre site is surrounded on three sides by water, with several miles of shoreline. One of the reasons the developers pushed west, away from the confines of Hilton Head Island, was to make greater use of the abundant land. The adjacent 1,200-acre nature conservancy adds greatly to the feeling of quietude and remove that are regrettably lacking at some of the neighboring on-island enclaves.

Fully half the holes on the Dye design feature views of the Atlantic. The housing presence is less obtrusive than on the Nicklaus Course, on the inward nine in particular. While the outward nine follow a conventional routing, the inward journey is a windswept, wide-open walk beside the Colleton River and featuring exhilarating views of the Chechessee River and Port Royal Sound.

Dye's creation is not only different from Nicklaus's, but dissimilar to any other golf experience in the area—no mean feat considering there are some five dozen other courses within an hour's drive. Mounding and sand dominate the landscape, often concurrently. The wide fairways are pristine, but the rough is a particularly nasty strain of club-grabbing centipede and zoysia grass. Because there are few trees to block the breeze or throw shadows, the whipping wind and the

Above: 12th hole
Opposite: 6th hole

abundant sunshine on the turf result in firm and fast conditions, which is another anomaly in a region where conditions are often ball-plugging soft.

Practically since he began his design career in the 1950s, Pete Dye has attempted to thwart the technological advances in the game. This certainly holds true at Colleton River, as the observant golfer will occasionally spy little-seen tee boxes set far behind what appear to be the tips. On holes like the par-4 ninth and 15th, these hidden boxes add as much as 60 additional yards to holes that were staunch in the first place. So if ever there is a need to stretch the proceedings to 7,400 yards, the possibility exists. But the conventional black tees at 6,900 yards are more than enough golf course for the overwhelming majority.

The front nine par-3 holes are both jaw-droppers. The third, fairly lengthy at 190 yards, plays to an elevated green with water left and seemingly as many sand pockets as a golf ball has dimples. It's a visual novelty, as most are small and innocuous, about the size and depth of a child's wading pool. The 6th hole is a shade over 170 yards, with a single bunker. However, this multitiered, three-dimensional monster has elevated grass berms interspersed throughout the sand stretching all the way from tee to green. It's known locally as "the moonscape," and it's unforgettable. Either of these one-shot holes lends a vivid impression, but considered jointly, they are a powerful one-two punch.

The short 14th hole is worth noting. At only 335 yards, big hitters might impulsively attempt to drive the green. Fronted by a bunker and a huge, flag-hiding mound, this isn't the percentage play. A fairway wood or long iron played to the right leaves a short pitch and circumvents the mound. The problem occurs when a ball leaks too far to the right, and ends up in the marsh that looms to the right of the fairway.

Dye once commented, "Of all the courses I have ever designed, I like Colleton River as much as any. I don't know what more you can ask for." It's a rhetorical question, but the lucky members of Colleton River Plantation can offer a concrete answer—a recently restored, traditional Lowcountry-style course by Pete's old protégé Jack Nicklaus, which serves as the perfect golf counterpart, the yin to Dye's yang.

18th hole

Above: 13th hole
Left: 10th hole

Pete's flying back to the U.S. on the Concorde one time, and he gets on the airplane straight from the field. He's in his usual state of clothing disarray. He notices the guy next to him is waving his hand back and forth, so Pete figures he's pretty ripe after a long day in the dirt. Being the polite Midwesterner that he is, he says, "Mister, I'm sure you paid a fortune for your plane ticket, but somebody else is picking up my tab. So if I'm offensive in some way, I'll move, and find a seat toward the back of the plane." The guy says, "No, it's not that. It's the fruit flies." Pete looks down at his satchel, where he had previously stored some fruit that was beginning to rot. He opened it up, and a whole bunch of fruit flies start buzzing around the Concorde!

Joe Webster III, *course developer; owner of the Dye Preserve in Jupiter, Florida*

PGA Golf Club The Dye Course

Is Pete Dye lucky, or does he make his own luck? One of the main reasons he's become such an acclaimed architect is that some of the most unforgettable moments in modern golf history have occurred on his designs.

There was Arnold Palmer, at the height of his kingly powers, triumphing at the then brand-new Harbour Town Golf Links at the inaugural Sea Pines Classic on Hilton Head in 1969. John Daly in 1991, unknown and untested, shocked the golf world at Dye's Indiana masterpiece Crooked Stick, zooming from the ninth alternate position to PGA Champion in four unforgettable days. But that was a mere precursor to the 1991 Ryder Cup, contested a month later at another brand-new venue, the unforgettable Ocean Course at Kiawah Island. That Ryder Cup, the most mesmerizing international golf competition ever held, is still the drama standard by which all other team golf matches are judged. In addition, Dye courses have held U.S. Women's and Senior Opens, U.S Amateurs and Mid-Amateurs, Senior PGA Championships, and LPGA Championships.

Is it pure happenstance? Or is it that iconic moments generally occur on iconic venues, and golf heroes are birthed on heroic courses?

Thus, it only made sense that Pete Dye was approached by the powers-that-be and asked to design a golf course at the PGA Golf Club, a classy, well-run, and extremely popular fifty-four-hole resort facility in Port St. Lucie, Florida.

The Dye Course was the final piece of the puzzle. Tom Fazio designed what were then known as the North and South courses in 1996. Dye's effort opened in 2000. The original duo is rather traditional in feel, but the Dye Course is unusual by Florida standards—almost bereft of water, linksy, open, windswept, and thought-provoking. It features wide fairways pocked with heart-sinking pot bunkers and large greens with severe pitch and roll.

Housing is mostly minimal. Mid-fairway barber poles provide a sense of direction in an otherwise spare landscape. The map says Port St. Lucie, but it often feels like playing the links of Portmarnock, outside of Dublin, with the snare-drum

18th hole

Opposite: 6th hole

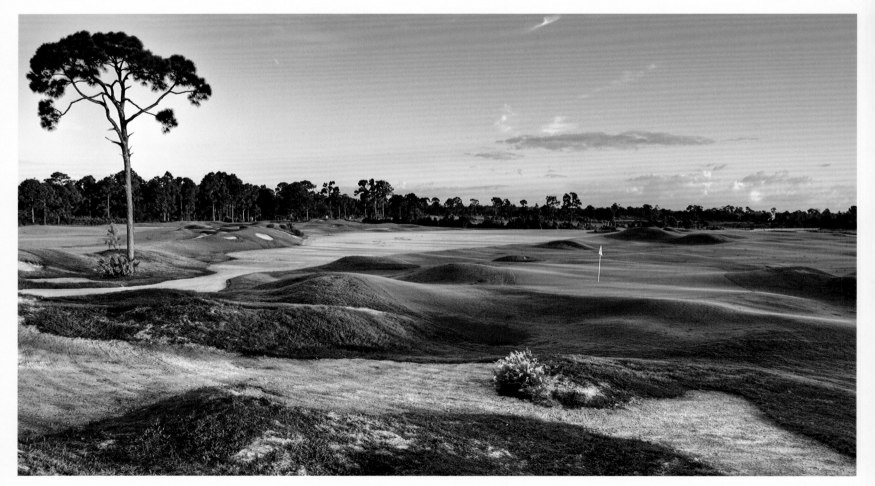

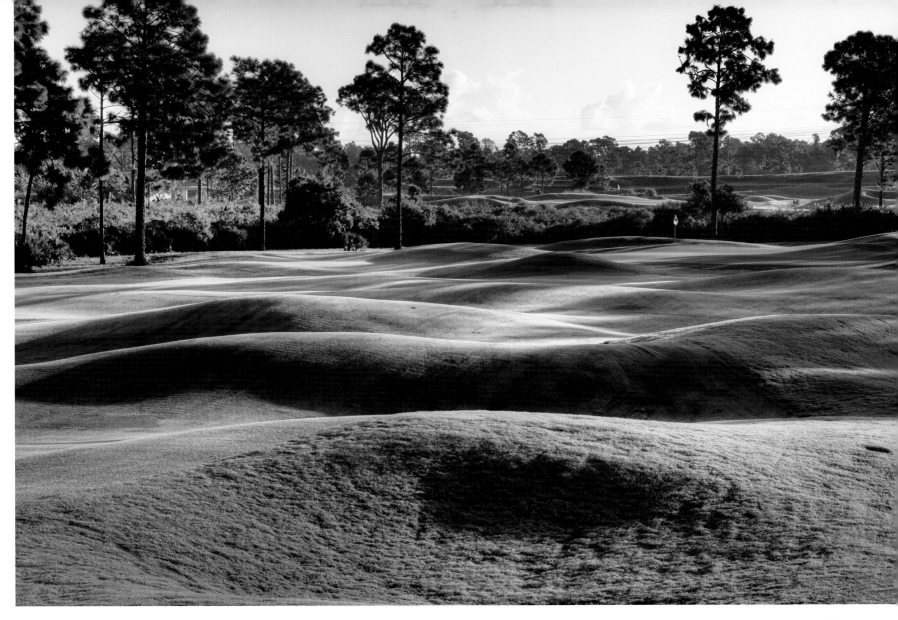

14th hole

fairways, scatter-shot pot bunkers, and out-of-nowhere mounding covered with pampas grasses.

As has occasionally happened in his career, Pete Dye was recalled several years after the course debuted to mollify disgruntled golfers who felt the original design was too penal. In this case, there were too many waste areas impinging on the landing areas near the greens. They were filled with coquina sand that scratched pitching clubs, bruised egos, and defiled scorecards. Dye added some dedicated turf, enlarging the green grass footprint of the golf course and quieting his critics.

Oftentimes the moonscape of bunkers, mounds, and penal rough somewhat short of the green will inhibit an aggressive golfer from going for a par-5 in two, or torture a misplayed approach on a par-4. But if a player is skillful or lucky enough to avoid the assorted pitfalls, bogeys are simple and pars well within reach. Greens are mostly open, and water practically a nonfactor.

Only holes 3, 4, and 5 have water in play, and in each case there's a waste area buffer that can help slow down a ball headed for a lagoon. So while the ball retriever will likely be holstered through the whole round, unfortunately the same cannot be said for the sand wedge.

Much like Pete Dye, Tom Fazio is also one of the modern masters of golf course architecture. But it's instructive to note that when *his* two contributions to the PGA Golf Club were renovated in 2006, they were renamed the Ryder and Wanamaker courses respectively—the first in honor of Samuel Ryder, the patron saint of the Ryder Cup, and the second in honor of Rodman Wanamaker, the New York City department store magnate who inspired the birth of the PGA of America, and whose name graces the trophy handed to the winner of the PGA Championship every August. But Pete Dye's effort is simply called The Dye Course. This subtle tribute speaks volumes, showing in no uncertain terms the esteem in which Pete Dye is held by the PGA of America.

West Bay Club

With P.B. Dye

Tiny Estero, midway between Naples and Fort Meyers in southwestern Florida, isn't quite as developed and doesn't yet have the population density of either. That fact, along with its location at the extreme western edge of town, make West Bay Club one of the more distinctive golf experiences in the region.

This Pete and P.B. Dye co-design from 1998 is more natural and roughhewn than many of the neighboring facilities. Not much earth was moved at West Bay Club. Directly west of the property is a thick and impenetrable jungle—the Estero Preserve. West of the preserve is Estero Bay, which connects to the Gulf of Mexico. North of the property is the Estero River. So the demanding nature of the playing experience is somewhat mitigated by lush surroundings and abundant wildlife. For indifferent ball strikers lacking the precise iron play necessary to negotiate these ultrademanding greens, birdies will be rare. But eagles (of the bald variety), wild boar, bobcats, herons, snowy egrets, and alligators are all present, affording plenty of distractions if the golf becomes frustrating.

And it will, as this is a stern test. Not even 6,900 yards from the tips, but with a 145 slope, and with 6,400-yard middle markers sloped at a staunch 138. There is a surfeit of water and encroaching wetlands on virtually every turn, though fortunately it is almost all marked as lateral hazards. West Bay Club remains blessedly uncivilized, in the best sense of the word. Nearly 60 percent of the 858 acres that comprise the property will remain undeveloped and untouched.

Not only is the golf course an Audubon Signature Sanctuary, but taking it one step further, the Clinic for the Rehabilitation of Wildlife (acronym—C.R.O.W.) has released hundreds of wild animals on site, figuring they'll thrive in the protected environment.

To continue the wildlife theme, the course really begins to bare its fangs on the par-3 3rd, a shade below 200 yards to a long and very narrow green, with lateral hazard left and bunkers right. It sets the tone for a foursome of truly tough one-shot holes with hazards aplenty and greens that tilt and whirl.

Tough as the one-shot holes can play, the par-5 holes are a slight break. The outward nine has a pair that is relatively straightforward. Two good whacks and a chip or pitch will usually do. The second nine has more drama in the way of ponds, mounds, and swales, but these three-shot holes represent the best chances to record pars or better.

As the course moves farther west midway through the front nine, the housing presence, not great to begin with, fades appreciably. Subtle mounding, palmettos, other hardwoods, and a general discretion in housing style make the real estate presence far less intrusive than in most areas of Florida. But unfortunately, a pair of behemoth condo towers loom over the start and finish of the golf course, actually casting shadows across the final fairway at day's end.

Calling West Bay Club a 50–50 collaboration between father and son isn't quite accurate. P.B. Dye was on site more than his dad, and some of the younger Dye's more extreme architectural concepts make the course an ultrahardy test. After all, Pete's mellowed some with age, but P.B. is still in his prime.

The concluding trio is considered the toughest in southwest Florida, no small reputation in this extremely golf-centric part of the world. The over-water par-3 17th and dogleg finisher demand full attention, but it's the 16th that's tougher than the tax code. This two-shot beauty is 460 yards from the back-of-the-box, 425 from the blues. The drive must be far enough left to afford a peek at the green. The uphill approach must carry a fronting marsh to a green so steep all that's missing is a chairlift. For the short or medium hitter, it's really a station-to-station par-5. Afterward, the view from the mounding behind the green, looking west toward untold acres of jungle leading to the Gulf helps assuage the angst built up by the hole. But not completely.

3rd hole

Opposite, top: 7th hole
Opposite, bottom: 17th hole

Avalon Golf and Country Club

Greater Youngstown, Ohio, has long been one of the country's most economically depressed regions, with median housing prices among the lowest in the nation. But Avalon Golf and Country Club has gone from exactly zero members to more than 3,000 since the dawn of the millennium. Midlevel country clubs, long the bastion of the privileged, are struggling to fill membership rolls from coast to coast. Yet in one of the least prosperous areas in the continental United States, this multicourse facility is thriving. How has this come to be? It is mostly owing to visionary businessman Ron Klingle, but also in part to Pete Dye.

"We've discovered a new way to run a private country club," explains Klingle, who was trained as a chemical engineer before embarking on a lifetime of entrepreneurship. "Now we're trying to perfect it."

Klingle is the chairman and CEO of Avalon Holdings, a $50 million, publicly traded company that deals with waste management and other environmental issues. Among his other assorted business interests, he's now expanding his golf portfolio, which includes the Pete Dye–designed Avalon Lakes, a late-1960s original which the old master completely renovated in 1999. He also owns two other area courses— Squaw Creek and Buhl Park.

"I bought Avalon Lakes in 1991, when it was still the public facility it had always been," explains Klingle, who originally hails from just over the Pennsylvania state line, a few miles east of Youngstown. "Pete came out to refurbish our greens, which had drainage issues. Instead, we decided to completely renovate the whole course, and while it was closed for a solid year, I made the decision that we would go completely private."

But he went private with a streamlined twist. Klingle eschewed the concept of initiation fees completely, instead relying exclusively on dues to keep the operation afloat. Within a few years, he had attracted some 500 members, who themselves were attracted by the flexibility of the rate plans, the variety of amenities he was offering, and the gem of the redesigned Dye original. A few years later, the members of nearby Squaw Creek asked to come under the Avalon umbrella, struggling as they were to maintain a vital membership. A few years later, the same thing happened at Buhl Park, just across the Pennsylvania border. "I told the folks at both places I couldn't afford to both purchase the club and

2nd hole

4th hole

sink the necessary monies into renovation. So in both cases, the members basically gave me the club, which allowed me to drastically improve both the infrastructure and amenity packages."

"Country clubs have traditionally lost money," explains the self-admitted struggling golfer, who happens to be a scratch businessman. "Their concept is dated, which is why so many are in trouble nationwide. They charge a lot to join, in both initiation and dues. Food and pro shop goods are expensive, they're often stuffy, and there are not enough people around, but you have to employ a full staff for whoever might be there. Avalon is affordable golf. Our prices are reasonable, the mark-ups in the pro shops are minimal, our lounges, restaurants, and grill rooms are always busy, and the food and service are first rate."

So is Avalon Lakes, the superb Dye design that is the marquee course in this fifty-four-hole lineup. It's a mature parkland, tree-lined but not tree-choked through the opening holes. As the front nine concludes, the water features come into play dramatically. The 8th is a peninsular par-3 with water lurking in every direction. Missing short is the only option. The 9th is a delicate par-4, water fronting the putting surface. The 11th is a heroic three-shot hole with a lake menacing the tee shot and then paralleling the line of play to the green. Dye's design is flexibility personified. The course can play to a gargantuan 7,500-plus yards or be minimized to less than 5,000. Some of the length disparities border on the comical. The tips on the opening hole are 495 yards. That's a solid par-5, but this is a par-4. But the front tees on the same hole are a whisker above 300.

Avalon Golf and Country Club is the antithesis of the old-school golf club, where there's nothing on the property but eighteen gorgeous holes, a locker room, grill room, and pro shop—no tennis courts or swimming pools need apply. Instead, Klingle offers a diverse series of amenities above and beyond golf, including pools, spas, fitness, tennis, and a whirlwind of social activities. "Most of our members have never belonged to a private club before. We attempt to give them what they want, be it arcades for the kids, movie nights, whatever. I consider this a resort-style country club. I'm attempting to emulate the all-sports, all-activities concept of the Greenbrier or Homestead, but on a community-wide basis. Perhaps someday we'll have skeet shooting or equestrian events. The future is wide open."

Klingle admits that a large part of the appeal, perhaps the single most important reason people join, is because of the signature Avalon Lakes course. "There's no doubt that our members' greatest pride comes from the fact that Pete Dye is the architect of our main course. You can't overstate how important he's been to the history of golf course architecture. We're lucky to have had his involvement."

Surely the legions of satisfied members say the same thing about Ron Klingle.

9th hole

We had worked on the renovation plans for our golf course for nearly a year. Finally, it was the eve of construction, and I was sitting next to Pete in a golf cart, looking at what was soon to become our 4th hole. I had asked him to replicate a wonderful water-laden par-3 he had designed at the Pete Dye Golf Club on our property, one of my favorite holes in the world. Pete looked at the topo map, gazed across to the raw land, then looked back at the topo map. Then he crumpled the plans into a little ball and shoved them into the glove box, saying, "We don't need water here. I think I'll build a redan green instead." I was crushed, but what can you say to the world's greatest architect after he makes a decision? All I said was, "What's a redan green?" He gave me a wink, and said, "You'll know after I build it." Later on, we were driving by the 8th, and Pete said, "You'll get your water hole here." Bottom line: The 8th is a remarkable par-3, easily the most talked-about hole on the course. Pete never referred to any of the plans during construction, and his renovation job of the original golf course is absolutely incredible.

Ron Klingle, *owner of Avalon Golf and Country Club*

Barefoot Resort The Dye Club

Pete Dye has occasionally been forced to race the clock, attempting to finish a golf course in time for a concrete deadline. The best example is Kiawah Island's Ocean Course, which was completed just days before the 1991 Ryder Cup matches. But despite that sprint to the finish, it's doubtful Mr. Dye ever endured quite the "competition" that he had nearly two decades later and 135 miles farther north.

On the day The Dye Club at Barefoot Resort opened in the spring of 2000, so did courses envisioned by Tom Fazio, Davis Love III, and Greg Norman. This all-star quartet, offering tremendous variety and quality, is the main reason why Barefoot Landing has become such a hot topic in resort golf. In a stagnating Myrtle Beach golf economy, with contraction and course closings becoming commonplace, the "Barefoot Four" continue to command top dollar, enjoying full tee sheets and rising revenues. All of the courses have fine attributes, but the Dye effort is—no surprise here—the least conventional and most talked about.

In brief, the Love course is best known for its faux plantation ruins, a Disneyesque crumbling construction and conversation-starter that minimally impacts a couple of front-nine par-4s. The Norman course has just sixty acres of dedicated turf, a Southwestern feel, lots of pine straw, and four holes abutting the Intercoastal waterway. Fazio's effort, as is usually the case, is an exquisite visual experience. The man is a green-grass Impressionist in addition to being an architect. And then there's the Dye course, the most memorable of the bunch.

It's a completely different visual sensibility from the trio of more traditional Lowcountry-style courses just a half mile away. It's a moonscape, a Scotland-comes-to-Myrtle sensibility with tawny fairways, odd angles, ubiquitous waste areas bracketing the fairways, and Dye's trademark humps, hollows, and mounding. The housing presence is slowly being added, but despite this "taming of the landscape," the Dye course is the most elemental of the four.

It's also the most difficult, and especially tough on first-timers, with lots of visual deception. The landing areas are more generous than they appear from the tee, bracketed with waste areas. Newcomers inevitably tighten up and steer their pellets into the sandy maws they were so desperate to avoid when staring down from the tee box.

10th hole

6th hole

Despite the abounding sand, the first par-3 is relatively simple, at least in comparison to its brethren. The remaining trio menace with encroaching water (the 6th), a precipice (the 15th), and wetlands (the 17th), leaving a minimal margin for error. The course concludes with a virtual carbon copy of the final hole at the Stadium Course at TPC Sawgrass, a sweeping dogleg par-4 with water lurking left from tee to green.

This high-profile design has seen lots of high-profile players and has served numerous times as the venue for the "Monday after the Masters" charity event sponsored by South Carolina rock icons Hootie and the Blowfish.

The celebrities and PGA Tour pros rave about the course. One year, Hall-of-Famer Tom Kite was relaxing in the grill room post-round, talking about how fabulous the golf course was and how he really wanted to tackle it from the tips. Apparently the 1992 U.S. Open champion contemplated the matter more carefully while finishing his drink—the back-of-the-box tee markers, stretching 7,300 plus yards, a slope rating bumping up to 150—because he soon changed his mind. "On second thought, maybe the blue tees are tough enough."

Barefoot Landing will likely continue to thrive in the decades to come, because it's rare for golfers to find such an impressive assortment of courses in such close proximity. Each of the four offers its own experience. But the most different, dynamic, and unquestionably the most demanding was executed by Mr. Dye.

2nd and 3rd holes

There was a big press conference when we announced that we were building four courses simultaneously at Barefoot Resort. There were several hundred in attendance. Besides the press, each of the design principals had an entourage of assistants with them. One by one they stood up and introduced themselves and their entire staff. Mark Love, the president of Love Course Design, stood in for Davis. Greg Norman's chief design associate was there, as was Tom Fazio. They all were talking about how they were going to build enjoyable, playable resort courses that would appeal to all levels of golfers.

Then Pete took the microphone. He said, "I'd like to introduce you to my entire staff. Alice, please stand up." After the laughter died down, he said, "This business can be tough, so I keep the staff small. In case business slows down, I only have one employee I need to lay off." He went on to say, "I know all about these guys and their staffs, because at one time or another, most of them have worked for me. And one other thing. My golf course won't be like theirs. It's going to be so damn hard, people are going to hate it!" And Pete was true to his word. The course is one of the hardest in the state. But once people play it, they can't wait to come back and try it again.

Sam Puglia, *owner of The Dye Club at Barefoot Resort in North Myrtle Beach, South Carolina*

Lost Canyons The Sky Course

Less than a mile from the suburban sprawl of Simi Valley, northwest of Los Angeles, the ubiquitous retail scenery of Borders Books and Bed, Bath & Beyond quickly gives way to rising elevation and a stark alpine setting. The landscape changes dramatically, and in the looming Santa Susanna Mountains, Pete Dye has dramatically changed the landscape of golf in greater L.A.

Course contraction is a fact of life the whole golf world over, and Lost Canyons is an example. The thirty-six holes are being halved; the Shadow Course will give way to housing. But the original Sky Course, a fabulous and stirring golf experience, will remain, converting to what will likely become a much-coveted private membership. Part of the contraction is owing to the preponderance of daily-fee courses that opened in the area at about the same time Lost Canyons made its debut, almost all of which are significantly less expensive to play. But the contraction is a minor upheaval in comparison to what's come before.

Self-effacing at all times, Pete Dye is given to crediting "the man upstairs" whenever he produces a slam-bang design on a sterling piece of property. But the good Lord giveth, and also taketh away, as in its short lifetime Lost Canyons has dealt with natural disasters of Biblical proportions.

A major wildfire swept the 1,600-acre property less than three years after the Sky Course opened in 2000. There was advance notice of the impending blaze, and management ran the irrigation system full force, saving greens, tees, and fairways. But the inferno roared through the bridges spanning ditches throughout the property, and they were all destroyed. The course reopened more than a year later. Within months, torrential rains came and the hillsides, denuded by the wildfire, couldn't absorb the flow of water. All the bridges were lost once again. For years, the rap on many Dye courses was that they were unplayable. Lost Canyons, bereft of bridges, brought literal meaning to the expression.

The course that exists today is a stunner. Major elevation changes, writhing fairways, treacherous greens, and not a home or condo in sight. It's hard to believe the course is but three miles from a major east-west artery.

If the setting seems familiar, it may be because the TV show *MASH* was filmed in the area. Golfers not ultra-deft with their wedges may soon need a MASH unit—the greens can cause psychological, if not actual bodily harm. The fact that there is a quartet of par-4s in the 300–325 yard range is meaningless, as is the fact that the virtually treeless canyon the course is routed through helps funnel tee shots to fairways that are generally wider than they appear from the tee. Because if a player can't hit the proper portion of these roiling putting surfaces, some as ribbed and wavy as ribbon candy, then forty-plus putts in a round are a distinct probability.

Some of the greens will be decontoured as the club morphs from public access to private, and the softening will be a welcome change. Set in the shadow of White Face Mountain, whose slopes are covered with sage and chaparral, the golf

Sky Course, 2nd hole

course has a drastic, minimalist setting. But there's no need for the greens to be as drastic as the topographical surroundings. The playing fields themselves needn't be as harsh and unforgiving as the mountains that surround it.

It's a fun golf course, and an exhausting one, mentally and physically. The downhill tee shots are thrilling, the steeply uphill approaches on the short par-4s fill a player with uncertainty as to actual yardage.

There are plenty of superlative holes, but the course crescendoes with the final duo. The 17th is a par-3 with a long, narrow green, twenty-mile views beyond, and death to any shot pulled left. The finale is a par-4 steeper than the Hannenkam downhill. Even at 450-odd yards, a solidly struck tee ball will leave but a short iron home. Even those with "warning track" power will feel like a power hitter. It's a rousing conclusion to a powerfully compelling golf course.

The Hideaway Golf Club The Pete Course

With Perry Dye

The Hideaway. How perfect is the name? There's no signage on the busy roadway just outside the gates. There are untold thousands of "snowbirds" in and around Palm Springs and La Quinta who probably have no idea the club exists. They literally don't know what they're missing within this 600-acre Shangri-La.

Never mind the game of choice for a moment. Instead, a description or two as to why this place is a gourmand's, in addition to a golfer's, delight. Breakfast features both sliders and smoothies. The former are mini ham-and-egg biscuit bites, the latter blended fruit drinks. From mid-morning until mid-afternoon, a chef prepares the "Snicky-Snack" of the day, made fresh and served to order, near the 1st and 10th tee of The Pete Course. It might be lamb chops, fish tacos, mini pizzas or tostadas. On course, adjacent to restrooms, are a wide range of drinks, energy bars, and premium ice cream treats. Every comestible is complimentary, or at least built into monthly dues, so you've got to pace yourself.

Palate aside, The Hideaway is a sensory feast for other reasons. The drive from the gatehouse is completely bracketed by orange trees, and their fragrance permeates the air. Hemmed in by the looming Santa Rosa Mountains, the courses are flecked with flowers like gazinia, verbena, and sweet alyssum—so many that the grounds look as much like a botanical garden as they do a world-class golf facility. The dazzling multitudes of pansies, gardenias, lilies, geraniums, etc., comprise what are known as "Hideaway Hazards."

Normally it's Pete Dye who causes headaches for golfers, but in this case the members made things tough for themselves. The Dye effort debuted in 2001 and was followed a year or so later by a course designed by former European Ryder Cupper Clive Clark. The members were so taken with the multitudinous plantings on the Clark course, they requested that the wide swaths of grass that earmarked The Pete Course be replaced with fescues and wildflowers.

The end result is a golf course both enchanting and demanding, as landing areas are now significantly reduced. Even longtime members of the professional staff admit getting around the course with a single ball is a distinct improbability. The Hideaway Hazards are always played laterally, saving the distance, if not the stroke. But no ball contained therein can be advanced. Unless it's reachable by hand from the fairway or cart path, it must not be touched. That's how serious the membership is about keeping the surroundings pristine.

But for all the beauty abounding, the situation becomes ugly when balls leak into water hazards, which, unfortunately for the average player, are mostly on the right-hand side of the fairway. Better to miss into the flowerings, where no distance penalty is assessed.

Each of the 400-plus homes at The Hideaway has a golf course view. But despite the opulence of these desert digs, they don't intrude on the playing experience, being angled away from the fairway corridors and somewhat concealed by plantings. Furthermore, because the course itself is so

8th hole

17th hole

strikingly lovely, a player's eyes rarely stray to the surrounding mansions.

Just as the club is practically invisible from the road, the converse is also true: The road is invisible from the golf course. High berms and mounding, tree plantings and other vegetation, and a stone wall all conspire to separate the nearby roadway from encroaching on the course.

The conditioning is meticulous. Fred Couples, who worked as a design consultant with Pete Dye at Lost Canyons north of Los Angeles, calls the greens at The Hideaway the most

difficult in the area. No faint praise, with ten dozen courses in the Coachella Valley. It's not because there are crazy knobs and swales, it's more the subtlety of the breaks. There is a lot of nuance, which makes for a perfect member's facility. Because the course is built on a sand base, the drainage is ultra efficient. Mostly a moot point, as only about four inches of rain fall annually. But when that rare deluge appears, the course plays firm and fast again quite quickly. It's just another delightful touch at a club that has no shortage.

The Dye Preserve Golf Club

There are dozens of private golf clubs in Palm Beach County, Florida, offering nearly 1,200 holes in all. What makes the eighteen at The Dye Preserve so special? Why does this low-key bastion of the game differ from the competition? Because it's a golf club, period, and emphatically not a real estate development. And though it sits in a very high-end ranch-and-horse community, the club has no official connection to its neighborhood.

Take the clubhouse. Most area golf clubs-slash-real estate developments construct glass-and-brass palaces, 50,000-square-foot testaments to extravagance. But The Dye Preserve clubhouse is almost invisible from the road. It's just 15,000 elegant square feet, constructed of wood harvested in Costa Rica and weathered in Mexico, then constantly waxed. The day the clubhouse opened, it looked as if it had been standing for a century.

Then there's the membership—ardent, dedicated golfers who generally eschew golf carts. Some 80 percent of the rounds played here are literal walks in the park, always in the company of caddies. These purists also grace the membership rolls at virtually all of the nation's premier golf clubs. Augusta National, Shinnecock Hills, National Golf Links, Oakmont, Pine Valley, Winged Foot, and dozens of other first-line courses are where Dye Preserve members play when they are away from south Florida. Friends refer friends, quality rules over quantity, and the membership grows slowly but steadily.

This uniquely desirable project is the brainchild of Joe Webster III, a longtime developer and friend of Pete Dye. Webster worked at Sea Pines Resort on Hilton Head and was then one of the principals at Long Cove. "When we first bought this property, there was a below-basic golf course sitting here. I think it was constructed for $600,000. Pete came in and rebuilt the golf course in 1988. We called it Cypress Links, and it was a fine facility." Shortly thereafter, the entire private club dynamic changed throughout Palm Beach County. "In the early 1990s, a club membership could be had for five or ten thousand dollars. By decade's end, that figure had skyrocketed to six figures."

Webster realized that to avoid being trapped in the bottom echelon, and to be able to compete in a market going more upscale by the moment, he needed to begin anew. "Basically, we started from scratch. We tore down the original clubhouse. We got Pete in here again, and asked him to redo and really enhance the golf course, and create an unforgettable setting that would help us stand out dramatically in this golf-saturated environment." Without question, the third iteration represents the high-water mark on this wonderfully spacious property west of Jupiter.

The golf course represents a softer, more user-friendly side than one normally associates with Pete Dye. "We aimed at making a different kind of golf course here," the designer says. "I tried to give the course a clean, well-defined look. South Florida is dead flat, so the golfer needs some help to see the shape of every hole from the tee." Fairways are wide, greens are sizeable, water is in play, but usually adjacent to buffer zones like ball-grabbing St. Augustine grass or narrow waste areas, either of which can stop a pellet prior to submersion. The gnarly St. Augustine grass really provides a look that screams "Old Florida" and does a wonderful job of framing and defining fairways throughout the facility. It's tricky to hit out of initially, but local knowledge dictates that you play the ball a bit farther back in the stance to ensure clean contact and a reasonable advancement of the ball.

Teeming with wildlife, almost free of housing, each of the eighteen holes is engaging. But perhaps the most interesting sequence is midway through the opening nine. The 3rd is a medium-length par-3 with water left, followed by a sweeping dogleg par-4, the toughest hole on the course. The tee shot must be played well left, far from the forest, to have a look at the green. The next is a tricky par-4 less than 300 yards, with water menacing the entire left side. It's an evil little construction, and even chronic slicers have been known to come to grief with stunning regularity by pulling the ball into the drink. The par-5 that follows is a straightaway, but while the flag can be seen as a player addresses his or her second shot, it disappears behind mounding prior to the short-iron approach.

When he built his brand-new golf course in 2002, Joe Webster felt it needed a brand-new name. The visionary behind the project chose to honor his longtime friend and business associate, a man whose skills he has admired for decades, and name the course The Dye Preserve. Alice, witty provocateur, was comically aghast. "You'll never sell any memberships," she cautioned, half-kidding. "Don't you know how many people curse my husband's courses?" But one delightful amble around this pristine property will sway even the most vehement Dye naysayer.

Opposite: 6th hole

17th hole

Promontory Ranch Club The Pete Dye Course

With Perry Dye

It's a common enough feeling in Park City, Utah. Poised on a precipice, your heart does a drumbeat as you contemplate the steeply twisting corridor falling away beneath your feet. You take a deep, steadying breath and prepare to negotiate the plunging terrain.

But it isn't winter, it's summertime. You're wearing a polo shirt and Bermuda shorts, not goggles and Gore-Tex. You were transported by golf cart, not chairlift. You're on the third tee box of the thrilling Pete Dye Course at Promontory Ranch Club, one of the intermountain West's most prestigious golf addresses.

This rugged, corkscrew par-5 is the standard-bearer for a course that offers an extraordinary combination of panoramic views, nosebleed tee shots, serpentine canyons, and shot-making challenge. Welcome to the new world of high-end Utah golf, as exemplified by this high desert dynamo.

The name Promontory has dual meaning. Historically speaking, the Golden Spike connecting the Union Pacific and Central Pacific lines to create the first transcontinental railroad was driven into the track at Promontory Point, some 120 miles north of Park City, in 1869. But for the modern-day golfer, the name has more immediate resonance. The golf course property, particularly on the inward, valley nine, has magnificent rock outcroppings, or promontories, at virtually every turn.

The dual meaning of the name dovetails with the course's dual personality. The outward nine meanders through a sunlit meadow, the southern exposure offering thirty-mile views. The back nine is located over a ridge and is nestled within a contained valley. "The difference between the front and back is like night and day," says Pete's son Perry, a noted course architect in his own right. "With 350 feet of elevation change from top to bottom, it's just a gorgeous site." Perry, a Denver resident, worked on the project along with two of his cousins, Matt Dye and Cynthia Dye McGarey. "It's very difficult to get a piece of land with mountain views, ski slope views, and lake views, which we are fortunate enough to have. Between the sunlit plateau of the opening nine and the protected, less windy back nine, it's a tremendous juxtaposition."

"I feel this course has really made a statement out in Utah," adds Pete. "The arid climate is great for golf, and the tremendously long vistas that are part of the landscape make the course stand out."

The greens stand out, certainly. They are full of contour, slope, and movement, mimicking the rolling terrain that completely envelops the property. "It would be totally incongruous to have dead-flat greens on terrain that offers such elevation change," explains Perry.

Owing to more than a half-century's prominence as a winter wonderland and its more recently earned status as an Olympic venue, Park City has always been better known for skiing than for golf. But estimable venues such as the Dye Course at Promontory continue to sprout from the high desert landscape. Jack Nicklaus entered the fray some five years after the Dyes, designing a signature course of his own against a mountain backdrop in the development's scenic Painted Valley. With ten square miles of land available, there are several other courses in the Promontory pipeline. These very welcome green-grass additions help put the town's recreation options somewhat back into balance.

Opposite: 15th hole
Below: 2nd hole

Woodland Country Club

Redesigned by Pete Dye, with Tim Liddy

When he was just getting started in golf course design in the mid-1950s, Pete looked for advice from Indianapolis native Bill Diddel, who had designed numerous courses in the state. He admired the straightforward, some might suggest simplistic technique that Diddel employed. The older man eschewed fancy irrigation systems and flashy bunkering, and created his courses as naturally as possible. Pete saw him as a mentor, and told him he hoped to design courses in the same no-frills way. Diddel, with an eye toward the future, was blunt in his reply. "If you try and do it like I did, you'll starve."

Though he's slender as a flagstick, it's safe to say Pete never missed a meal, other than those he skipped during the untold eighteen-hour workdays he has put in over the decades. When the time came, he was delighted with the opportunity to renovate Woodland Country Club, north of Indianapolis in the town of Carmel, fifty years after the Diddel design opened in 1952.

Pete's instructions to his crew were to keep things simple, as Mr. Diddel would have done. The front nine of Woodland retains this sensibility. It's a lovely parkland setting, has some parallel fairways, and is just slightly encroached upon by commerce and roadways. But the second nine, bolstered by an expansion using additional acreage that had previously been fallow, has more of the Dye flair. Longer, harder, and hillier than the outward journey, the concluding half shows more than a hint of Pete's devilish personality.

The renovation came about because the club had to relinquish an easement to the town of Carmel, compromising the first several holes. So it was decided to sell fourteen acres on the northeast side to a developer, and use the proceeds to fund the reconfiguration of the golf course, including more than fifty acres of woods, creeks, and hills on the southwest side adding some back-nine dramatics.

Woodland is playable for all levels of golfers, befitting a suburban country club. Retirees, women, and children can enjoy the layout, with its mostly wide fairways, open greens, dearth of water hazards, and few forced carries. But step to the back box, 7,200-plus yards, or even the penultimate markers at almost 6,900 yards, and the skilled player will be battling the entire round. Trouble comes in the form of luxuriant rough and sizeable, though thankfully just occasional, patches of fescue. There are tree-lined holes, fairways with slants, and hillocks that impede the view of the putting surfaces and encourage uneven lies. The greens pitch and yaw just enough

2nd hole

18th hole

to make putting a puzzle. Pete once called the gasp-inducing 18th the hardest finisher he ever built. Apparently an episodic bout of amnesia prevented his recall of the final holes at Kiawah's Ocean Course, Harbour Town, and the Stadium Course at TPC Sawgrass, to name but three. Nonetheless, it's a heavyweight in welterweight's clothing. Not even 400 yards from the tips but narrow as an army cot, with water menacing the entire right side and a yawning bunker ready to devour the steady diet of left-side bailouts from the tee.

Another conversation starter is the 500-plus-yard par-5 11th, a three-shot hole for all but the strongest players. The left side of the fairway is banked more steeply than the nearby

Indianapolis Motor Speedway, and second shots that appear to be screaming toward the underbrush or O.B. stakes will carom effortlessly back to the fairway. With this unexpected reprieve, a skillful wedge over the creek fronting the elevated green may well yield a birdie putt.

In a town with no shortage of premium golf experiences like Crooked Stick, the Brickyard, Wolf Run, and Country Club of Indianapolis, Woodland flies well below the radar. But while it remains unfamiliar to many, those in the know realize it is one of the finer courses in the capital city, thanks to the sensitive yet exciting Dye redesign.

Bridgewater Club Golf Course

With Tim Liddy

The Bridgewater Club is big. In every sense of the word. It's a housing development, "perhaps the most successful I've ever been associated with," says Pete Dye, and that's saying plenty. The houses are uniformly massive. As are the fairways. As are the comprehensive practice facility, the elegant clubhouse, and the footprint of the golf course, taking up nearly one-third of the 750-acre development. With all the size abounding at this Carmel, Indiana, showplace, it's hard to fathom that the project began as a small but noble idea for youth golfers.

A longtime friend of the Dyes named Doc O'Neal initiated the project. Doc had much in common with Pete—both were excellent amateur golfers, former presidents of Crooked Stick, and insurance men, though Doc stayed in the profession while Pete left, literally to pursue greener pastures as a golf course architect. "Doc had a real interest in promoting junior golf," explains Alice Dye. "He envisioned a clubhouse, a short-game facility, a nine-hole, executive-length course, and a practice range, all to promote junior golf in greater Indianapolis."

Doc was slightly ahead of his time. The idea was well intentioned, but eventually his plan was merged into a larger, more ambitious project that included the surrounding showpiece neighborhood and a championship golf course authored by Pete Dye with the assistance of Tim Liddy.

"It's a former tree farm, and the property is absolutely lovely," says Alice Dye. "The club caters primarily to families, and the golf course reflects that sensibility. It's an open piece of property, with minimal forced carries, and is extremely friendly to women and junior players."

Alice, the first-ever woman president of the American Society of Golf Course Architects, explains that the Dyes' aversion to forced carries goes well beyond Bridgewater and is essential to their design philosophy. "Our forced carries are usually limited to par-3 holes. We know where you're starting from, and assuming the golfer has chosen the appropriate tee box for their ability, it shouldn't pose a problem. But we avoid forced carries from fairways to greens, because we don't know where you're attempting to hit from. A long driver will have a lofted club in hand, but a shorter hitter will be forced to attempt a shot with a long iron or wood. That's why we tend to avoid them."

Once on course, one cannot avoid the fact that this is one of the most prestigious neighborhoods in Indianapolis. It's a stately parkland setting, and part of its appeal is the strict guidelines surrounding tree removal. Most of the nouveau mansions encircling the course look as if the paint is still drying and the bricks are still settling. But because the

10th hole

15th hole

hardwoods are protected and flourishing, the golf course reflects a maturity beyond its true age.

While the course is mature, the same cannot be said for many of those who regularly enjoy it. O'Neal's original passion for junior golf is alive and well. About 300 junior players, an astonishing number, take part in a summer program emphasizing lessons, clinics, and tournaments.

The course is handsome throughout, with two dozen lakes and ponds dotting the landscape. The most notable water hazard is on the inward nine, and changes the character of this otherwise uniform course just a bit. The crafty little par-4 14th precedes a sharp-angled par-3. These two holes benefit greatly from the intimidating presence of a rock-lined lake fronting both greens, with thousands of mini boulders bolstering the

shoreline. A well-executed pitch is required on the former, and a solid mid-iron on the latter. The par-3 tee shot must carry not just rocks, but also an imposing tableau of marsh grasses.

Design associate Tim Liddy recalls how pleased Pete was during an initial tour of the property. "He was very impressed that the owner had the foresight to plant so many beautiful maple, ash, and oak trees before the housing element went in, and told him so. Then we turned the corner and saw a grove of Lombardi oaks, which are about the lousiest trees you'll find on a golf course. Pete turned to the owner and said, 'I guess you're not as smart as I thought you were.'"

But those who've chosen to make their home at the Bridgewater Club and enjoy this fine golf course on a regular basis are very smart indeed.

11th hole

Wintonbury Hills Golf Course

With Tim Liddy

Perhaps it's nothing more than a statistical anomaly, but the fact is that among the 850 or so golf courses within the six New England states, only one is officially credited to Pete Dye.

The reason Dye has even that much presence: In 1995, discussions were held regarding the construction of a high-end, municipally owned golf course in the town of Bloomfield, Connecticut, just a few miles north of the capital city of Hartford. The area had plenty of high-quality private clubs, but worthwhile public-access options were scarce.

Veteran golf writer and longtime town resident Brad Klein was consulted about the potential new course. "I've always thought highly of Pete Dye's work," says the *Golfweek* magazine architecture critic. "I called him, said I knew that once in a blue moon he would design a course for just a dollar. I told him if he didn't provide the same service for my town, I'd write bad reviews of his courses for the rest of my career. He laughed, said he'd be happy to do it, and was up in Bloomfield within a couple of weeks' time."

Klein pursued Dye for reasons beyond their years-long friendship and his admiration for Dye's talent. "I knew that the publicity we'd generate by having an architect the caliber of Pete Dye on board would allow us to get the bonds through and the financing we needed to make the course a reality."

It took six years to get the proper permitting and find the appropriate site, which at one point moved from one end of town to the other. Even with Pete on board for a buck, and design associate Tim Liddy working at a substantial reduction from his normal fee, the total construction tab—including land, clubhouse, maintenance barn, and equipment—was just over $11 million, about two million of which went for engineering costs and environmental studies.

The difficult nature of the chosen site was a major reason for the laborious process entailed in making the golf course a reality. Fully ninety acres of the 290-plus-acre site were wetlands, and the permitting process involved local, state, and federal authorities. A power line that ran down the center of the property was a headache, as was the fact that half the acreage had to be leased from local water authorities. "It seems that in New England, especially, nobody wants to let you build anything anymore," recalls Klein.

But build it they did, eventually, and the course has met and exceeded the expectations of its proponents and regular patrons. Only 225,000 cubic yards of dirt were moved, an inconsiderable amount in the modern era. Wintonbury Hills has had minimal impact on the wetlands, both in the building process and in the playing. In a three-year study conducted

5th hole

Pete came up for an early site visit to a municipal course he agreed to design in my hometown of Bloomfield, Connecticut. The location was very mucky, filled with wetlands, and he tromped around with his dog, Sixty, for better than three hours. Finally he came back, and the welcoming committee waiting for him included the mayor, town manager, the engineering team, and the local environmentalists, among other dignitaries. We were all gathered, waiting for his assessment of the land. But before he said a word about the site, he spent nearly an hour picking about two dozen ticks off his dog. We couldn't wait to hear his opinion, but his priority was cleaning up his dog, which was all he was really talking about as he worked. Eventually he gave us his opinion, which was succinct, to say the least. "Yeah, I think we can make this work." He certainly did make it work, and the golf course is one of the better public-access courses in western New England.

Brad Klein, *veteran golf writer*

14th hole

postconstruction, an environmentalist hired by the town documented 160 different bird species and twenty different mammals making their homes on the golf course. Only fifty-five acres of managed turf, large swaths of fescue grasses, and numerous bird-boxes throughout the property showcase the soft-upon-the-land sensibility that Dye and Liddy envisioned and delivered on the property.

When approached from the frontage road, Wintonbury Hills looks like little more than a flattish, farmland-style tract of land, with the aforementioned power lines seemingly crossing the opening holes. But what are not readily apparent are the 100-foot elevation change, the hardwood corridors featuring birch, oak, and walnut trees, and the proximity of the expansive Tunxis Reservoir, which gives an entirely different sensibility to the property midway through the inward nine.

The course features bent-grass throughout on tees, fairways, and greens—the last a puzzle offering the sturdiest defense against par. It's a real nature walk, or can be, although a trio of 400-foot-long bridges that traverse wetland areas between the playing corridors keep most players tethered to golf carts.

It was iconoclastic comedian George Carlin who famously riffed on some of life's most intriguing oxymorons—incongruities like jumbo shrimp and military intelligence. To that list one might also add "upscale muni." But Wintonbury Hills, the town-owned, all-are-welcome golf facility that in many ways plays and feels like a private club, is exactly that. And the citizenry of leafy Bloomfield, Connecticut, and environs can thank the diligence of Brad Klein and other concerned town citizens, as well as the architectural acumen of Pete Dye and Tim Liddy, for making it so.

Big Fish Golf Club

With Tim Liddy

"Anyone who's achieved anything of note in this area has done so by dint of hard work. The area may be beautiful, but nothing comes easy." So says Matt Vandelac, founder, co-owner, and director of golf at the lyrically named Big Fish Golf Club, located in the remote Hayward Lakes region of northwestern Wisconsin. It wasn't easy to finance or build. It took plenty of effort to get the architect he coveted. But perseverance eventually paid off and Big Fish became a reality, one of the finest golf experiences in rural Wisconsin.

Vandelac hails from the twin cities of Minneapolis and St. Paul, located some two hours to the northwest of Hayward Lakes. Earlier in his career he was the project manager at Stoneridge Golf Club in "the cities," designed by Dye protégé Bobby Weed. "He did a great job with Stoneridge, and my first thought was to try and secure the services of Bobby for our golf course. Then I figured, why go for the student if I might be able to get his teacher?"

It wasn't easy to secure the services of Pete Dye, particularly in Wisconsin, where he had previously hit a Grand Slam—the four unforgettable courses he authored at Destination Kohler.

"I'd get Pete on the phone, ask him to do the golf course for us, and he was noncommittal. He'd say, 'Call me again tomorrow at 7 A.M.' I'd call him again, and he'd say the same thing. I kept calling him at 7 A.M., day after day, and eventually he relented." Dye, no stranger to eighteen-hour days in the field, appreciates persistence.

Towering white pine forests, crystalline lakes, and flourishing wildlife are all hallmarks of the Hayward Lakes region. Vandelac's dream was to build a destination golf course in this little-trafficked area, one that he had grown to love on numerous visits with his wife and family. "The region has attracted hunters, fishermen, boaters, and campers for generations, but the area is also hilly, with sandy soil, and I knew it would be perfect for a championship golf course."

Vandelac introduced a high school friend, Jack Datt of Newport Beach, California, to the town and golf course, and Datt purchased the majority share in the facility. Like Vandelac, Datt is committed to the vision of firm and fast conditions and is ecstatic with the results of Dye's work.

The 300-acre site chosen for the course was practically bipolar. Half was a perfectly flat cornfield, the other was rolling, ravine-filled, and heavily wooded. Dye and design associate Tim Liddy used a light touch on the terrain. It's a pristine nature walk, thrilling but well short of terrifying. Players are stimulated by the surroundings, not intimidated by the course demands. The Hayward Lakes region usually makes a visitor's pulse go down, not up, and Big Fish was built with that same sensibility in mind. A common pro shop occurrence is a proud daily-fee visitor crowing about a career-best or near-best score managed on this beautifully inviting golf course.

Few parallel fairways, holes meandering in every direction on the compass, one-shot holes playing both uphill and down, and a rhythmic combination of right-to-left and left-to-right tee shots and approaches are all part of the playing experience. Sugar maples, evergreens, and oaks frame the landscape. There's no shortage of wispy fescue grasses, but management made a conscious decision to minimize the irrigation in these areas. So it's thoroughly playable, the ball can be advanced easily, and the waving fescue is rarely a club-grabbing nightmare for the casual golfer.

There are seventy feet of elevation change on the property, the most notable example being the par-5 13th hole, easily reachable for big hitters, tumbling downhill some fifty feet from tee box to green.

"It was amazing to see a legend like Pete Dye, a man in his late seventies at the time, with a hundred courses or more on his résumé, get into this project the way he did," recalls Vandelac. "We had wonderful specimen trees surrounding the final green, and Pete cut them down, one by one, until they were all gone. I wondered why, until he told me he wanted players who had just concluded their round to have an unimpeded view of the entire front nine, so they could relive the golf adventure they had just experienced."

The irony is that despite the peppering of lakes and ponds throughout the region, the nearest significant body of water is two miles from the course. But the name Big Fish still makes sense, because besides its distinctive ring, ease of spelling, and the lack of confusion it inspires in the customer base, the Hayward area is where the world record muskie was caught some years ago. There's no other course in the upper Midwest that has a name even remotely similar.

"There are a dozen or so other courses in this region, but they are all mom-and-pop shops, pretty basic, without name designers," concludes Vandelac, who proudly acknowledges that his Dye-designed golf course is undoubtedly the Big Fish in an otherwise small pond.

9th and 18th holes

I once suggested to Pete that it would be great to get all of the shapers and design associates he worked with over the years, guys who went on to architectural careers of their own, back together to do a "tribute course" of all his great holes. He looked at me for a second, shook his head, and with a straight face said, "Nah, it'll never work. You couldn't get them all out of jail at the same time."

Matt Vandelac, *director of golf and co-owner of Big Fish Golf Club*

Hampton Hall

Thirty-five years after he first made his mark in the Carolina Lowcountry, Pete Dye came back to greater Hilton Head for the fourth time. His design sensibility at Hampton Hall in nearby Bluffton is a 180-degree reversal of what he produced at Harbour Town Golf Links in the late 1960s.

"This is an entirely different golf course from what I've done previously in this location," explains Dye. "There was much more room here than is typically found in the Hilton Head area, and we've employed a great variance in the length, with five sets of tees, and in the width of this golf course."

While Harbour Town features writhing fairways, encroaching trees, and tiny, flat greens, Hampton Hall is the polar opposite. These fairways are capacious, and though there's plenty of water in play, balls either hooked or sliced will often remain, however precariously, on the playing field. The course also has massive, undulating putting surfaces. There can be a three-club difference depending on a front or back pin location. The slope and contour are as severe as a Tilt-a-Whirl in some cases, and putting from the wrong side can be every bit as exhilarating (or dizzying, depending on one's perspective) as the carnival ride of the same name.

"Most courses in the area are tree lined, and golfers have to navigate their way carefully. The strategy is dictated from the outset," Dye continues. "But here the golfer can choose which side of the fairway affords the best angle into the greens, and because of the challenges of most of the putting surfaces, choosing the proper angle into the green is very important."

The outward nine is configured in a tight clockwise routing, while the inward journey is counterclockwise and a bit more spread out, green to tee, than the front nine. But despite the confidence that will be inspired by these expansive tee-box vistas, Hampton Hall is no wide-open pastureland where personal bests or career low scores will be recorded by anyone stepping to the opening hole.

The course is lengthy, pushing 7,500 yards from the tips. Most players will have all they can handle at 6,800 yards, or better yet, 6,300 yards, sloped at 132 and 128 respectively. The greens themselves can be a puzzle, and getting to them in regulation isn't a foregone conclusion. The architect has employed a never-ending series of high-profile bunkers, both in the fairways and near the putting surfaces. All of these sand pits have low entry points but are bolstered by intrusive grass berms that impede the line of play between the ball and the target. For example, from the tee box toward the green at the lengthy par-5 3rd hole, it looks as though there are a dozen random earth piles awaiting removal. But the reality is that these are scattered bunkers, easy to roll into, tricky to blast out of, a curiously maddening design feature.

Many Pete Dye designs use visual intimidation. They are actually easier to play than what appears from the tee. Hampton Hall, at first glance a ball-basher's delight, is something else entirely.

Opposite: 13th hole
Below: 8th hole

The Gasparilla Inn Golf Course

How low-profile is this discreet island paradise, located about midway between the cities of Tampa and Naples on Florida's Gulf Coast? Consider this fact: Despite having lived in Florida on a part-time basis for seventy-some-odd years, Pete Dye had never once visited this sliver of land between Port Charlotte and the Gulf of Mexico, though his home near Delray Beach is a simple three-hour drive.

For much of its nearly century-long existence, The Gasparilla Inn did no advertising at all. The occasional media mentions it received came courtesy of wedding announcements in *The New York Times*, when a society couple chose the island as their nuptials venue. This was and remains Old Florida, with no condominiums, high-rises, neon, or franchises besmirching the nearby village of Boca Grande, the island's only center of commerce.

"Before we hired Pete to come renovate the course, our visitors were more inclined to fish for tarpon, play tennis, and relax. Golf was mostly a secondary pursuit," says Will Farish. He and his wife, Sarah, are the current proprietors. She is the only daughter of longtime Gasparilla Inn owner Bayard Sharp, himself an heir to the DuPont fortune. Sarah Farish inherited the property after her father's 2002 passing.

"Our goal was to refurbish the entire facility, and the golf course, which was flat, nondescript, and with serious drainage issues, was our first priority." All that changed when Pete made his way cross-state to their Gulf Coast Eden for his first look around. "We have a home near Pete and Alice on Florida's east coast in Gulfstream, close to Delray Beach. We wanted their opinion on how we could improve things," continues Farish, the former United States Ambassador to The Court of St. James and a friend to England's Queen Elizabeth.

When Dye first saw the property, with its vintage inn, swaying palms, and water on all four sides, he declared it an architect's dream. But on closer inspection, he disparaged the thick row of Australian pines at the edge of Charlotte Bay as ridiculous, remarking that it was akin to building a seaside course and then obstructing the view by building a brick wall. The trees quickly disappeared, as did all vestiges of the original course.

Originally slated as a touch-up, the end result was a complete blowup. The course closed in April and reopened for Thanksgiving weekend of 2004. The seven-month shutdown included a lengthening from barely 6,100 yards to nearly 7,000, several new lakes dug, and the fill used to provide notable contour to the fairways. Waste bunkers, some studded

with palm trees, were added to provide fairway definition. An entirely new set of puzzling greens emerged, with scattered pot bunkers and greenside swales adding an intimidation factor to the approach shot. What thankfully remains from the 1930s-era original are water views from virtually all points on the course, though true proximity is on holes 14 through 16, with the 13th green and 17th tee acting as waterside bookends.

Furthermore, Dye provided serious enhancement to the infrastructure, installing a series of sump pumps and an irrigation pond, the former to eliminate flooding, the latter to release water as needed during dry periods.

He's the antithesis of a tree-hugger, as evidenced by his instantaneous decision to remove the aforementioned pines from the shoreline. All told, about two-thirds of the trees on property prior to the renovation were removed, many at the hands of the architect, some as the result of Hurricane Charlie, which rumbled across the property that summer.

Dye rarely gets the credit he deserves for his environmental sensitivity, but several magnificent banyan trees that were uprooted during the storm were replanted at great effort. More telling was his decision to regrass the course with a salt-tolerant turf-grass variety called Seashore Paspalum, which was especially welcome in the delicate ecosystem of this minimally developed barrier island. The superintendent can now eliminate weeds and other infiltrating vegetation with natural compounds like sea salt and baking soda, without relying on noxious chemicals.

"Before the renovation, it was The Inn itself that would attract visitors, some of whom would occasionally play golf," says Farish by way of conclusion. "Now we have a notable golf course that is attracting avid players on its own merit, and these are the type of visitors who also enjoy staying with us at The Inn. We have Pete Dye to thank for this welcome turn of events."

11th hole and driving range

TPC Louisiana

With design consultants Kelly Gibson and Steve Elkington

Some fifteen miles west of Bourbon Street, unquestionably the most famous thoroughfare in the beautiful city of New Orleans, lies the Pete Dye–designed TPC Louisiana.

Because this facility was built on the west bank of the Mississippi, in the Jefferson Parish town of Avondale, it was spared some of the devastation that Hurricane Katrina wrought farther east. Nonetheless, the property was denuded of 2,000 of its 10,000 trees, and thirty acres of fairway grass were submerged under standing water, owing primarily to the fact that there were no workers available after the evacuation to remove the debris clogging the drains. It closed the day Katrina hit in late August 2005 and didn't reopen for nearly another year.

Some 250 acres of swampy marshland filled with cypress trees were the raw canvas on which Dye worked. The nearby Mississippi River was dredged for the sand needed to provide fill for the fairways. Now the property is self-contained, surrounded on three sides by drainage canals. "Seems the commissioner only gives me swamps and rock piles to work with," said Dye, laughingly. "But I appreciate the confidence he has in me. And I still love digging in the dirt." No doubt the Dye hire was influenced by his work some twenty-five years prior at a similar swamp site near Jacksonville, Florida, which was artfully engineered into the TPC Sawgrass complex, the flagship of the Tour, and one of the most popular courses in the world.

"Pete told me his goal is to challenge the players mentally, on the optics of the hole, and keep them uncomfortable, a little off balance," says New Orleans native Kelly Gibson, a long-time Tour player who consulted on the project with 10-time Tour winner and former PGA Champion Steve Elkington. A core strength of the course is the daunting nature of the par-3s. Dye wasn't keen to have the talent-rich "flat-bellies" peopling the Tour assault his one-shot holes with mid or short irons. Consequently, they all play well over 200 yards from the back tees. "One day during construction we were playing the 17th into a stiff breeze," recalls Gibson. "I hit 3-wood, Pete hit a driver, and neither of us reached. I commented that perhaps

the hole was too hard. He said there's no rule that says a player needs to reach a green in regulation."

The three major physical features of the site are the preponderance of cypress trees, numerous wetland areas, a tremendous amount of fairway bunkering, some thirteen acres of sand in total, and more than seventy additional pot bunkers, besides. Dye built modestly sized greens, no more than 5,000 square feet. He set the bunkers away from the putting surfaces with chipping areas between. "No need to have the bunkers right up against the greens. We want to have a different look, maybe a little optical illusion, and a different strategy to the holes."

The trees are a commanding presence throughout, never more so than on the petite 13th, a potentially drivable par-4 of 377 doglegging yards from Tour tees and 350 from the Dye tees. In mid-fairway is a large cypress surrounded by "cypress knees"—half a dozen chest-high, even head-high roots surrounding the trunk and sticking out of the turf in a semicircle. Because cypresses often grow in swamps, their roots reach upward to breathe. This effect on the TPC's 13th hole is eerie at minimum and undesirable in the worst case—should one's tee shot come to rest among these most unusual natural hazards.

Dye hasn't just held on to his design acumen at an advancing age, but his golf skills also. On opening day in 2004, the then seventy-eight-year-old set the course record (from the appropriately named Dye tees, the penultimate markers set at 7,000 yards) with a smooth 74. What makes the feat even more impressive is that he easily bettered his age with borrowed clubs, no golf shoes or golf glove, and eschewing a cart entirely, choosing to walk instead. His course record stood for seven months. However, while the challenging yet tranquil golf course he fashioned from the richly verdant Louisiana Bayou is a stern enough test for the PGA Tour pros who happen by annually, it is also enjoyable from shorter distances for the daily-fee golfer the rest of the year. Unlike his short-lived course record, it will endure and delight for decades to come.

We were walking the back nine during construction, and I was trying to convince Pete to save the magnificent cypress tree located at the corner of the dogleg on the 13th hole, which was slated to be taken down. He said, "Son, you can't be a tree-hugger and survive in the course design business." I continued to plead my case. I said that the tree was probably 750 years old, and it would be a shame to take it down. We kept walking up the fairway, and he smiled a bit, and then said, "You're telling me that tree is 750 years old, and I'm telling you that I'm seventy-five years old. One of us is leaving today, and it's not me!" We walked a bit farther, and I asked him to look at the tree from a different angle. Finally he was convinced. He said, "You know, you're right. I think we'll keep it." I'm happy to say the tree not only survived Pete Dye, but several years later, it also survived Hurricane Katrina.

Kelly Gibson, *former PGA Tour pro; TPC Louisiana design consultant*

5th hole

"He's one of the most generous and one of the finest men I know," begins Pete Dye. "I consider him a very close friend, and it has been a pleasure working for him over the years, at Kiawah Island, on Hilton Head, and certainly in Blacksburg, Virginia."

The architect's high opinion of Bill Goodwin of Richmond, Virginia, is most certainly shared by countless others—many of whom are enjoying the Dye-designed River Course at Virginia Tech, some twenty minutes from the college's main campus. An alumnus of Virginia Tech and an avid golfer, Goodwin owns both the Kiawah Resort and the Sea Pines Resort in South Carolina. He and his wife, Alice, who have also donated significantly to the University of Virginia over the years, wanted to provide the Virginia Tech golf team and the university community an opportunity to enjoy the game on a championship venue. So he funded the project and hired his favorite architect to refurbish and fortify the existing routing.

"The ambience of the course is unbelievable," continues Dye, who moved some 400,000 cubic yards of dirt during the two-year renovation process and relocated the playing corridors to take greater advantage of a nearby waterway. "The course plays adjacent to a two-and-a-half-mile stretch of the beautiful New River. We now have fourteen holes with water views, including eight that play directly to the river's edge, which is definitely in play. The other great thing about it is that the river keeps things cooler in summer and a bit warmer in the winter."

Despite all the earth moving, the course is relatively flat. Dramatic elevation changes are close at hand; players can see the ridgelines and cliffs in the rise of the Blue Ridge Mountains directly across the New River from the golf property, but not on the course itself. Likewise, the acreage is surrounded by trees, but the course has very few. Without the hardwood presence, the wind whipping off the river often ratchets up the difficulty scale.

The university community not only benefited from Dye's vision, but also by his hands-on attention. He worked in concert with Chris Lutzke and Keith Sparkman, both of whom have been indispensable to Dye for more than twenty-five years. The trio paid particular attention to the bunkering and green contours. "Both of those aspects of the golf course are outstanding, as fine as you will ever see," says Dye.

"There's an old railroad that runs at the base of the mountain across the river," he continues. "It adds even more character to the property. If you think about it, some of the best courses in the world are near railroad tracks," citing examples such as Prestwick, Pine Valley, and Yeamans Hall.

Dye is no stranger to building big-time courses for big-time universities. Michigan, Arizona State, and especially Purdue, near his Indianapolis home, have all benefited from his contributions. But it's arguable that no college course he's created, perhaps no college course that *any* architect has created, is as uniquely lovely as what Dye has done in Blacksburg. "It is really a thrill to build a golf course that you know young people are going to enjoy, and hopefully improve their games on, and I've always enjoyed being part of a university community."

"I've been fortunate in that several of my designs have hosted the NCAA Championships, including Purdue," he concludes. "I hope the same thing happens at this Virginia Tech course someday."

Opposite: 18th hole
Below: 17th hole

Tuscany Reserve Golf Course

With Greg Norman

Most gates at gated communities resemble a tollbooth barrier—a pole that rises at a right angle to let cars pass through. But the Tuscany Reserve, ritzy even by posh Naples, Florida, standards, has an actual wrought-iron gate, fit for a castle, at its entry point. It sets a tone of astonishingly high standards from the first glance, one that repeats consistently throughout this meticulous Pete Dye–Greg Norman co-design.

All 140 acres of turf on this roomy, 460-acre landscape are SeaDwarf Paspalum grass, a revolutionary strain that grows horizontally, not vertically, so it's totally bereft of grain. It knits together like a vine, and every blade is the exact same strain—like a crew cut on the greens, a buzz cut on the fairways and tees, a Beatles' 'do in the rough.

The development is in the farthest reaches of northern Naples, practically bordering the town of Bonita Springs, and is reputed to have the most expensive infrastructure of any project east of the sumptuous Bellagio Hotel in Las Vegas. The earth requirements alone necessitated that 1,000 loads of fill be brought in daily, a total of 6,000 loads per week, over nine straight months. All that dirt only adds up to fifty-eight feet of elevation at its highest point, near the first tee. But it still makes Tuscany Reserve the pinnacle, and not just of opulence, in Collier County.

Concrete slabs an attention-getter? Only when the bridge railings and walls fronting the greens are chiseled and carved, then hand painted to look like the work of a nineteenth-century Tuscan stonemason.

So what type of golf course did this "money is no object" mentality provide? An impressive one. The architects did not "divide and conquer," or split the workload. It's a collaborative effort. But the back nine, with scattered-buckshot bunkers, many small and canted upward, look more like Dye. The opening nine, with gentle, flash-faced bunkers and greens that morph seamlessly into collection areas below, look more like the work of Norman.

"I have learned a great deal from Pete Dye over the years," offers "The Shark." "Pete has always been an innovator, pushing the boundaries on everything from turf varieties to new types of bunker sand. I was delighted to have the opportunity to work with him."

Though they've been known as demanding architects throughout their solo careers, building courses much tougher than average, at Tuscany Reserve they tempered each other's severities. They are keenly aware of their audience and have built a roomy and friendly golf course that will eventually be enjoyed by hundreds of families, not U.S. Open hopefuls or wanna-be Tour players—though the nascent development already does have a bona fide Tour player in Rocco Mediate, who lives with his family in grand style adjacent to a back-nine green.

Why the co-design? Word is that the two architects were the first and second choices of the search committee of WCI, the huge development company behind the project. Rather than choose one over the other, the committee asked both if they were willing to collaborate—which was a simple solution and gives the course a unique imprimatur.

If all goes as planned, there will eventually be some 560 homes, though the majority will be on the periphery of the playing fields, with long-range views of the rolling parkland property. Housing-lined fairways are thankfully not part of the picture. Among the cleverer design features on this immaculately conditioned, serpentine routing are the disappearing bunkers. Looking from the tee box toward the green, one sees what appears to be a sandy minefield, but on looking back down the fairway after planting the flag, the hazards have all vanished.

Two final notes: The greens are equipped with the ultramodern Sub-Air system, basically PVC pipes that are buried beneath the putting surfaces. This sophisticated system pumps warm air to the roots during cold conditions, cool air to de-stress the grass when it's hot, and extracts moisture from the roots after too much rain. There is even multidirectional water flow in the peripheral canals, so depending on need, the superintendent can redirect water from one retaining pond to another with the touch of a button. Man can't contain nature, but with the vast resources of WCI behind it, Tuscany Reserve is doing a respectable job of controlling it.

Opposite, top: 1st hole
Opposite, bottom: 13th hole

Boca West Club The Dye Course

Renovation

It's 6:30 on a pitch-black January morning. A golfer might think he is the only person stirring as he makes his way to a seemingly buttoned-up clubhouse. But because the golfer is about to enjoy a round at the bustling Boca West Club in South Florida, he would be dead wrong.

The golf cart staging area is a hive of activity, with thirty-odd golf operations employees already working. Some are loading carts, others are behind the pro shop desk, taking tee time reservations. Several are heading to each of the four courses' first tees as rangers. Their day begins at 5:30, as they get ready for the daily average of 800 golfers that the club sees through the winter season. This club has 70 golf operations employees, owns nearly 300 golf carts, and stores 4,000 bags. Take your typical golf operation, ramp it up by a multiple of at least five, and you have Boca West.

It was into this busy, dynamic environment that Pete Dye came in 2006, hired to redo a Joe Lee design from the 1980s. Some members were initially apprehensive, concerned that a typical Dye design would prove too daunting for their skill level. But, fully engaged in the redesign at age eighty, Pete understood his audience completely, assuring those who voiced their concerns that he would build a golf course that he himself could play and enjoy. In an eight-and-a-half-month renovation, with the course going from all grass to all dirt and back to grass again, that is just what he did.

Dye actually softened the original Joe Lee design, removing a goodly number of bunkers fronting greens, allowing the run-up shot to be played where previously an aerial assault was required. He added some long, narrow bunkers running parallel to encroaching lagoons, the better to stop a ball that might otherwise be heading to submersion.

However, he had not quite lost his cantankerous streak. He added some retaining ponds that threaten balls to the right on straightaway holes like the par-4 11th and doglegs like the par-5 16th. He tossed bunkers scattershot all over the final fairway, where previously there were only a few. He even conceived an island green par-3, albeit of sand instead of water, on the sporty 12th. But many of the changes he authorized were less apparent, alleviating drainage issues, revamping the direction and length of a few holes, and making the course easier to get around.

Dye's overhaul is the final renovation at Boca West in its current iteration. Previously, Arnold Palmer renovated the original pair of Desmond Muirhead courses from the 1960s.

Jim Fazio updated the third course, a Robert Von Hagge–Bruce Devlin co-design from the 1970s. One course is considered the tournament-worthy championship layout, the second now offers a classic country club setting, with waterfalls and abundant flowerbeds, and the third is the shortest and tightest, demanding precision iron play.

In Dye's case, the parcel of land in the northwest corner of Boca West's 1,450 acres—where Joe Lee's original design was located—wasn't ideal golf ground. But Pete managed to tie a dozen far-flung neighborhoods, some in fairly close proximity to the bustling Florida Turnpike, into a seamless and mostly tranquil whole.

He did so by installing high berms; large grass mounds that block the Turnpike from view midway through the opening nine. He figured that if he could block out that major artery, then obstructing the golfer's view of the inner roadways at Boca West would be a piece of cake. So he raised the profile behind numerous greens, effectively blocking out the neighborhood streets and passing cars that were previously visible.

Housing is ever present throughout Boca West, but on the Dye course most of the playing corridors are quite generous. As he's done so often in his career, his design makes one concentrate on the playing field proper and not on peripheral elements. With coquina-sand waste areas studded with soaring palm trees as buffers between the occasional parallel fairways, stands of oak and pine dotting the property, gentle undulations on mostly sizeable greens, and the reassuring width of the fairways, it's altogether a very pleasant ramble.

"We wanted Pete Dye here because his name is so well known in the game. To my mind, it's like having a modern-day Donald Ross as your course architect," offers director of golf Brad Luken, whose tenure at the club dates from 1982. "Both the members and administrative staff are extremely pleased with how the course has turned out. And furthermore, while many architects come to a multicourse facility and are intent on outdoing the courses already in place, Pete has no ego in that regard. He just wants to build the best course possible on the land he's been given, and provide the membership with a course they can enjoy."

In the full swing of the winter season, despite a hundred moving parts, Boca West is a well-oiled mechanism. And Pete Dye, thanks to the subtle but challenging course he created, has become an important and much-admired cog in the machine.

12th hole

I see Pete and Alice Dye occasionally at functions around the country, and also around town in South Florida where we both have homes. One time Pete and I were talking about the severity of his courses, and I made the comment that there were times when a shot did not have to be very far off line to have no chance of recovery. Pete responded, "Golf is not a fair game, so why should I design my courses to be fair?"

This statement has stuck with me over the years and given me insight into Pete as a designer and a person. It also is the reason his golf designs are so unique, interesting, and controversial.

Beth Daniel, *LPGA Hall of Fame member*

Mission Hills Golf Club, China The Dye Course

With Lee Schmidt and Brian Curley

Golfers' opinions are like their short games—everybody has one, though most are faulty. But some things are beyond debate. Taiwan's Taipei Financial Center is at this time the world's tallest building. North Korea's 150,000-seat May Day Stadium is the largest yet built. And the dozen courses at Mission Hills Golf Club in Shenzhen, China, make it the most expansive golf complex now on earth.

Hong Kong native and life-long golfer Dr. David Chu is not only a forward thinker, but a big thinker as well. He was one of the first entrepreneurs to invest in the People's Republic of China in the late 1970s, and took more than 600 million dollars of the fortune he amassed from his corrugated-paper conglomerate to build a golf complex with literally no equal anywhere in the world.

It makes sense—China is the most populous country on Earth and the fourth largest in terms of landmass. So why not build a 4,500-acre complex with a 300,000-square-foot "bungalow" of a clubhouse dwarfed by its 680,000-square-foot sibling. Add 2,000 golf carts, 3,000 female caddies, and floodlights on four of the twelve courses allowing play until 2:00 A.M. Mission Hills is clearly not your granddad's golf resort.

"Having the chance to take my dad's style of architecture to the Far East has been, is, and always will be a fabulous opportunity," says Perry Dye, who has built some forty courses throughout Asia. "Our style is so much different than the runway style of courses that have been built here in the past, that are basically flat from tee to green. Until we began working there in the mid-1980s, there were very few Scottish-style— in other words three-dimensional—courses. Most everything previously had the same horizontal archetype. It's a real tribute for the Dye family to be part of the world's largest golf resort, especially considering the other architects who are involved. When Dr. Chu put together his roster of designers, including Jack Nicklaus, Greg Norman, Nick Faldo, Ernie Els, Vijay Singh, Annika Sorenstam, and José Maria Olazabal, among others, we were honored to be on the list."

Scottsdale, Arizona–based Schmidt-Curley Design worked with the Dyes, routing the course through the thickly forested landscape of the resort. "Both Lee and I cut our teeth working with Pete on designs from Casa de Campo to PGA West, Kiawah, Las Vegas Paiute, and many more. His influence on modern design is enormous and his impact on our lives is even greater," states Brian Curley, who continues to visit the property on a monthly basis.

Left: 18th hole
Below: 13th hole

Mission Hills commenced operations in 1995, the first course delivered by Jack Nicklaus. In ensuing years Dr. Chu hired the Schmidt-Curley team to master-plan another eleven courses, including the penultimate, the Dye design, which debuted in 2007. It's a 6,800-yard par-72, less about ball-bashing and more about shot-making, much like several of his celebrated coastal designs such as Harbour Town and the Stadium Course at TPC Sawgrass. The difference here is the south China, as opposed to Southeast, location.

The Dye Course traverses rolling hills and has many typical hallmarks, including small pot bunkers, long tee-to-green waste areas, and railroad ties. Perhaps the course's greatest defense are its wildly undulating greens, most prevalent on several short par-4s. "We worked on almost all the Mission Hills courses, and there was always a big effort to vary each design," says Curley. "Collectively with the Dyes, we decided to really push the envelope of odd and quirky features. The Dye Course easily has the wildest greens of the twelve-course complex, including the 15th, where extreme contours within a tennis-racket shape have earned it the nickname 'flyswatter.'"

"We felt that our collection of courses would not be complete without including a design from perhaps the greatest golf course designer of the last fifty years," concludes Dr. Chu. "Just as Mission Hills is influencing an entire generation of golfers in China, Mr. Dye's work influenced an entire generation of golf course architects. We can only hope that Mission Hills will have as lasting an effect on the game in China as Mr. Dye's work has had worldwide."

4th hole

15th hole

4th hole

Heron Point Golf Club

Redesigned with Tim Liddy

At most every multicourse facility in which Pete Dye has a presence, his contribution reigns supreme. At Kiawah Island, the marquee Ocean Course is king of the quintet. In the California desert, at PGA West, the same can be said about the Stadium Course, which lords it over the other contenders in mystique and reputation. At places like South Carolina's Barefoot Landing and south Florida's PGA Village, it's the Dye designs that have a special aura, a singular reputation that sets them apart from the other courses on property. And, of course, the same holds true on the southern tip of Hilton Head Island, in the Sea Pines Resort, where Harbour Town has always been top dog.

Now classic Dye is on display with state-of-the-art Dye, thanks to his complete transformation of the old Sea Marsh course, long considered the "third wheel" of Sea Pines' golf offerings. His returning presence nearly forty years later showcases Dye the Visionary in bold strokes. Consider this fact: The George Cobb–designed Sea Marsh course predated Harbour Town Golf Links by a scant two years—1967 for the former, 1969 for the latter. But while Harbour Town continues to flummox the PGA Tour pros every spring, and remains Hilton Head's singular "must-play" golf course for tens of thousands of eager tourists, Sea Marsh was nothing more than a tired anachronism from a bygone era.

Management could and did trot out terms such as "family friendly" or "playable resort offering" for decades. But the fact is that Sea Marsh was something of an afterthought for resort golfers, who flock to Harbour Town and also enjoy Cobb's Ocean Course as a second option. However, thanks to Dye's sterling redesign, the newly renamed Heron Point is destined for far greater popularity in the years to come.

One can make the argument that Heron Point is still a family-friendly golf course. That is if the family name is Nicklaus. Dye has enacted a multitude of changes including shrinking (greens), enlarging (bunkers), heightening (fear factor), adding (water volume), lengthening (overall yardage), and tightening (fairways). But the variety of changes can be summed up in a single word: fortifying. What was previously a benign ramble, a lazy afternoon walkabout with wife, kids, or grandkids in tow, is now one of the staunchest resort tests on all of Hilton Head.

"There is no resemblance to the former course," says long-time Sea Pines director of sports and golf operations Cary Corbitt. "It is a total reconstruction, no different than taking a virgin piece of land and sculpting a new golf course."

"Golf courses are like me. They get older," jokes Pete Dye. "Every golf course, no matter where you are, after a while you've got to come back and just totally rebuild them. Heron Point was past due. Now it's a great combination of holes. We didn't change the routing itself, but a lot of the holes will have more shot-value than they did before."

Much of Dye's shifting of tees and greens was made to facilitate greater sunlight on the course and to improve suspect turf conditions. Superintendents have been known to say, "You can't grow grass in a closet," and the shadowy turf bordering sun-blotting hardwoods have proved over forty years' time to be equally dark and uninviting. So some 700 trees were removed from what was an overgrown property—though the thinning is minor in comparison to the many thousands of trees that still remain.

"The general customer playing resort golf today doesn't want to see 'resort friendly.' The days of so-called resort friendly are out the window. Players want to be challenged," says Corbitt, who has more than thirty years tenure at Sea Pines.

To be perfectly fair, not every change was made to strike fear into the heart of a 15-handicapper. Some lovely visuals have been added, including board-work in the guise of vertical railroad ties, each plank separated by strips of grass. There's only one forced carry on the course, the water-laden, par-3 4th. Dye shrank and moved some lagoons so as not to overly penalize the lesser player who can't negotiate a forced carry down the center line. Most of the unpleasantness has been shuttled to the periphery of the angled fairways, because the architect feels that while a straight shot should go unpunished, a ball drifting left or right toward water or sand is fair game.

In summation, though he is as slender as one of his signature railroad ties, in this case Pete Dye played the role of Charles Atlas. He took the proverbial ninety-eight-pound weakling of a golf course and bulked it up big time, made it worthy of respect. Resort guests will be kicking up sugary sand from a multitude of bunkers hither and yon, hoping to hold elfin greens that tilt and pitch at sharp angles. But, as in the case of the weakling who became a muscleman, nobody will be kicking sand in the face of Heron Point anymore.

Pound Ridge Golf Club

With Perry Dye

C.C. and Florence Wang escaped China and settled in Manhattan after World War II. Through hard work they built a thriving pharmaceutical distribution business, and in so doing built comfortable lives for their two children. Their son, Kenneth, graduated from M.I.T. and became a successful businessman, growing and diversifying the family enterprise. Their daughter attended Sarah Lawrence College and the Sorbonne in Paris, and spent many years as an editor at *Vogue* before embarking on her own design career. Today, her name is synonymous with haute couture, and she's become an international arbiter of taste and style. Her name is Vera Wang.

Her brother's creative instincts turn more to fairways, not fashion. But Ken Wang thinks some of his big sister's intuition regarding what people want, what is pleasing to their eye, has rubbed off on him. So his long-awaited Pound Ridge Golf Club, designed by Pete Dye with his son Perry and with healthy doses of creative input from Alice, is at last a reality.

"In the mid-1970s, my father built a weekend home in the Westchester County town of Pound Ridge. Afterward, he began toying with the idea of buying the local public golf course," Ken recalls. "We loved to play, but didn't feel we were country club types. We also thought it would be an interesting land investment."

By 1980, the Wangs had purchased the remnants of a 350-acre, eighteen-hole course in Pound Ridge that had straddled the New York–Connecticut state line. A previous developer had purchased the parcel, turned the Connecticut portion into housing lots, and sold the remaining 170 acres, with nine holes intact, to the Chinese entrepreneurs. Ken and his dad operated the modestly priced daily-fee facility as a sideline to their main business for well over two decades before breaking ground on a total redesign.

Though the Dyes were onboard from the mid-1990s, it took nearly a decade to obtain the proper permits and to please the environmentalists and homeowners in the surrounding neighborhoods before they actually began renovating in 2005.

"I would've left our simple nine-hole course as it was, and wouldn't have considered taking on the project without Pete Dye as the architect," says Ken, who counts the Ocean Course at Kiawah Island, and especially the Stadium Course at TPC Sawgrass, as among his favorite Dye creations. "I'm a mathematician by training, a numbers person. And I remember the first time I set foot on Sawgrass's Stadium Course, it immediately struck me as an exercise in precision. Every hole was like a giant puzzle, each decision Pete forced you to make was starkly apparent and exact. It was marvelous. I became aware

that despite his longstanding reputation as a 'no-plans' guy, he has this incredible sense of rigor, and nothing is left to chance. His genius lies in not having it show. That's why I insisted on having him as our architect."

While 170 acres is usually plenty for a golf course, the steep, rock-strewn terrain and the consistent presence of wetlands shrank the usable footprint. "We knew it was rocky," admits the owner. "We just didn't know how rocky it actually was." Perry Dye adds, "The best way to describe this land is a combination of woods, wetlands, and rock. While it was very difficult to build, the finished product provides an unforgettable day of golf."

Many large boulders remain on the property, adding to its distinctive character. Nowhere is this more evident than on the par-5 13th, where the focal point off the tee is a cottage-size boulder between the tee and the landing area. The short over-wetlands 15th is another example. This par-3 green has been literally carved into a hillside, with a broad expanse of exposed rock acting as a backboard for any tee shot too boldly struck. "It looks like marble," says Perry. "I've never seen anything like it." Nor have daily-fee golfers around Westchester County seen anything quite like Pound Ridge.

"This course has no housing component. That's rare enough these days, but because real estate values in Westchester County are among the highest in the nation, this project is even more special," continues Perry, who's made dozens of site visits over the years. "The permitting process took nearly a decade, and the complexion of the golf business took a dramatic downward turn in that time frame. But Ken Wang was consistent in his vision of what he wanted this place to be."

"I felt the course would be most worthy as a stand-alone facility, with no encroaching houses," says the owner. "And while it would have been easier and more profitable to include home sites, I'm glad we did it this way."

Perhaps sister Vera, who encouraged Ken to bring the land to its full potential, will consent to design an ultra-exclusive line of golf shirts and skirts that can only be acquired at the Pound Ridge Golf Club. Ken isn't holding his breath, but his long-deferred dream of owning the area's premier public golf course has finally come to fruition and will likely flourish regardless of whose label adorns the pro shop's soft goods. "Westchester County has some of the finest private courses in the world," he concludes, referring to classic gems like Winged Foot, Quaker Ridge, and Westchester Country Club. "But ours is by far the most upscale course that is accessible to any golfer who would like to play."

15th hole

My wife, Libby, and I were vacationing at Casa de Campo with USGA Executive Director David Fay and his wife, Joan. Coincidentally, Rees and Susan Jones were there as well. Pete and Alice invited us all to dinner one night at their lovely home overlooking the Caribbean Sea. We had a wonderful meal in their thatch-roofed dining room on an idyllic evening.

Now, I was well aware of Alice's career as an amateur golfer, particularly in the senior ranks. Toward the end of the evening, being a bit over-served with red wine, I decided to blow some smoke at Alice.

"Alice," I said, "with all your accomplishments playing the game, have you ever achieved that signal honor for a woman golfer?"

"What's that, George?" she asked.

"Have you ever shot your age?"

"Why, no, George," she said, "I'm only fifty-seven."

I've never been more embarrassed— nor have I ever seen Fay with a bigger grin on his face.

A few months later, I was playing with Pete at the opening of one of his courses in Orlando. During the back nine, a cart approached us from a distance. Pete saw it first. "Here comes that old bag of a wife of mine," he said.

In fairness to Alice, she took my gaffe with great humor, and never failed to kid me about it in later years. One day I got a card from her. "George," it said, "wanted you to be the first to know—I did it—shot sixty-five yesterday!"

George Peper, *twenty-five-year editor-in-chief of* GOLF Magazine

Antigua Golf Resort, Guatemala

With Perry Dye

"This course is going to set off a real golf boom in Guatemala," says a chuckling Perry Dye. "It brings the national total from five courses to six."

Even with this recent addition, there's still only one course for every two million citizens in this Central American nation. But the Dyes' effort shows that while quantity is sorely lacking, quality golf has definitely arrived.

The golf course shares its name with the former capital city in the nation's central highlands. Antigua, about an hour's drive from the modern capital of Guatemala City, is a sixteenth-century Colonial Spanish town, famous for its well-preserved Baroque architecture and spectacular ruined churches. "It is one of the most beautiful old cities you can imagine," says Perry, "with cobblestone streets and incredible historic landmarks. It's like St. Augustine, Florida, except this city is flanked by three massive volcanoes—called Acatenango, Agua, and Fuego."

All three volcanoes soar more than 12,000 feet above the horizon, and while the first two have long been dormant, Fuego (meaning "fire") still emits a daily stream of smoke. Agua and Fuego make spectacular bookends to the exciting new golf course that sits in a valley between them.

The hilly property lends itself to cart golf, though the exacting terrain didn't keep an eighty-something-year-old design legend from walking the property repeatedly on his initial visit. "This will be a five- or six-hour round of golf," Pete decided. The developers were perplexed, knowing the course under construction was challenging, but not impossible. "It's not the difficulty factor that will slow them down," Dye continued, "but the golfers will be taking photos on every hole!" Pete's statement came after Perry had done massive clearing of the land.

"My first site visit began in jungle so thick you couldn't see ten feet in any direction," Perry recalls. "We were in there with machetes, trying to clear a path. José Miron was asking me how I visualized the hole, and I told him that until we could clear the head-high weeds, plants, and grasses, I couldn't visualize a thing!"

The aforementioned Miron, a golf fanatic who had previously developed a successful country club in Guatemala City, was called in to consult on the possibility of a golf course in the burgeoning development. Brothers Roberto and Rolando Roesch, an architect and engineer, respectively, were the idea men behind creating a vacation- and second-home community near the town of Antigua. Two hundred and fifty villas

5th hole

Left: 7th hole
Below: 8th hole

2nd hole

and residences and 380 building lots surround the golf course on the 3,800-foot-high property, which is little more than ten miles from the center of the historic old city. The elevation makes the climate ideal for golf, with daytime temperatures never exceeding 90 degrees or dipping below 65. There is currently a small boutique hotel on premises, with the potential for a much larger name-brand one somewhere down the line.

"The site was so topographically difficult because of the valleys, ravines, and hills throughout," Miron points out. "I knew the best man for the job was Pete Dye, who has always been my favorite designer. While the course itself is now cleared, it is surrounded by forest and jungle just beyond the line of play. The ponds, creeks, and spectacular views of the volcanoes will make this one of the most memorable and exciting golf courses in this part of the world."

Antigua is Central America's first course with bluegrass rough, and bent grass tees, fairways, and greens. Speaking of the latter, though they are mainly flat, the greens are deceptive and are often built into the side of a hill. "A good caddie is imperative, because the greens are going to be ultra-tricky to read," Pete says. "Players will often lose sight of the horizon, and won't know if they are putting uphill or down."

Antigua has inspired other developments in the region, and soon there will be additional Dye designs sprouting in neighboring countries like El Salvador and Honduras. Will these courses-to-come one day be remote outposts on some type of Guatemalan Golf Trail? One never knows, but with the peripatetic Dye family motivated and enthused about making their mark in this part of the world, it would be folly to bet against it.

French Lick Resort   The Dye Course

It's safe to assume that until the late 1970s, not one Bostonian in 10,000 would have had even an inkling of a tiny Indiana town named French Lick. But that was before Larry Bird came to town, resurrecting the moribund Boston Celtics franchise, and in a thirteen-year NBA career becoming one of the most iconic sports figures in New England history.

The self-described "Hick from French Lick" came from a town that had welcomed mainly Midwesterners to its resort and spa for generations. Nestled in the Hoosier National Forest, what was then known as the French Lick Springs Hotel had long been an attraction because of the many mineral springs found nearby.

Where resort-goers congregate, golf is sure to follow. Tom Bendelow conceived the first course in 1907. Donald Ross came to town and delivered his vision in 1917—a course that was fully restored by architect and Dye disciple Lee Schmidt in 2006. And now Schmidt's mentor has added a second eighteen-hole course to what has become the French Lick Resort & Casino. It is a high-elevation beauty. The melding of masters both old and new only adds to the rich tapestry at this somewhat-under-the-radar but eminently worthwhile destination.

"I'm thrilled to death with it," says Dye. "The views are wonderful. You can see for thirty miles from almost every green and tee. It's also a self-contained course on a ridge, with no housing component at all." Long before Dye the designer came to town, he was there as a competitor. "The Donald Ross course already on property is a classic. Walter Hagen won the 1924 PGA Championship there, and I was fortunate to win the Midwest Amateur Championship on that same course in 1957!"

The Bendelow eighteen was halved to make space for the casino, and reappeared in its current nine-hole iteration as a tribute to the early American architect in 2007. It sits in a wide valley adjacent to the resort itself. The beautifully restored Ross Course, full of character and with the original wicked green contours, is found a short distance away. With literal top billing at the highest point in southern Indiana, Dye's new effort is truly King of the Hill.

Dye has made great use of the available acreage. The surroundings are rugged forest, but he fashioned the playing field proper on gently rolling terrain on the ridgeline. The course is walker-friendly, but the adjacent topography is full of scary elevation changes, and wayward shots will tumble down deep wooded ravines into oblivion. He also excavated numerous sandstone boulders during construction, which have been used to buttress certain tee boxes and water hazards, though water isn't really a factor in the playing.

The Ross Course has been widely admired for nearly a century. But the old classic is now sharing billing with its modern counterpart. A longtime member of the facility's professional staff offers this opinion: "I don't know of any other public-access venue that presents the opportunity to play one course designed by the preeminent classic architect, and another one designed by the preeminent modern architect."

The renaissance of the hotel and its numerous amenities is due to the efforts of Bill Cook, who made his vast fortune in medical devices before diversifying into numerous other fields of endeavor. He also believes in giving back to the community, and the refurbishing of the old hotel in French Lick is a prime example of his interest in the welfare of southern Indiana.

Larry Bird and Pete Dye have plenty in common. Neither is afraid of hard work. Each brings a dedicated single-mindedness to his craft. Because of their skills, each achieved a worldwide fame neither ever thought likely. But for all of his greatness, his unshakable status as one of the best ever, Bird's legacy is now the stuff of memory. His genius is available only on video, or in the mind's eye of tens of millions of grateful fans. But because of the enduring nature of Pete Dye's work, his craftsmanship and creativity continue to be enjoyed by all who venture to southern Indiana and take a tour of his new course at the venerable but recently polished resort.

One came from, and one came to, French Lick, and the town has gained great prominence because of them.

17th hole

5th hole

The Links at Sleepy Ridge, 15th hole

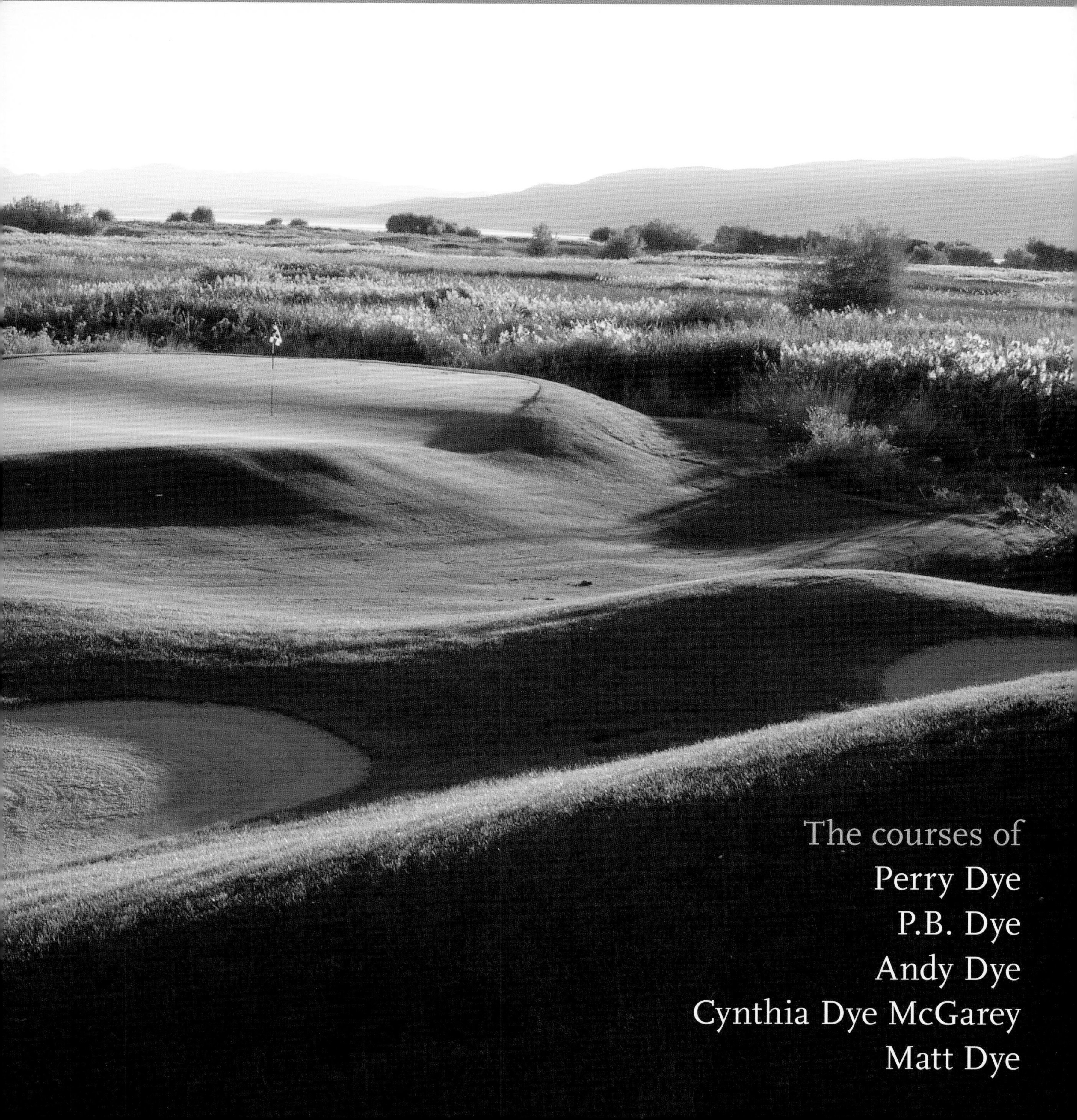

The courses of
Perry Dye
P.B. Dye
Andy Dye
Cynthia Dye McGarey
Matt Dye

Auburn Hills Golf Course

Perry Dye

As befits a state often referred to as America's Bread Basket, most of the 200-plus Kansas golf courses are as flat as a baking sheet. "It's one of the toughest architectural environments in the nation," says Perry Dye. "There's little or no elevation change, so visual interest has to be manufactured, as it doesn't occur normally. The trick is making the golf course appear as part of the natural environment, without looking forced." An earth-moving magician like his father, Perry turned the trick with ease at Wichita's Auburn Hills.

While there's some topographical interest in the northeast portion of the state, near Kansas City and Topeka, the central portion has very little. A typical mid-Kansas course has pushed-up tees, pushed-up greens, relatively flat fairways, modest green-side bunkering, and minimal water. Auburn Hills, in south-central Kansas, is something else entirely. Fourteen distinct water hazards, many of which serve as catch basins for storm water runoff from the adjacent neighborhood, necessitate precision from the tee. Wetlands abound. Sculpted terrain and peripheral mounding provide definition, sight lines, and containment of errant shots. Though there is only twenty feet of elevation change on the entire property, Dye's clever mounding and visual misdirection make the landscape seem to rise and fall far more dramatically. While the water is mostly a peripheral presence, cross-bunkering bisects several fairways, forcing golfers to lay back or go up and over. The inward nine has a significant housing presence, but the first half has little. With its difficulty, beauty, and unique playing characteristics, Auburn Hills quickly became the marquee municipal course in the city.

It had been almost a quarter-century since the last modestly priced "muni" opened in Wichita, and it's safe to say that demand was outstripping supply. Well over 200,000 rounds were being played annually on the quartet of courses already in play, and a stylish new entry was long overdue. But the realization of the course was of benefit well beyond the tee time–starved legions of local golfers.

"I wanted to help revitalize the west side of town, which is my home area," explains Wichita native Jay Russell, a land developer with partner John McKay. "We owned the acreage adjacent to a burgeoning neighborhood, but we didn't have the funds to build a golf course. We decided to donate the land to the city, and promised we would continue to build a minimum of fifty houses a year in the area if they would build the golf course. When all was said and done, Wichita golfers have a beautiful new course to enjoy, the city got the land they needed at no cost, another great amenity, and the added tax revenue of the homeowners who moved to the area. My partner and I enjoyed the increased value of housing lots in what is now a golf course neighborhood, and the ability to construct many more homes than we would have otherwise. We've been building nearly 100 homes a year, double our original commitment. This was a win-win, and a great example of a private-public partnership."

It's not just Wichita residents who are benefiting. Clyde Cessna spent most of his life in Kansas, and the aviation pioneer built his company headquarters in Wichita. The state's largest city is also home to Koch Industries, and boasts plants by Boeing and Raytheon, among others. The private pilots who bring their Cessna planes to Wichita for annual maintenance, not to mention the globetrotting executives who pop into town on business, also enjoy Auburn Hills.

One could appreciate Dorothy's confusion had she been clambering to the tee box at Auburn Hills, and observing its uncharachteristic mounding, wetlands, and lakes, instead of making that unscheduled landing in Munchkinland. Her famous words from *The Wizard of Oz* would have been equally appropriate, albeit erroneous: "Toto, we're not in Kansas anymore."

Opposite: 14th hole
Below: 15th hole

Desert Pines Golf Club

Perry Dye

Here is a short story about a short golf course. Or, as Perry Dye puts it, "Desert Pines offers a full golf experience on a smallish piece of ground."

The course is an oasis of green in an otherwise arid landscape, and was built in a troubled neighborhood in east Las Vegas. "When we first got on property, there were about two dozen vagrants we needed to remove. There were crack vials and drug paraphernalia everywhere."

Despite the comprehensive cleanup, the course is still something of a shooting gallery. Hemmed in all sides by divided highways and a freeway, Dye constructed an impressive, albeit three-quarters-scale golf course on just 90 acres of ground, instead of the standard 120. Fairways are less than 30 yards wide, not the typical 40. Accuracy off the tee is imperative to play this course effectively. The "long-and-wrong" crowd will be in for a tough slog.

More than 3,000 imported pine trees lend a Carolina Sandhills vibe to the stunted acreage. It's a combination of mature trees, pampas and love grasses, and fairway-bracketing mounding that help to separate holes and to keep the course from turning into some sort of green-grass war zone, with wayward pellets zooming about in all directions. "We put down bales and bales of pine straw at the beginning, to give it more of that Carolina flavor," explains Perry, laughing at the memory. "But we didn't anticipate how the lack of humidity would dry it out. Vandals would sneak on the course and set it ablaze, so we got rid of it."

The presence of Desert Pines has also rid the neighborhood of some of its less savory elements. It's a thriving daily fee operation, booked steadily, with a bustling practice facility. The latter features a towering mesh netting that completely encircles the driving range at a height of more than 100 feet, keeping those "range rocks" from bounding onto nearby fairways, or worse, bouncing onto adjacent thoroughfares.

This isn't to give the impression that Desert Pines is some sort of executive length course—not in the least. Playing to a par of 71, it's a respectable 6,800-yard test from the tips, the middle markers nearly 6,500 yards. But the holes are totally shoehorned within the confines of the property. An example: The 7th, 8th, and 17th greens are separated by one of the four major water hazards on property. But in the absence of water, with an overland route, the flagsticks on each of these greens could be removed within a single minute's ramble by even the most leisurely of walkers.

Speaking of the developer who hired him, Perry Dye concludes, "In my experience, Billy Walters has done plenty of crazy things. One of the nuttiest was attempting to put a Carolina-style golf course in the middle of one of this city's bleakest neighborhoods. But you know what? It worked out, and the area is far better because of the presence of Desert Pines."

Opposite: 3rd hole
Below: 2nd hole

Fisher Island Golf Club

Renovated in 2007 by P.B. Dye

Much like the P.B. Dye–designed golf course snaked skillfully through its interior, South Florida's Fisher Island is a tiny diamond. Formed when Miami's newly built ship channel separated its 200-plus acres from the mainland in 1905, and eventually owned by the Vanderbilt family, who put up an estate house and some cottages, the island has gradually become the most expensive piece of property in the nation. The average new condominium price on this triangular property situated between Biscayne Bay and the Atlantic Ocean is about $5 million. Any truly livable space is well over a million, though the international cadres of owners (more than forty foreign countries are represented, predominantly South Americans and Europeans) have been known to purchase undersize studio apartments for their nannies or housekeepers at prices in the mid-six figures. So, coming back into this ultramoneyed atmosphere after a long absence, why would P.B. consent to revamp his original golf course design for the price of a turkey burger, delicious as they may be, from the golf course grill? Just another example of how the Dyes do things differently.

"When I was asked to come back almost twenty years later, the first thing I noticed was that the integrity of the putting surfaces had been lost," says P.B., whose offices are based in Florida. "The prior rebuilding job was not up to speed, and the regrassing of the greens was done poorly. Up to 30 percent of the green surfaces had disappeared, and a significant portion of the pin placements had been lost, along with many of the greens' contours. I told the board that I had been paid for this golf course once, and didn't need to be paid again. I just said, 'Let me do them over for you, and do them right.' So we restored the putting surfaces to their original size and shape."

Dye greens are quite often a course's focal point, but within the truncated space available on Fisher Island, their importance was paramount. This sporty, ultrascenic par-35 meanders among sculpted Scottish-style bunkers. The undulating fairways wriggle between lagoons and lakes. For many players the visual highlight is the par-4 7th, playing waterside along Miami's shipping channel, where the yachts and cruise ships sail. But on this course in particular, the major defense is the greens, which is why it was so important for them to be redone properly.

6th and 7th holes

4th hole

The impetus to bring P.B. Dye back for consultation was precipitated by another architect's plan to reconfigure the 8th hole in a way that didn't jibe with the course character. "This fellow wanted to take a very clever, potentially drivable par-4, with sand and water trouble everywhere, and stretch it to conventional length," explains an involved board member. "We thought that before we agreed to any major course changes, we should involve the man who conceived things in the first place."

Dye's work, which he describes as "a comprehensive face-lift," went well beyond the putting surfaces. The outmoded irrigation system was replaced and a hardy new turf called Paspalum Supreme was planted on top of a twelve-inch cap of sand, creating a uniformly great growing surface. "To ensure the integrity of the golf course, I brought in the original construction superintendent to make sure the restoration was done professionally," P.B. says. "It was, and has thankfully remained, a very fun golf course to play."

P.B.'s attraction to the original job isn't hard to understand. "First of all, it's in the heart of Miami, which is unusual enough. Even in the late 1980s, the property we built on was really valuable, well over a million dollars an acre." Though the architect had previously been instrumental in helping his father build some of his most celebrated courses on vast tracts of land (Tennessee's Honors Course and West Virginia's Pete Dye Golf Club are two such examples), this was a different situation entirely. "It was a real challenge to fit nine holes and a driving range in just forty acres. And it was also great fun to use all the designing tricks I know that are usually spread across eighteen holes, and fit them into nine."

"Fisher Island is a unique location, there's nothing really like it," he concludes. "A place like that deserves a golf course that's equally special, and I was happy to resurrect the original and bring it back to the standard that made it so good in the first place."

Opposite, top: 5th hole
Opposite, bottom: 7th hole

La Estancia Golf Resort

P.B. Dye

What would inspire a developer to build a smaller-scale golf resort practically in the shadow of the iconic Casa de Campo? For decades, the Dominican Republic's southeastern city of La Romana has been home to what's widely acknowledged as the Caribbean's finest golf experience. But the developers built La Estancia just a ten-minute drive from the gates of Casa de Campo, with its world-renowned trio of Pete Dye–designed courses.

The developer explains that La Estancia is a project that dovetails very nicely with its neighbor. P.B. Dye has a built-in flair for the dramatic anyway, and the raw canvas he worked with here afforded ample opportunity to make a brash statement. La Estancia is located across the Chavon River and somewhat upstream from the über-scaled Dye Fore course at Casa de Campo and offers much the same sense of grandeur. The second hole is a thrill-fest of the highest order. At the precipice tee box, the golfer is perched several hundred feet above the riverbed. But expansive stands of trees reach up from the river, their thick canopies spreading out below the level of the fairway. One is faced with the exhilarating task of arching the tee shot over all of this deciduous danger, and finding safe purchase on the short grass beyond. The "canyada," as it's referred to locally, winds through the right side of the opening nine and the left side of the inward nine.

Consider the seemingly mile-long par-5 12th, with the forebodingly deep ravine delineating the left side of the playing corridor. Any of the three shots required to reach the elevated, well-bunkered green that is hooked, or pulled left, will never be seen again. The 14th is another beast, one that will have golfers shaking in their spikes. Play safely to the right on this dogleg left par-4, and you have practically zero chance of reaching the green in regulation. Attempt the tight line, over the corner of the ravine, and hope to carry the ball to the short grass, because the alternative is a hard rebound off the steep slope to the inside of the dogleg, and down into the same dark ravine. Even on the holes where the fear factor is reduced, there is plenty of movement in mostly large greens, deep swales, and flag-obscuring drop-offs for those who can't find the putting surfaces with the approach.

Several of the game's best-known architects were interviewed for the job, but P.B. Dye was ultimately selected because of his knowledge of the area, the terrain, and the Dominican people. Both architect and developer also credit longtime design associate Mike O'Conner, who spent years working extensively on numerous Pete Dye projects, including luminaries such as Old Marsh, PGA West, and the quartet of courses in Kohler, Wisconsin.

Asked about the potentially daunting prospect of designing in such close proximity to one of golf's best-loved venues, P.B. says, "I don't feel like I compete with my dad, and I don't feel like I'm in his shadow. I believe we walk side by side." Dye the Elder can't help but be impressed with his younger son's stupendous achievement on the nether side of the Chavon River.

10th hole

Above: 1st hole
Left: 14th hole

Laguna National Golf and Country Club, Singapore

Andy Dye

Pete's eldest nephew, Andy Dye, laughs as he recounts the differences between his famous uncle and his father, the late Roy Dye, who lost a hard-fought battle with cancer in 1994. "Dad was a Yale grad, a marine, a chemical engineer," says the eldest of Roy's eight children. "He planned his courses meticulously, with total precision, and didn't suffer fools. Pete, conversely, gets along with everybody, and his talent for working without blueprints or maps is legendary. But they were partners, best friends, and shared the same heart and family values. They were perfect in the classic 'good cop, bad cop' routine when dealing with difficult clients."

Andy, like his siblings Cynthia and Matt, followed their dad and uncle into the family business. He has lived and worked extensively in the Far and Middle East for nearly twenty years, rearing eight children of his own. His kids have a remarkably wide view of the planet, having lived, studied, and fanned out to Singapore, the Philippines, Croatia, France, Spain, Panama, and the Ivy League. He is justifiably proud of their achievements, as he is of his most highly regarded work, Laguna National, in the equatorial city-state of Singapore, one of the wealthiest and most densely populated nations in the world.

"I was living in Singapore, and finishing up the Masters Course at Laguna National, when my dad was very ill," says Dye, now based in Dubai. "One afternoon we got an incredible tropical storm, with amazing lightning, crashing thunder, and as soon as it ended, there was this beautiful rainbow. I knew in my heart my dad had just died. I called my mom as soon as I got home, and before she could say a word, I told her I knew that dad had passed."

Perhaps it was his father's inspiration. Maybe it was the culmination of effort and experience after thirty-plus years in the business, and the right piece of land at the right time. Whatever the factors, the Masters Course is the high mark of Andy Dye's career and the most prestigious, best-known course in Singapore. The course has hosted what is now known as the Singapore Masters since 2002, which has been won by Colin Montgomerie, and a title that has just eluded Ernie Els, among other luminaries.

Top and bottom: Masters Course, 8th hole

Masters Course, 3rd hole

The engineering of the course is as impressive as the end result. In certain ways it's reminiscent of the famed Stadium Course at TPC Sawgrass, and the analogy goes well beyond the risk/reward nature of the holes, the omnipresent water, the varied length and direction of the holes, and the very tough, water-laden finish—an amphitheater effect where a player's fortunes can turn in an instant, in full view of the spectators. Dye had to begin by building the site platform a full two meters above sea level, for drainage and viewing purposes. In essence, he had to pull the golf course up out of the ground, much the way his uncle Pete pulled his Sawgrass masterpiece up and out of the north Florida swamps. Andy Dye imported 3,000 trees onto the barren site—frangipani, rain trees, and willows among them, to provide fairway delineation. The fill from the assorted lakes that were dug on property supply much of the course contour, and long fairway bunkers, doglegs, and elevated greens combine to provide the numerous challenges.

"The original owners were so intimidated by the daunting nature of the Masters Course, they had me take my foot off the gas pedal completely when I built The Classic, the other course on property," continues Dye, who is renovating, modernizing, and fortifying both courses. "The Classic was very straightforward, not as penal or demanding, which is what the previous owners thought would be attractive, so members could shoot lower scores." Management was flummoxed to see that despite the new addition, the tougher course maintained a two-to-one ratio in terms of popularity.

They learned an eye-opening lesson, one that is built into the DNA of Pete and virtually any architect named Dye. "They didn't understand that the tougher the course, the more it attracts golfers who try to conquer it."

Classic Course, 12th hole

Left: Masters Course, 6th hole
Below: Masters Course 18th hole

P.B. Dye Golf Club

P.B. Dye

Not every golf course architect is fortunate enough to receive what might be the ultimate honorific. Having a course named for the man who built it is rare, but it's even more so for it to happen in the architect's prime, as opposed to his twilight. But that's exactly the tribute afforded P.B. Dye when he created one of his typically gorgeous yet treacherous courses on 250 acres of rolling farmland near Frederick, Maryland.

The mailing address of the P.B. Dye Golf Club is Ijamsville, Maryland, but the town is only a speck on the map and is incorporated within the larger community of Urbana, about an hour from the nation's capital. "P.B. was attracted to the project beyond the beautiful piece of land we had acquired," explains Won Yu, general manager of the semiprivate facility. "He had recently added a second nine to the original nine-hole course his grandfather had created in his hometown of Urbana, Ohio. P.B. thought it was neat he could build another course in a town named Urbana."

It's hard to believe that this pastoral location, framed by Sugarloaf Mountain at the northern end of the Blue Ridge Range, is just about twenty minutes from the infamous Washington Beltway. The rustic beauty of the region belies the fact that the nation's bustling capital is so near.

Despite the serene setting, the golf course is hazardous, and not just because once in a while a D.C.-based foreign diplomat or ambassador shows up to play, with a Secret Service detail in tow. The fescue-laden terrain, peppered with hardwoods, rolls and dips constantly. While the elevation changes from tee to green are fairly dramatic, they are as level as a chessboard compared to the wildly undulating greens, which are big and bending, with waist-high swales, shelves, drop-offs, and triple-tiers, among other terrain nuisances, all requiring a deft touch with a putter. "I'm a golfer's worst nightmare," P.B. is fond of saying, "a bulldozer operator with a scratch handicap and an Irish sense of humor." The first descriptive is particularly apt. As much of a do-it-yourselfer as his famous father, P.B. sculpted the greens himself, days and days in the driver's seat of the heavy equipment, weeks and weeks spent on site. The Dyes don't delegate much, at least in comparison to other marquee architects, and to them, spending substantial time on the job is more than a duty. It's their preferred method of doing business.

Even the casual, ten-rounds-a-year golfer may recognize the architectural influence on the property, and what many consider the singular distinguishing feature of Dye courses. There's a kaleidoscope of railroad ties in place—framing the green on the par-3 2nd hole, on the 3rd tee, and, most memorably, scattered like buckshot on the approach to the daunting par-4 16th.

The staircase-style greens may be the course's staunchest defense. The tough par-4 6th, the uphill par-3 8th, and the puzzling par-5 12th are as tiered as a wedding cake, and excellent examples of the younger Dye's truly mischievous side. Several of the par-5s will frustrate the average hitter. On the 7th and 12th, wetland hazards bisect the fairway about 100–130 yards from the green, which is generally where a typical second shot will land. Bashers will have no problem launching over the vegetation in their attempt to reach in two blows. But those who can't hammer it home will have to lay up with a mid-iron short of said hazards, then loft the third shot over the trouble.

Whang Shin and his business partner, Won Yu, describe themselves as golf addicts who wanted to turn their passion into their business. "It's always a delight to build a golf course for owners who really know and love the game," says P.B.

The architect took his employers to the Pete Dye Golf Club in West Virginia, one of his father's most famous designs, during construction of the as yet unnamed course being built in Maryland. Because honor is one of the most important touchstones of Asian culture, it was there that his guests first got the idea of naming their new facility after the man building it.

"P.B. worked extremely hard to make this golf course so special. But he was in grave health throughout construction," relate Yu and Shin. "We thought it would be appropriate to name the golf course out of deference to him, and in turn, we felt honored when he chose to accept our request."

Eight members of the Dye family have been stricken with colon cancer, including P.B., his dad, two of his cousins, his uncle, grandmother, aunt, and great-great grandfather. "Hereditary cancer is easier to catch, and easier to correct," explains the architect, leaving out the fact that it's never easy to deal with. "The P.B. Dye Golf Club was the first course I completed after undergoing my cancer surgery. So it's special to me regardless, name aside. After you kick cancer, it's great to be hired again. It makes you feel like a winner, and having the course named for me just reinforces that."

Above: 11th hole
Right: 16th hole

Playa Paraiso Golf Club

P.B. Dye

In the previous century, Cancun conjured one of five basic images: Spring break–style bacchanalia, languid beach vacations, world-class diving and/or snorkeling off the nearby island of Cozumel, eco-adventures, or a jumping-off point to explore the ancient Mayan civilization.

Golf was well off the radar, but all that changed with the Jack Nicklaus–designed Moon Palace Golf Club. Since this first destination course opened in 2002, other marquee architects have joined the fray in the Mexican Caribbean, including Robert Trent Jones Jr., Greg Norman, Tom Fazio, Tom Weiskopf, and, most notably, P.B. Dye.

Don Miguel Fluxa is the sole owner of the Iberostar Hotel Chain, which encompasses nearly 100 separate properties in twenty-odd countries, some 25,000 hotel rooms in all. But he never authorized a golf course until inviting P.B. Dye to meet with him in Spain. "A man like Mr. Fluxa is used to blueprints, detailed architectural renderings, PowerPoint or autoCAD presentations." So recalls a high-ranking company executive, who didn't realize that the interviewee, who was recommended to the boss by a mutual acquaintance, besides never having turned on a computer in his life, was also a chip off his old man's "Who needs a blueprint?" block. "P.B. walked in, Mr. Fluxa asked about the plans, and the architect replied, 'Plans? What the hell fun would that be?' He improvised, and proceeded to borrow a piece of plain paper and a pencil, sketched out where he'd put some mounding, some bunkers, and where he'd route fairways. But somehow, he got the job anyway."

And with no regrets on either side of the ledger. The younger of Pete and Alice's two sons made some thirty-five site visits to Mexico's Riviera Maya, about a half-hour drive from Cancun, which is at least thirty more visits than a typical marquee architect will make. Lots of the big names will limit their personal involvement to the groundbreaking, one or two visits during the construction phase, and then one additional trip for the ribbon-cutting. But P.B. was 150 days on the ground, including twenty-five on a bulldozer, fifty more on a tractor shaping greens, and his wickedly playful style imbues a course like no other on the Yucatan Peninsula.

"As far as I'm concerned, Mr. Fluxa runs the most incredible, all-inclusive, upscale hotels you can find," says P.B., who has since become something of Iberostar's in-house architect, with additional courses designed in Brazil and the Dominican Republic, and more on the drawing board. "And when he calls me, all I say is, 'Yes sir.'"

All a player will say at Playa Paraiso is, "Oh, boy!" That's a typical response when dealing with massive swales camouflaging mostly hidden greens, 90-degree doglegs, palm trees smack in the middle of greenside bunkers, and drivable par-4s where an offline shot will lead to double bogey or worse. And perhaps most notably, the three-tiered, 10,000 plus square-foot 7th green, the largest in Mexico, where most any player not named Faxon, Roberts, or Crenshaw who finds himself a few hundred feet from the flag and on the wrong level will likely consider even a three-putt a triumph of skill and touch.

There's only the one golf course on property, but five separate hotels dot the Iberostar landscape; four-star, five-star, and "Grand Turismo," which features the type of rare opulence where each room is serviced by an individual butler. All-inclusive is the watchword, not just for hotel guests, but even for walk-up pro shop business. For a couple of hundred dollars, a golfer is not only privileged to enjoy eighteen holes at the most unusual course in the Yucatan, but also unlimited food and drink before, during, and after the round. And for every frat-boy foursome determined to drain every cerveza or tequila shooter on the premises and gorge themselves

Opposite: 10th hole
Below: 9th hole

2nd hole

commensurately, management reports there are a hundred groups who are modest in their consumption. Good thing, too, as negotiating the golf course successfully is not a task for the inebriated or overstuffed.

"It's action-packed, and lots of fun. People want to play it over and over," says the designer. And while management reports that the typical customer comment is along the lines of, "I've never seen anything like it," it's almost never followed by, "and I hope I never see anything like it again." Positive comments outnumber negative ones by a ratio of nearly a thousand to one

Playa Paraiso began, like every other tract of land in the area, as a flat piece of ground. The other course designers hired in the region kept their designs literally low profile. But P.B. Dye incorporated some sixty feet of elevation changes, providing a roller coaster effect both topographically and thrill-wise. "When my dad designed Harbour Town in the late 1960s, he saw that lots of Hilton Head's courses were built up. He did the opposite, carving the holes at ground level, into the Lowcountry landscape. I did the exact same thing here. The competing courses were low-to-the-ground, so I did the opposite!"

The architect doesn't regret a single visit he made to the site. "It's like being a kid in a sandbox, only bigger, with bigger Tonka toys to play with. I loved every minute, it was a ball."

6th hole

Puntacana Resort & Club

P.B. Dye

There are some two dozen golf courses either built or under construction in the far eastern portion of the Dominican Republic. P.B. Dye's La Cana, at the Puntacana Resort & Club, was one of the first.

The architect downplays any comparisons to his dad's famous work down the coast at Casa de Campo, where the stunning Teeth of the Dog immediately put the island on the worldwide golf map in 1970. "That's a golf resort which includes a man-made beach," explains P.B. "This is a fabulous beach resort to which golf was later added. That's why La Cana has a totally different look and feel than Teeth of the Dog, or any of the courses at Casa de Campo."

Despite the differences in the terrain, there are some striking similarities in the stories. P.B. Dye, who has been visiting the Dominican Republic since childhood and speaks passable Spanish, built La Cana at the age of forty-three, the same age his father was when he produced the iconic Teeth of the Dog. "Not only was I the same age as my dad was when I built my first seaside course, but just like him, I also ended up with a house on the 7th tee."

Famed clothing designer and Dominican native Oscar de la Renta was a longtime resident of Casa de Campo, and a neighbor of the Dyes. When the fashion icon became a shareholder at Puntacana Resort & Club, and moved over to that resort, he recommended P.B. to visionary developer Frank Rainieri. He wasn't immediately convinced, but when the architect came up with a workable, logical sketch of a golf course routing just one day after walking the dense jungle earmarked for the course, Rainieri knew he had the right man.

La Cana features beautiful coral-buttressed tee boxes and a quartet of surfside holes, with the remainder offering fleeting ocean glimpses. The course plays tag with the ocean a time or two during the outward nine before meandering inland, and then returns for a crescendo along the palm-studded beach on the lovely 17th and 18th holes. For a course best known for its only intermittent proximity to the beauty of the Caribbean Sea, it's somewhat paradoxical that most of the danger in the playing comes in the form of sand. There are also a few wicked greens, plenty of massive mounding, and some steep greenside drop-offs. "We had to manufacture everything. Including the soil," says the architect. Two million cubic meters of pulverized limestone were spread on a dead-flat site to create some noteworthy contouring both in the fairways and around the greens.

18th hole

Long before most of the rest of us had an inkling about getting green, Frank Rainieri was an environmentalist. He endeavored to keep as much of his 15,000 acres of jungle in as natural a state as possible, and that philosophy goes beyond eco-friendly buildings and minimal tree-cutting throughout the property. On La Cana, there are just six inches of topsoil on top of a limestone base. This saves on both water and fertilizer. The course is the first in the Caribbean to use Paspalum grass, which can be irrigated with recycled water.

One of the most unusual features of the facility is the beachside clubhouse. Now, the reader may have noticed that clubhouse mentions in this book have been few and far between. But this one is worth mentioning.

"At most resorts, the golf and the beach aren't together," explains Frank Rainieri. "So the husband disappears for half the day, and often feels guilty. His wife feels abandoned and sometimes gets angry, because she's left with the kids. Here we have the spa at the clubhouse, right next to the beach. Dad plays golf, mom gets a massage, the kids are by the water, and everyone's happy. And they all reconvene in the afternoon!"

"There are three major factors that make up our resort," he concludes. "Families, beach, and golf. I'm a family man myself, and want a family-friendly resort. There are golf courses all over the world, but there are few beaches as beautiful as ours. If we're going to inspire families to come to this beautiful part of the world, where our rooms and villas are lovely and the beach is fantastic, we need to give them a great golf experience also. I've always been hands-on, and I appreciate the fact the P.B. is the same way."

American businessman Ted Kheel is one of the original founders of the entire development, and made Frank Rainieri a partner at project's inception. His bargain-hunting acumen resulted in the purchase of thirty square miles of jungle at an effective cost of about $10 per acre. "We've been very pleased with the work of P.B. Dye," says Kheel, whose land investment has appreciated an astounding 100,000 times its late-1960s value, as individual acres currently sell for a million or more. "We've hired him to build another golf course here, so I'd say that sums up our feelings about him very well."

Royal Links

Perry Dye

In Las Vegas, nothing is quite as it seems. Visitors suspend their disbelief, and while at heart they know their chosen hotel isn't really a pyramid or a castle, a pirate ship or a circus tent, in Paris, Venice, or Manhattan, they play along with the theme. Same holds true at one of the city's most unusual golf experiences, Royal Links, as conceived and executed by Perry Dye.

"Golf entrepreneur Billy Walters approached me about the concept of doing a British Open replica course," recalls Perry. "I thought, why not? It's Vegas, and anything goes! When all is said and done, the architecture of Las Vegas will probably go down in history as some of the most memorable and flamboyant that's ever been created. Why not push the same envelope with a golf course?"

Much as his parents had done some thirty years earlier during their seminal trip to the British Isles, when they studied the finest links courses extensively and then began incorporating these design elements into their Stateside work, Perry and his architect cousin Cynthia Dye McGarey went overseas to study the dozen-odd courses in the British Open rotation.

"What I found was that I was studying holes and design concepts I had been incorporating for thirty years anyway," explains the Denver-based Perry. "I had been expanding and working off my dad's ideas, which were based largely on what he had learned over there with my mother in the 1960s." Perry saw plenty of so-called bell holes, short par-4s with mounding blocking the approach shot, where players ring a bell signaling their exit from the green. He saw the S-shaped fairways, stacked sod-wall bunkers, and greens tucked into glens and hollows as opposed to elevated above the fairway. He then came back and implemented this vision in the Nevada desert.

Royal Links is a bit Disneyesque, with its faux baronial castle of a clubhouse loosely modeled after the Royal and Ancient Clubhouse at St. Andrews. To hammer the point home, it's fronted by a giant Claret Jug, the coveted trophy awarded annually to the winner of the British Open. Some touches are too theme park, like the English-style phone booth or the Swilican Bridge.

While the holes are inspired by some of the best known in the British Isles, they aren't meant to be exact replicas. Some fare better than others. The 10th at Royal Links is a decent facsimile of St. Andrews' famous "Road Hole," though here, instead of boldly driving over the corner of the Old Course Hotel, a player must attempt to drive over a strategically placed billboard. Troon's famous little par-3 "Postage Stamp" comes off reasonably well, as do several others, culled from courses like Turnberry and Prestwick. The point is that this is more of an artist's rendering and less of a carbon copy. The course sits in east Las Vegas, on some of the lowest, flattest ground in the entire valley, so the elevation element is often missing, as are the appropriate scale of the holes, the blind shots, the wacky, built-by-the-hand-of-God greens, and other touches unique to classic U.K. golf.

And while individual holes may or may not be faithfully replicated, the feel of the property as a whole is linkslike. It's mostly open vistas with over 100 bunkers, not a drop of water, home, or condo to be found. Wheat grasses do a serviceable job of imitating the fescue and heather across the pond.

It's a bit kitschy, to be sure. But tourists, the majority of whom have likely never made it to the actual courses that inspired this tribute, flock to Royal Links and love it. Just inside the pro shop door is a massive guest registry, thick as two city phone books and as large as a breadbox, which has recorded the comments of golfers since the course opened on New Year's Eve of 1998. A comprehensive perusal turns up but a single negative comment, if it can even be construed as such. Amid the hundreds of hosannas contained therein, some vitriolic grumbler penned the following: "The clubhouse needs comfy couches." If that's the worst that can be said, then Perry Dye's golf homage to all things British is truly the people's choice.

9th hole

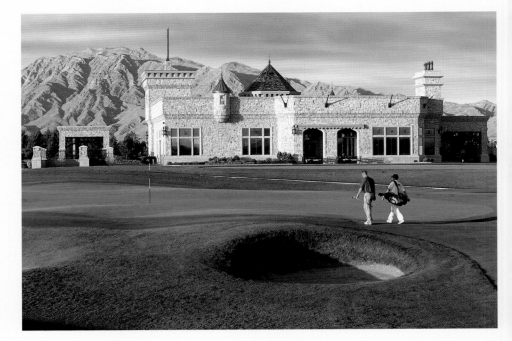

The Links at Sleepy Ridge

Matt Dye

Some thirty miles south of Utah's Salt Lake City are the nearby cities of Orem and Provo. Orem is home to a sporty golf course called the Links at Sleepy Ridge, while Provo has a higher-profile entity in Brigham Young University, better known as BYU.

NFL Hall of Fame quarterback Steve Young is likely the best-known athlete the school has ever produced. The great-great-great grandson of Mormon pioneer Brigham Young himself, Steve Young thrilled packed college stadiums in the early 1980s before embarking on his storied professional career. Across the city limits in Orem, another relative of a well-known, if not such an exalted, figure is impressing golfers. Matthew Dye, the late Roy Dye's son and Pete's nephew, is the architect of record at perhaps the most in-demand daily-fee course in sprawling Utah County.

"Sleepy Ridge was designed to be a player-friendly, maintenance-friendly course for the local market," says Matt, who lives in San Diego. "The wetlands and the natural lakes provide the scenic beauty, and the generous width of the fairways keeps the course from being overly difficult."

Still, Matt Dye shows some of his famous uncle's gleeful antipathy toward golfers. Working on a combination of old farmland, swampland, and wetland reserves, he has succeeded in taking a site with little inherent drama, and producing an attractive and occasionally penal test of golf. The course isn't overly long, barely 7,000 yards in total, and with the ball flying farther owing to the average elevation of 4,000 feet, it plays shorter still. But there are numerous junctures where trouble lurks. Wetlands border the western side of the property early in the opening nine, wreaking havoc with a hook. These same wetlands also bisect the playing fields several times, necessitating up-and-over tee shots and approach shots to notably sloping greens. Many of the putting surfaces are elevated, and offline approaches can carom off the banks and disappear into the lateral hazards that occasionally encircle the greens.

The inward nine has more character and difficulty. It's actually a shade shorter than the outward journey, but from the back tees, several of the early holes require a prodigious blow to find the safety of the fairway. For example, the 10th is a par-4 dogleg of just 415 yards from the tips, but in an early iteration, the tee ball needed to carry some 250 yards to reach the short grass. Fortunately, the hole has been reconfigured, and that overly daunting carry has been reduced to a more manageable 180 or so yards. The succeeding hole is more of a design puzzle. Not even 360 yards from the tips, but again, the tee ball must be launched some 200-plus yards in the air to carry a water hazard that intrudes on the landing area and then menaces the entire right side of the hole. For those without the requisite firepower to bomb it and then hit a flip wedge onto the green, the tee ball needs to be bunted about 180 yards to stay short of the water, and then the approach requires another 180-yard shot to the green.

While the greens are elevated, most of the tees are not. The combination of the relatively flat topography and the omnipresence of the wetlands necessitate directional poles on nearly every fairway. Sleepy Ridge will keep a golfer off balance from a visual perspective through most of the round. But for the regular visitor or neighborhood homeowner well versed in the lay of the land, it's a somewhat taxing but exciting test of the game. "It's gratifying that the course has quickly become the most popular facility in the area," says the architect, with understandable pride.

15th hole

Sweetbrier Golf Course

Matt Dye

Disco Duck. It's highly unlikely those words have ever before been published in a golf book. However, in this instance they are applicable. Readers of a certain age may recall the mid-1970s novelty song of that name. It was the brainchild of a then Memphis-based disc jockey named Rick Dees, who shortly thereafter became one of the nation's top radio personalities. "Disco Duck" sold six million copies and was featured, albeit briefly, in the seminal disco movie of all time, *Saturday Night Fever*. It earned Dees millions.

Some twenty-plus years after his runaway hit single, Dees, a Southerner at heart, invested some of his riches into Sweetbrier Farm, a couple thousand acres located in the geographical center of Kentucky, midway between Louisville and Lexington.

He was familiar with the region because his wife, Julie, hailed from neighboring Indiana and had enjoyed family vacations in the area in her youth. "The people of this area are so wonderful, and the rolling hills are so beautiful, when I arrive, my blood pressure immediately drops to practically zero," explains Dees.

After purchasing the abundant acreage in 1996, Dees toyed with the idea of building a golf course. His was a modest vision—just a driving range and three-hole practice ground,

but after meeting Matt Dye, the up-and-coming architect and nephew of Pete, his plans became grander. Though both Dees and Dye are based on the West Coast, their first face-to-face meeting was at Sweetbrier. "Matt fell in love with the property. He convinced me to do something a bit more ambitious, and was keen on having this as his first-ever solo design credit. We got together two weeks later, and the detailed routing plan he had devised for a nine-hole championship course just blew me away. I loved it. So we went for it."

An avid player who's been a longtime member of Hollywood's famed Lakeside Country Club, Dees has had many memorable golf experiences over the years. "I once caddied for Mark O'Meara in a practice round at the Masters," recalls the man who has been named *Billboard* magazine's "Number One Radio Personality in America" more than a dozen times. "In fact, I like to think when he won the Masters more than a decade later, he might've been recalling some of my course insights from that practice round! But the highlight of my golf career is owning Sweetbrier."

An avid student of golf architecture, Dees exclaims that the concept of having a Dye-designed golf course "sent chills down my spine. I think it's a masterpiece. Matt went above and beyond in creating it."

1st hole

"We found this wonderful parcel in the middle of Rick's property," recalls Matt Dye. "It was ninety acres of rolling hills, with about sixty feet of elevation change. There was no need to move any dirt during construction. Considering that a typical eighteen-hole course is laid upon 120 acres, you can get a sense of the spaciousness of Sweetbrier. The playing corridors are very wide. It feels like a farm field with some golf holes sprinkled about, as opposed to a golf course surrounded by a farm. It's wonderful to play."

Alas, few folks get the privilege. Dees estimates the course does less than a hundred rounds a year, though some of his celebrity friends like Jack Nicholson and Tim Allen have happened by. "I get out as often as I can from spring through fall,

and even have remote radio and TV studios on site. But it's hard to get the Hollywood elite out to Kentucky," he adds ruefully, "so I still do most of my interviewing and radio shows from L.A."

"'Disco Duck' has been a wonderful calling card for me, well beyond the financials," concludes the radio/television host–turned gentleman farmer–turned course proprietor. "It opened up many doors, including meeting my wife, winning a People's Choice Award, and facilitating my move to Los Angeles in 1980." And with the ripple effect in place, allowed him the wherewithal to one day construct the Sweetbrier Golf Course, his small slice of heaven, carved deep in the Kentucky bluegrass.

White Horse Golf Club

Cynthia Dye McGarey

In the late 1980s, longtime Washington State resident Bob Screen was looking for a few acres to board his daughter's horse. But when he discovered a beautiful woodland parcel west of the Puget Sound, gently rolling terrain that had previously provided a century's worth of timber for the Boise Cascade and International Paper companies, his plans became more ambitious.

Screen was a longtime marketing and advertising executive who had never before been in the golf business. But he sought an informed opinion as to the land quality from someone who had. "I had read a story in the Seattle paper quoting PING founder Karsten Solheim, who said he didn't think our area had enough high-quality public golf. I decided to solicit his judgment of this land directly," recalls the developer. "I knew that Karsten was a Seattle native and had a sister who ran a local restaurant. I went over there to inquire how to best reach him, and amazingly, he was actually sitting there when I walked in. I introduced myself, and within fifteen minutes' time we were on our way to tour the property."

Solheim wasted little time in telling Screen he thought it was some of the best golf course terrain he had ever encountered. And so began an eighteen-year odyssey from discovery to finished product. Screen bought the land in 1988, and permitting began in 1991. A decade-long fight with local environmentalists who wanted to stonewall the development ensued. By the time the lawsuits were settled, construction was begun and the golf course was ready for play, the calendar read 2006. But the legion of avid players who immediately anointed the course as one of the area's finest undoubtedly think it was worth the wait.

Unlike her famous earth-moving family, Cynthia Dye McGarey didn't have to create the playing corridors with ten-ton bulldozers. She just had to identify them, routing the fairways through the sandy soil. The 450-acre property is on the Kitsap Peninsula, near Puget Sound, between the Cascade and Olympic mountains. This scenic ridgeline between the small towns of Indianola and Kingston is no longer timber country, owing to recent population growth and the rapid appreciation of land values. Instead, some 220 homes will eventually be found on the property. McGarey incorporated housing setbacks at forty feet, but the natural buffer zone between the homes and the playing corridors is made up of old-growth cedar, spruce, hemlock, and Douglas firs, so the housing presence does little to dull the golf course ambience.

Although she's worked extensively in Asia, White Horse is McGarey's first solo United States design. Her hands-on

Above: 4th hole
Opposite: 13th hole

approach mirrored those of her male relations. "Cynthia was on the ground for thirty-two weeks, which in my opinion is an amazing level of commitment," says Screen, who makes his home on Bainbridge Island. The course has a distinct Northwest feel, with more than 100 feet of elevation change throughout and towering hardwoods in every direction. The fairways are wide, but flat lies are few. Bunkers are plentiful, greens are often perched, swales and run-offs surrounding the putting surfaces are deep. "When I saw what Cynthia had done as the project manager at Promontory, in Park City, Utah, I was very impressed. The decisions she was making there underscored her competence. I had no reservations about hiring her after seeing her work in Utah. Her understanding of the game and the level of detail she provided were both extraordinary. In my thirty-plus-year business career I worked with numerous competent women who ran circles around most men. Their ego doesn't get in the way like it does with most of us, and Cynthia is one of those kinds of women."

She is as pleased with the end result as are the dedicated patrons of the mid-priced facility, which was constructed for fewer than $4 million. "I was kind of surprised that Bob hired outside the state of Washington, and hired a woman to boot," says the architect. She feels the biggest hindrance to future success is not necessarily her gender, but her maiden name. "I feel like it's more difficult for any member of our family to get business. When your uncle is the premier architect today, all the clients prefer him, not you!"

Even though the course is now one of the leading lights in the greater Puget Sound region, Screen's original intention wasn't necessarily geared toward golf. "I bought that land because I knew it was a good value. I had been traveling more than 100,000 air miles annually and eventually wanted to get off those airplanes and down onto the ground." A beautiful piece of ground it was, and has been fashioned into an equally beautiful golf course.

Dye Courses Worldwide

Alabama	Country Club of Birmingham, West Course	Birmingham	Pete & P.B. Dye	1986
	Musgrove Country Club	Jasper	Pete Dye & Jerry Pate remodel	1992
Arizona	Ancala Country Club	Scottsdale	Perry Dye	1990
	ASU Karsten Golf Course	Tempe	Pete & Perry Dye	1989
	El Rio Golf & Country Club	Mohave Valley	Matt Dye	2004
	Red Mountain Ranch Country Club	Mesa	Pete & Perry Dye	1986
	Stonebridge Golf Club	Paradise Valley	Roy Dye & Gary Grandstaff	1983
Arkansas	Village Creek Golf Resort	Wynne	Andy Dye	Coming Soon
California	Bartley W. Cavanaugh Golf Course	Sacramento	Perry Dye	1995
	Carlton Oaks Country Club & Golf Course	Santee	Perry Dye	1989
	Carmel Valley Ranch Resort	Carmel	Pete Dye	1980
	Cypress Golf Club	Los Alamitos	Perry Dye	1992
	Dos Lagos Golf Club	Corona	Matt Dye	2006
	Furnace Creek Inn & Ranch Resort	Death Valley	Perry Dye	1997
	Hideaway Golf Club, Pete Dye Course	La Quinta	Pete Dye	2001
	La Quinta Resort, Citrus Course	La Quinta	Pete & Alice Dye	1987
	La Quinta Resort, Dunes Course	La Quinta	Pete Dye	1981
	La Quinta Resort, Mountain Course	La Quinta	Pete Dye	1980
	Lost Canyons Golf Club, Shadow and Sky Courses	Simi Valley	Pete & Perry Dye	2000
	Mission Hills Country Club, Pete Dye Challenge Course	Rancho Mirage	Pete & Alice Dye	1988
	Moreno Valley Ranch Golf Club (3 courses)	Moreno Valley	Pete Dye	1988
	PGA West Private Golf Courses	La Quinta	Pete Dye & Arnold Palmer	1987
	PGA West TPC Stadium Course	La Quinta	Pete & Alice Dye	1986
	Rancho Santa Fe Farms Golf Club ("The Farms")	Rancho Santa Fe	Pete, Perry, & Alice Dye	1988
	Temeku Hills Golf & Country Club	Temecula	Perry Dye remodel	1995
	Trump National Golf Club	Rancho Palos Verdes	Pete & Perry Dye	1999
	Westin Mission Hills Resort, Pete Dye Resort Course	Rancho Mirage	Pete Dye	1980
	William Land Park Golf Course	Sacramento	Perry Dye	1999
	Yucaipa Valley Golf Club	Yucaipa	Pete Dye & David A. Rainville	2000
Colorado	Copper Creek Golf Club	Copper Mountain	Pete & Perry Dye	1986
	Cotton Ranch Club	Gypsum	Pete & Perry Dye	1997
	Country Club of Colorado	Colorado Springs	Pete & Roy Dye	1973
	Broken Tee Englewood (3 courses)	Sheridan	Perry Dye	2008
	Glenmoor Country Club	Cherry Hills Village	Pete & Perry Dye	1985
	Green Valley Ranch Golf Club	Denver	Perry Dye	2001
	Kingspoint Golf Course	Aurora	Perry Dye	Coming Soon
	Plum Creek Golf and Country Club	Castle Rock	Pete & Perry Dye	1984
	Riverdale Golf Club, The Dunes Course	Brighton	Pete & Perry Dye	1985
Connecticut	TPC at River Highlands	Cromwell	Pete Dye remodel	1982
	Wintonbury Hills Golf Course	Bloomfield	Pete Dye & Tim Liddy	2003

Florida	Amelia Island Plantation, Oak Marsh Golf Course	Amelia Island	Pete Dye	1973
	Black Bear Golf Club	Eustis	P.B. Dye	1995
	Club at Olde Cypress	Naples	P.B. Dye	1999
	Delray Dunes Golf and Country Club	Boynton Beach	Pete Dye	1969
	Dye Preserve Golf Club	Jupiter	Pete Dye	2002
	Eagle Pines Course at Walt Disney World	Lake Buena Vista	Pete Dye	1992
	Fisher Island Resort	Fisher Island	P.B. Dye	1989
	Gasparilla Inn & Club	Boca Grande	Pete Dye remodel	2004
	Grand Harbor Golf and Beach Club, Harbor Course	Vero Beach	Pete Dye	1987
	Harbour Ridge Yacht & Country Club, River Ridge Course	Palm City	Pete & P.B. Dye	1989
	John's Island Club, North Course	Vero Beach	Pete & Perry Dye	1973
	John's Island Club, South Course	Vero Beach	Pete Dye & Jack Nicklaus	1970
	Loblolly Pines Golf Course	Hobe Sound	Pete & P.B. Dye	1988
	Medalist Golf Club	Hobe Sound	Pete Dye & Greg Norman	1995
	Monterey Yacht & Country Club	Stuart	P.B. Dye	1970
	Moorings Club	Vero Beach	Pete & Alice Dye	1970
	Old Marsh Golf Club	Palm Beach Gardens	Pete Dye	1988
	Palm Beach Polo & Country Club, Cypress Course	Wellington	Pete & P.B. Dye	1989
	PGA Golf Club at the Reserve, Pete Dye Course	Port St. Lucie	Pete Dye	1998
	Pinemoor Golf Club East	Rotonda West	Pete Dye	2004
	Pinemoor West Golf Club	Rotonda West	Pete Dye	2004
	Saint Andrews Club	Delray Beach	Pete & Alice Dye	1973
	Southern Hills Plantation Club, Pete Dye Course	Brooksville	Pete Dye	2005
	TPC at Sawgrass, Stadium Course	Ponte Vedra Beach	Pete & Alice Dye	1981
	TPC at Sawgrass, Valley Course	Ponte Vedra Beach	Pete Dye, Jerry Pate, & Bobby Weed	1987
	Tuscany Reserve Golf Club	Naples	Pete Dye & Greg Norman	2004
	Walkabout Golf Club	Mims	Perry Dye & Jan Stephenson	2002
	West Bay Golf Club	Estero	Pete & P.B. Dye	1998
Georgia	Atlanta National Golf Club	Alpharetta	Pete & P.B. Dye	1987
	Ogeechee Golf Club at the Ford Plantation	Richmond Hill	Pete & P.B. Dye	1987
Hawaii	Big Island Country Club	Kailua-Kona	Perry Dye	1995
	Luana Hills Country Club	Kailua	Pete & Perry Dye	1993
Iowa	Des Moines Golf and Country Club, North Course	West Des Moines	Pete Dye	1967
	Des Moines Golf and Country Club, South Course	West Des Moines	Pete Dye	1968
Illinois	Illinois Center Driving Range	Chicago	Perry Dye	1994
	Oakwood Country Club	Coal Valley	Pete Dye	1969
	Ruffled Feathers Golf Club	Lemont	Pete & P.B. Dye	1991
	Tamarack Country Club	O'Fallon	Pete Dye	1965
	Yorktown Golf Course	Belleville	Pete Dye	1963

Indiana	Birck Boilermaker Golf Complex, Kampen Course	West Lafayette	Pete Dye	1997
	Brickyard Crossing	Indianapolis Motor Speedway	Pete & Alice Dye	1993
	Bridgewater Club	Carmel	Pete Dye & Tim Liddy	2003
	Buck Point Golf Club	Liberty	P.B. Dye	2002
	Country Club of Indianapolis	Indianapolis	Pete Dye & Tom Bendelow remodel	1992
	Crooked Stick Golf Club	Carmel	Pete & Alice Dye	1964
	Eagle Creek Golf Club, Pines & Sycamore Courses	Indianapolis	Pete Dye	1975
	The Elks Country Club	West Lafayette	Pete Dye remodel	1975
	Forest Park Golf Course	Brazil	Pete Dye	1963
	The Fort Golf Resort	Indianapolis	Pete Dye & Tim Liddy	1977
	The Golf Preserve	Noblesville	Pete Dye & Tim Liddy	1999
	Greenbelt Golf Course	Columbus	Pete Dye	1972
	Harbour Trees Golf Club	Noblesville	Pete Dye	1972
	Maple Creek Golf & Country Club	Indianapolis	Pete & Alice Dye	1961
	Mystic Hills Golf Club	Indianapolis	Pete & P.B. Dye	1998
	Oak Tree Golf Course	Plainfield	Pete Dye	1962
	Plum Creek Country Club	Carmel	Pete Dye & Tim Liddy	1997
	Royal Oak Country Club	Greenwood	Pete Dye	1962
	Saddlebrook Golf Club	Indianapolis	Pete & Alice Dye	1962
	Stonebridge Club	Martinsville	Pete Dye	Coming Soon
	Tippecanoe Country Club	Monticello	Pete Dye remodel	1961
	West Baden Springs Hotel Resort	West Baden Springs	Pete Dye	2007
	William Sahm Golf Course	Indianapolis	Pete & Alice Dye	1963
	Woodland Country Club	Carmel	Pete Dye & Tim Liddy	2002
Kansas	Auburn Hills Golf Course	Wichita	Perry Dye	2000
Kentucky	Kearney Hills Golf Links	Lexington	Pete & P.B. Dye	1989
	Peninsula Golf Resort	Lancaster	Pete Dye	1997
	Sweetbriar Golf Club	Danville	Matt Dye	2002
Louisiana	Belle Terre Country Club	La Place	Pete Dye	1982
	TPC of Louisiana at Fairfield	Avondale	Pete Dye	2004
Maryland	Bulle Rock Golf Club	Havre de Grace	Pete Dye	1998
	Harbourtowne Resort Country Club	Saint Michaels	Pete & Roy Dye	1971
	P.B. Dye Golf Club	Ijamsville	P.B. Dye	1999
	Rum Pointe Golf Course	Berlin	Pete & P.B. Dye	1997
Michigan	Radrick Farms Golf Club, University of Michigan	Ann Arbor	Pete & Alice Dye	1967
	Wabeek Country Club	Bloomfield Hills	Pete Dye, Roy Dye, & Jack Nicklaus	1970
Minnesota	Izaty's Golf & Yacht Club, Black Brook Course	Onamia	Pete Dye	1999
Missouri	Boone Valley Golf Club	Augusta	P.B. Dye	1992
	Old Hickory Golf Club	St. Peters	P.B. Dye	2003
Mississippi	Pine Island Golf Club	Ocean Springs	Pete Dye	1972
North Carolina	Cardinal Golf and Country Club	Greensboro	Pete Dye	1973
	Country Club of Landfall, Pete Dye Course	Wilmington	Pete Dye, P.B. Dye, & Bobby Weed	1987

	NorthStone Country Club	Huntersville	P.B. Dye	1997
	Oak Hollow Golf Course	High Point	Pete Dye	1971
	St. James Plantation, The Founders Club	Southport	P.B. Dye	1991
Nebraska	Firethorn Golf Club	Lincoln	Pete, Alice, & Perry Dye	1985
New Mexico	Alto Lakes Golf & Country Club	Alto	Pete Dye, Milt Coggins, & R. Trent Jones	1968
Nevada	Desert Pines Golf Club	Las Vegas	Perry Dye	1995
	Las Vegas Paiute Resort, Snow Mountain Course	Las Vegas	Pete Dye	1995
	Las Vegas Paiute Resort, Sun Mountain Course	Las Vegas	Pete Dye	1996
	Las Vegas Paiute Resort, The Wolf	Las Vegas	Pete Dye	2001
	Royal Links Golf Course	Las Vegas	Perry Dye	1997
New York	Nassau County Club	Glen Cove	Cynthia Dye McGarey remodel	2007
	Pound Ridge Golf Club	Pound Ridge	Pete Dye	2008
Ohio	Avalon Lakes Golf Course	Warren	Pete Dye	1967
	Clear Creek Par 3	Franklin	P.B. Dye	1998
	Fowler's Mill Golf Course (3 courses)	Chesterland	Pete & Roy Dye	1971
	The Golf Club	New Albany	Pete Dye	1967
	Heritage Club	Mason	P.B. Dye	1996
	Heritage Golf Club	Hilliard	P.B. Dye	1993
	Little Turtle Golf Club	Westerville	P.B. Dye	1975
	Urbana Golf & Country Club	Urbana	P.F. "Pink" Dye	1922
			P.B. Dye remodel	1993
Oklahoma	Crimson Creek Golf Club	El Reno	P.B. Dye	1998
	Oak Tree Country Club, East Course	Edmond	Pete & Alice Dye	1979
	Oak Tree Country Club, West Course	Edmond	Pete & Alice Dye	1981
	Oak Tree Golf Club	Edmond	Pete Dye	1976
Pennsylvania	Iron Valley Golf Club	Lebanon	P.B. Dye	2000
	Montour Heights Country Club	Coraopolis	Pete & P.B. Dye	1987
	Nemacolin Woodlands Resort, Mystic Rock Course	Farmington	Pete Dye	1995
Rhode Island	Button Hole Golf and Learning Center	Providence	P.B. Dye, Ron Pritchard, & Brad Faxon	2000
South Carolina	Barefoot Resort, The Dye Course	Myrtle Beach	Pete Dye	2000
	Cherokee Valley Golf Club, Gauntlet Golf Course	Travelers Rest	P.B. Dye	1992
	Cobblestone Park, The University Club	Blythewood	Pete & P.B. Dye	1995
	Colleton River Plantation Golf Club, Pete Dye Course	Bluffton	Pete Dye	1998
	Cross Creek Plantation	Seneca	Pete & P.B. Dye	1991
	DeBordieu Club	Georgetown	Pete & P.B. Dye	1987
	Hampton Hall Golf Club	Hilton Head	Pete Dye	2004
	Harbour Town Golf Links at Sea Pines Resort	Hilton Head Island	Pete Dye, Alice Dye, & Jack Nicklaus	1970
	Kiawah Island Golf Resort, Ocean Course	Kiawah Island	Pete Dye	1991
	Legends Golf Resort, Moorland Course	Myrtle Beach	P.B. Dye	1991
	Long Cove Club	Hilton Head Island	Pete & Alice Dye	1980

	Northwoods Golf Course	Columbia	P.B. Dye	1990
	Port Royal Golf Club, Robber's Row Course	Hilton Head Island	Pete Dye redesign	1994
	Prestwick Country Club	Myrtle Beach	Pete & P.B. Dye	1989
	Windermere Club	Blythewood	Pete & P.B. Dye	1989
Tennessee	Honors Course	Ooltewah	Pete & P.B. Dye	1983
	Rarity Mountain	Jellico	Pete & P.B. Dye	Coming Soon
Texas	Austin Country Club	Austin	Pete & Alice Dye	1983
	Cibolo Canyons	San Antonio	Pete Dye	Coming Soon
	Cottonwood Creek Golf Course	Waco	Pete Dye & Joseph Finger	1985
	Hank Haney Golf Ranch	McKinney	Pete Dye & Hank Haney	1991
	Stonebridge Ranch Country Club, The Dye Course	McKinney	Pete & Alice Dye	1988
	Waterwood National Resort and Country Club	Huntsville	Pete & Roy Dye	1974
	Wind Creek Golf Course	Sheppard AFB	Pete Dye	1958
Utah	The Ledges of St. George Golf Club & Spa	St. George	Matt Dye	2006
	The Links at Sleepy Ridge	Orem	Matt Dye	2005
	Promontory Ranch Club, Pete Dye Course	Park City	Pete & Perry Dye	2002
Virginia	Chantilly National Golf & Country Club	Centreville	P.B. Dye remodel	1991
	The Gauntlet Golf Club	Fredericksburg	P.B. Dye	1995
	Kingsmill Resort and Spa, The River Course	Williamsburg	Pete Dye	1974
	Pete Dye River Course of Virginia Tech	Radford	Pete Dye	2005
	TPC of Virginia Beach	Virginia Beach	Pete Dye & Curtis Strange	1999
	Virginia Oaks Golf Club	Gainesville	P.B. Dye	1995
Washington	Gamble Ranch Golf Club	Brewster	Perry Dye	Coming Soon
	Plateau Club	Sammamish	Perry Dye	1997
	White Horse Golf Club	Kingston	Cynthia Dye McGarey	2007
Wisconsin	Big Fish Golf Club	Hayward	Pete Dye	2004
	Black Wolf Run, Meadow Valleys Course	Kohler	Pete Dye	1988
	Black Wolf Run, River Course	Kohler	Pete Dye	1990
	Hidden Glen Golf Club at Bentdale Farms	Cedarburg	P.B. Dye	1998
	Highlands at Grand Geneva Resort and Spa	Lake Geneva	Pete Dye & Jack Nicklaus	1970
	Whistling Straits, Irish Course	Sheybogan	Pete Dye	2000
	Whistling Straits, Straits Course	Sheybogan	Pete Dye	1998
West Virginia	Pete Dye Golf Club	Bridgeport	Pete Dye	1994
Austria	Golfclub Seltenheim Klagenfurt	Klagenfurt-Wölfnitz	Perry Dye	1995
Bahamas	Lighthouse Point	Eleuthera	Pete & Perry Dye	Coming Soon
Brazil	Búzios Golf Club and Resort	Armaçáo de Búzios	Pete & Perry Dye	1993
	Iberostar Bahia Resort and Golf Club	Praia de Forte	P.B. Dye	2007
Canada	Country Club of Montreal	St. Lambert, Quebec	Roy Dye remodel	1975
China	Beijing Daxing Capital Golf Club	Beijing	Cynthia Dye McGarey	Coming Soon
	Sanya Four Seasons Resort	Hainan Island	Cynthia Dye McGarey	Coming Soon

	Shenzhen Tycoon Golf Club	Shenzhen	Pete Dye & Cynthia Dye McGarey	Coming Soon
	West Coast Golf Club	Haikou, Hainan Island	Perry Dye & Cynthia Dye McGarey	2004
Dominican Republic	Bávaro Lakes	Bávaro	P.B. Dye	Coming Soon
	Casa de Campo, Dye Fore	La Romana	Pete Dye	2003
	Casa de Campo, The Links	La Romana	Pete Dye	1977
	Casa de Campo, La Romana Country Club	La Romana	Pete Dye	1990
	Casa de Campo, Teeth of the Dog	La Romana	Pete Dye	1971
	Iberostar Resort Course at Bávaro Beach	Bávaro Beach	P.B. Dye	Coming Soon
	La Estancia Golf Resort	La Romana	P.B. Dye	Coming Soon
	Puntacana Resort, La Cana Golf Course	Puntacana	P.B. Dye	2001
	Puntacana Resort, Hacienda Course	Puntacana	P.B. Dye	Coming Soon
El Salvador	El Encanto Villas y Golf	San José de Villanueva	Pete & Perry Dye	Coming Soon
France	Golf Club Barbaroux	Brignoles, Cote d'Azur	Pete & P.B. Dye	1989
Germany	Munich Golf Club	Munich, Strasslach	Perry Dye remodel	2006
Guatemala	Antigua Country Club at La Reunion Resort	La Antigua	Pete & Perry Dye	2008
Honduras	Black Pearl at Pristine Bay	Roatán	Pete & Perry Dye	Coming Soon
Israel	Caesarea Golf Club	Caesarea	Pete Dye & Tim Liddy	Coming Soon
Italy	Parco di Roma Golf Club	Rome	P.B. Dye	1994
	Sciacca Golf Resort	Sciacca	Cynthia Dye McGarey	Coming Soon
	Sibari Golf Resort	Sibari	Cynthia Dye McGarey	Coming Soon
	Simeri Golf Resort	Simeri	Cynthia Dye McGarey	Coming Soon
Japan	Alpen Golf Club, Bibai Course	Hokkaido	Perry Dye	1995
	Chukyo Golf Club, Ishino Course	Aichi	Pete & Perry Dye	1993
	Country Club Glenmoor	Chiba	Pete & Perry Dye	1991
	Country Club Momotaro	Okayama	Perry Dye	1991
	Edelweiss Golf Club	Saitama	Perry Dye	1989
	Golden Lakes Country Club	Tochigi	Perry Dye	1992
	Iwase Royal Golf Club	Ibaraki	Perry Dye	1993
	Kannami Springs Country Club	Shizuoka	Perry Dye	1988
	Kimisarazu Golf Links	Chiba	Pete & Perry Dye	1987
	Kogoya OGM Cherry Creek Country Club	Gifu	Perry Dye	1993
	Maple Point Golf Club	Yamanashi	Pete & Perry Dye	1990
	Mission Hills Country Club	Saitama	Perry Dye	1994
	Olympic Country Club	Yamanashi	Perry Dye	1990
	Olympic Staff Tsuga Golf Club	Tochiga	Perry Dye	1990
	Pete Dye Golf Club, Royal Course	Tochigi	Pete & Perry Dye	1988
	Pete Dye Golf Club, VIP Course	Tochigi	Pete & Perry Dye	1990
	Saitama Royal Golf Club, Ogose Course	Saitama	Perry Dye	1993
	Sapporo Bay Club	Hokkaido	Perry Dye	1995
	St. Lakes Golf Club	Mie	Pete & Perry Dye	1989
	Third Place Country Club	Mie	Perry Dye	1994

	Village Club, Daigo Course	Ibaraki	Perry Dye	1992
	West One's Country Club	Hyogo	Perry Dye	1993
Korea	Asiad Country Club	Busan	Perry Dye	2002
	Castlex Country Club	Jeju-do	Perry Dye	1993
	Club Vision Hills	Seoul	Perry Dye	2000
	Even Dale Country Club	Chojung Mineral Waters	Cynthia Dye McGarey	Coming Soon
	Hyosung Golf Resort	Seoul	Perry Dye	2005
	Nasan Country Club	Kisan-do	Perry Dye	1994
	Pine Nut 60 Golf Club	Gapyeoung	Cynthia Dye McGarey	Coming Soon
	Woo Jeong Hills Country Club	Ching-Nam	Perry Dye	1993
Malaysia	Poresia Country Club	Johor Bahru	Pete & Perry Dye	1993
Mexico	Cabo Riviera	La Rebera, Cabo	Perry Dye	Coming Soon
	Cabo San Lucas Country Club	Cabo San Lucas, BCS	Roy Dye	1994
	Iberostar Playa Paraiso Golf Club	Quintana Roo, Cancun	P.B. Dye	2005
	La Mantarraya / Las Hadas Golf Course	Manzanillo, Colima	Pete & Roy Dye	1984
	San Carlos Golf and Marina Properties	Nuevo Guaymas, Sonora	Roy Dye	1980
	San Gil Golf Club	San Juan del Rio, Queretaro	Roy Dye	1977
	Santa Fe Golf Club	Cuernavaca, Morelos	Pete & Roy Dye	1974
Netherlands Antilles	Santa Barbara Plantation	Curacao	Pete & P.B. Dye	Coming Soon
New Zealand	Carrington Club	Kaitaia	Matt Dye	2003
Panama	La Hacienda Golf Club	Panama City	Perry Dye & Cynthia Dye McGarey	Coming Soon
	Panama Bay Country Club	Panama City	Pete & Perry Dye	Coming Soon
Portugal	Comporta	Lisbon	P.B. Dye	Coming Soon
	Falesia D'el Rey	Obidos	Cynthia Dye McGarey	Coming Soon
Singapore	Laguna National Golf and Country Club	Singapore	Perry & Andy Dye	1991
Spain	Club de Golf Masia Beach	Barcelona	Perry Dye	Coming Soon
	Les Fontanelles	Valencia	Perry Dye	Coming Soon
	Real de la Quinta	Marbella	Perry Dye	Coming Soon
	San Roque Club, New Course	San Roque, Cadiz	Perry Dye	2003
	Toledo Golf Resort	Madrid	Perry Dye	Coming Soon
Switzerland	Golf Club du Domaine Imperial	Gland (Vaud)	Perry Dye	1993
Taiwan	Wing-On Resort and Country Club	Tainan County	Perry Dye	1993
Thailand	Khao Kheow Country Club	Chonburi	Perry Dye	1992
	Southern Hills Golf and Country Club	Hat Yai	Perry Dye	1993
	Subhapruek Country Club	Samut Prakam	Pete & Perry Dye	1992
	Thai Muang Beach Golf Club	Phang-nga	Perry Dye	1995
Turkey	Lykia Links	Antalya	Perry Dye	2008
United Arab Emirates	Jumeirah Golf Estates, Wind Course	Dubai	Pete Dye, Greg Norman, & Sergio Garica	Coming Soon

Index

Photo Credits

Dye Designs, Inc. & Rolling Greens Photography, Inc./Ken May: 12, 15 top & bottom, 16 top right, 17, 25, 36, 37, 38 top & bottom, 39, 44, 45, 46 top & bottom, 47, 48, 49 top & bottom, 68, 69, 70, 71 top & bottom, 86 top right, 87, 89, 90, 91, 92, 93, 96, 97, 98, 99, 124, 129 top & bottom, 143 top & bottom, 152, 158, 159 top & bottom, 160, 161, 171, 172, 173 bottom, 178, 179, 180 181, 190, 191, 192, 193 top & bottom, 206, 207, 212, 213, 214, 215, 220, 221, 257, 258, 259, 260, 261, 262, 263, 264, 265, 272, 273 top & bottom, 274, 275, 286 bottom, 287.

Rolling Greens Photography, Inc./Ken May: cover, 2, 10, 40, 41, 42 top & bottom, 43, 52 top left, 55, 56, 57, 58, 59, 60, 61, 62, 63, 64, 65, 80, 81, 82, 83 top & bottom, 164, 165, 166, 167 top & bottom, 168 left & right, 169, 170. 173 top, 174, 175 top & bottom, 176, 177 top & bottom, 186, 187 top & bottom, 188, 189, 194, 195, 196 top & bottom, 197, 254, 255, 276, 277, 278, 279 top left, right & bottom, 292, 293, 294, 295.

Aidan Bradley: 280, 281 top & bottom, 282, 283.

Tom Breazeale: 248, 249, 250 top & bottom, 251, 252, 253.

Patricia Buchanan-Bay: 242, 243.

Alan Chan: 52 top right, 53, 76, 77, 78 left and right, 79.

Rick Dees: 302 top & bottom, 303.

"D" Squared Productions, Inc. Murphy/Scully: 94, 95.

Tid Griffin: 198, 199 top, bottom left & right.

Chip Henderson: 208, 209, 210, 211.

Paul Hundley: 6, 7, 122, 123, 125, 207, 217, 218 top & bottom, 219 top & bottom.

John R. Johnson: 200, 201, 202, 203, 204, 205.

USGA/Russell Kirk: 144, 145, 146, 147.

Larry C. Lambrect, Courtesy of The Honors Course: 4, 5, 72, 73, 74, 75, 110, 111 top & bottom, 112, 113, 114, 115.

Rob Perry: 304 & 305.

David S. Soliday, Courtesy of Hampton Hall: 232, 233.

Tom Travis: 118, 119, 120, 121.

Peter Wong, Courtesy of Big Fish Golf Club: 231.

Courtesy of Atlanta National Golf Club: 126, 127.

Courtesy of Boca West Club: 247.

Courtesy of Bridgewater Club Golf Course: 224 left & right, 225, 226, 227.

Courtesy of Crooked Stick Country Club: 26, 27, 28, 29 top & bottom, 30, 31 left & top right.

Courtesy of Des Moines Country Club: 33 top & bottom, 34 top & bottom, 35.

Courtesy of Destination Kohler: 130, 131, 132, 133, 134, 135, 136, 137, 138, 139, 140, 141.

Courtesy of Fowlers Mill: 66, 67

Courtesy of Gasparilla Inn Golf Course: 234, 235, 236, 237.

Courtesy of Kiawah Resort The Ocean Course: 153, 154, 155 top & bottom, 156, 157.

Courtesy of Laguna National Golf And Country Club: 284, 285, 286 top, 288, 289 top & bottom.

Courtesy of Luana Hills Country Club: 162, 163.

Courtesy of Maple Creek Country Club: 22, 23, 24 top & bottom.

Courtesy of P.B. Dye Golf Club: 291 top & bottom.

Courtesy of Purdue University Kampen Course: 150, 151, 182, 183 top & bottom, 184 top & bottom,, 185.

Courtesy of The Links At Sleepy Ridge: 270, 271, 300, 301.

Courtesy of The Ogeechee Golf Club at the Ford Plantation Golf Course: 116, 117.

Courtesy of TPC Tour: 100, 101, 102, 103, 104, 105, 106, 107, 109, 239, 240, 241.

Courtesy of Tuscany Reserve Golf Course: 244, 245.

Courtesy of White Horse Golf Club: 304, 305.

Courtesy of Wintonbury Hills Golf Course: 228, 229.

Courtesy of Woodland Country Club: 223 top & bottom.

Editor
Margaret L. Kaplan

Designer
Brady McNamara

Production Manager
Anet Sirna-Bruder

Photo Research
Sandra and Ken E. May, Rolling Greens Photography, Inc.

Library of Congress Cataloging-in-Publication Data
Zuckerman, Joel.
  Pete Dye golf courses : fifty years of visionary design / by Joel
Zuckerman with appreciations by Jack Nicklaus, Arnold Palmer, and Greg
Norman.
    p. cm.
  ISBN 978-0-8109-7289-6
  1. Golf courses—Design and construction—Pictorial works. 2. Dye, Pete.
  3. Golf course architects—United States—Biography. I. Nicklaus, Jack.
  II. Palmer, Arnold, 1929– III. Norman, Greg, 1955– IV. Title.

  GV981.Z83 2008
  796.352'068—dc22
                        2008018674

Printed and bound in China
10 9 8 7 6 5 4 3 2 1

Abrams books are available at special discounts when purchased in quantity
for premiums and promotions as well as fundraising or educational use.
Special editions can also be created to specification. For details, contact
specialmarkets@hnabooks.com or the address below.

HNA
harry n. abrams, inc.
a subsidiary of La Martinière Groupe
115 West 18th Street
New York, NY 10011
www.hnabooks.com